KVM
Deepak

The
No-Salt,
Lowest-Sodium
Baking Book

THE
NO-SALT,
LOWEST-SODIUM
BAKING BOOK

❖ ❖ ❖ ❖ ❖ ❖

DONALD A. GAZZANIGA

and

JEANNIE GAZZANIGA MOLOO,
PH.D., R.D.

WITH A FOREWORD BY
DR. MICHAEL B. FOWLER

THOMAS DUNNE BOOKS
ST. MARTIN'S PRESS ❦ NEW YORK

THOMAS DUNNE BOOKS.
An imprint of St. Martin's Press.

THE NO-SALT, LOWEST-SODIUM BAKING BOOK. Copyright © 2003
by Donald A. Gazzaniga. Foreword copyright © 2003 by Michael B. Fowler.
All rights reserved. Printed in the United States of America.
No part of this book may be used or reproduced
in any manner whatsoever without written permission
except in the case of brief quotations embodied in critical
articles or reviews. For information, address
St. Martin's Press, 175 Fifth Avenue, New York, N.Y. 10010.

www.stmartins.com

Library of Congress Cataloging-in-Publication Data

Gazzaniga, Donald A.
    The no-salt, lowest-sodium baking book / Donald A. Gazzaniga and Jeannie Gazzaniga
Moloo ; with a foreword by Michael B. Fowler.—1st ed.
        p. cm.
    Includes index (page 215).
    ISBN 0-312-30118-9
    1. Salt-free diet—Recipes. 2. Baking. I. Moloo, Jeannie Gazzaniga. II. Title.

RM237.8.G37 2003
641.5'632—dc21

                                                                        2002034748

First Edition: March 2003

10 9 8 7 6 5 4 3 2 1

Dedicated to all who have helped this book come alive:
my wife, my doctors, my publisher,
and my new online friends at www.megaheart.com.

CONTENTS

Acknowledgments   *ix*

Foreword: Bread of Life, Salt of the Earth
    by Dr. Michael B. Fowler, F.R.C.P.   *xi*

The Importance of Dietary Fiber for a Healthier You
    by Jeannie Gazzaniga Moloo, Ph.D., R.D.   *1*

Bread Machines and Bread Baking   5

Ingredients   11

Ovens   23

The Effect of Weather on Bread Baking   25

Troubleshooting the Inevitable Failures   29

Low-Sodium Substitutes   33

Bread Making for People with Diabetes   37

Baking at Home   41

THE RECIPES   43

Bread   45

Muffins, Rolls, and Biscuits   103

Waffles   157

Cookies   161

Pastries   *193*

Toppings and Fillings   *205*

APPENDIX   *209*

Measurement Conversions   *211*

Supporting Research   *213*

Index   *215*

ACKNOWLEDGMENTS

This book would not have come about but for the people who helped me so much.

First, and foremost, my wife Maureen. She's put up with a lot through the years, but my efforts in the kitchen have been a bit much lately. Flour, sugar, raisins, and spices all over the place. Bread machines going, ovens on, dishwasher constantly working.

And then there's the testing of the breads. I'm afraid we both put on weight with this effort. So now we joke that we'd better sign on to Weight Watchers or hike from California to New York.

But above all that tongue-in-cheek stuff, she has been a great star in my life and without her this book would not have happened. Our love for each other has grown even stronger during these trying years. It shows in this book.

And before I forget it, it was Maureen who edited this book into the fine shape it was when presented to the publisher. Her keen eye and knowledge of cooking caught a lot of errors at a time when I thought the book was "perfect."

I can't leave my family out of this. "Mom" brought five great children into this world. Each has been extremely supportive and each has participated. The family I grew up in and the family we created have each contributed to my well-being and to this book with great recipes, and understanding. Our oldest daughter, Jeannie, has participated as an R.D. and a Ph.D. with the first book and with this one. Her contributions have helped make the first book highly successful. Our son Daniel designed and put together our www.megaheart.com Web site. Suzanne, a lawyer, has kept me from inadvertently stepping over the legal line with the Web site and the question-and-answer pages. That would be easy to do, since we laymen believe we understand all laws, and generally don't. Our dear Maria, who teaches Spanish in school, is here to translate into Spanish or from Spanish recipes for those who write in for them or send them to us. Our biologist, Kathleen, has been terrific as a recipe contributor and humorist. Well, they've all got a great sense of humor, and, trust me, that helps as much as low sodium does. To each, I owe my life and these books.

I must also thank those who kept me going medically. Without Dr. Fowler, Director of the Stanford Heart Transplant Clinic, I might not be here at all. It was he who prodded me to answer to my own bravado that I could indeed lower my sodium below 500 mg a day. When I first suggested that, it was considered by many as not doable. So, having put my foot in my mouth, I set out to prove it possible.

And guess what? It worked. My rather enormous heart downsized as they say in the corporate world, and my ejection fraction (EF) gained. In other words, the combination of family support, a very low sodium diet, great medical care, and exercise moved me away from a transplant to a healthier, more active life.

I owe others much, too, including doctors, nurses, R.D.s, and good friends.

And then there are Mike Shatzkin, Marin Gazzaniga, and Ruth Cavin, Thomas Dunne Books, a team of agents and editors who believed in me and the concept of a No-Salt series of books. To them, I bow and offer a huge "Thank you."

The list gets longer each day. It also includes thousands of visitors to www.megaheart.com who have improved their lives by cutting salt and sodium from their diets.

To each and all of you, I say, Thank You! You have helped not only me, but thousands of others who are already "downsizing" their hearts with the help of our No-Salt, Lowest-Sodium cookbooks.

FOREWORD

BREAD OF LIFE, SALT OF THE EARTH (BUT NOT IF YOU HAVE HEART TROUBLE)

BY DR MICHAEL B FOWLER, F.R.C.P.
DIRECTOR, STANFORD HEART TRANSPLANT CLINIC

Heart failure, in its different forms, affects more than five million Americans. Some common symptoms are significant weight gain, abdominal bloating, and swollen ankles. The patient will have an increased shortness of breath from moderate exertion, sometimes up to the point where almost any physical activity causes distress. Patients with some forms of heart failure may experience episodes of sudden breathlessness while they are sleeping; many feel uncomfortable lying flat. All of these symptoms are the result of fluid being retained in the body. Unless steps are taken to prevent it, the heart patient's body will retain sodium, and this in turn causes the retention of water. For this reason, two important factors in the treatment of heart failure are dietary advice and the use of diuretics to encourage the body to rid itself of excess water.

When a person with a healthy heart has an emergency that temporarily affects the organ, such as a major injury, a serious lack of water, or simply excessive physical activity, the body calls on a variety of alterations in its systems to compensate. The purpose of these is to provide short-term adjustments to protect the heart. Unfortunately, these compensatory systems are also activated when the heart is damaged, in an effort to provide a level of support to the ailing organ. But in the case of an ailing heart, they operate for extended periods and have an adverse effect on the heart and circulation that actually contributes in a major way to the progression of heart failure, to an increase in symptoms, an increased necessity of hospitalization and an increased risk of death.

The therapy for sodium retention, therefore, includes, along with the dietary advice and diuretic medication mentioned above, additional drug therapy directed at modifying the response to the injury that brought on the heart failure. These drugs do favorably modify the patient's tendency to retain sodium but do not address this problem directly.

Various diuretics remove the sodium that is the "congestion" in congestive heart failure and that is responsible for retained sodium and water in the lungs, liver, and ankles. They act on the kidneys and increase the amount of sodium in the urine, and the amount of urine excreted, thus removing excess sodium from the body. Various diuretics differ in strength, etc., and the dose of any is particularly dependent on the how severe the patient's heart failure is, the individual's tendency to retain sodium, and the amount of sodium taken in through the patient's diet.

But sometimes there are individuals for whom the use of diuretics seems to have little or no effect on water retention. These individuals will only respond to diuretic therapy when the sodium intake is reduced—and that necessitates a diet extremely low in sodium. (Those who follow a low-sodium diet but punctuate it with "binges" of high-sodium meals will respond only intermittently.) In fact, really effective sodium reduction almost always can only be achieved with the medication plus a significant reduction of sodium in the everyday diet.

Most patients with heart failure are advised to reduce their sodium intake, but few are taught how to achieve this goal. How do they choose the foods for a diet that is naturally low in sodium? The first step is to avoid all foods whose preparation or processing includes the addition of sodium. This reduces the sodium intake to what is naturally in the food itself.

Bread is a part of just about everyone's diet; unfortunately for heart patients up until now, it is also a food that has had sodium added during commercial production. While it is not very likely that modest daily quantities of bread will carry the risk of a sodium overdose, for some patients with heart failure even this degree of sodium intake can be a problem. For all patients with heart failure, any lessening of sodium in the diet cannot help but be a positive step. Now, heart patients, using the recipes in this book, need not limit the amount of bread they enjoy

The art of living well with heart failure is to optimize the balance of available medical therapies for your personal condition. It's important for patients to enjoy a variety of satisfying recipes without going beyond the sodium intake of a low-sodium diet since this is a crucial component of minimizing symptoms, reducing the need for hospitalization, and optimizing the effects of diuretics. Having bread-baking recipes specifically designed as part of a "no-added-sodium diet" will add one further resource to the eating habits of the millions of patients with heart failure, and all others who are trying to balance sodium restriction with diuretic therapy.

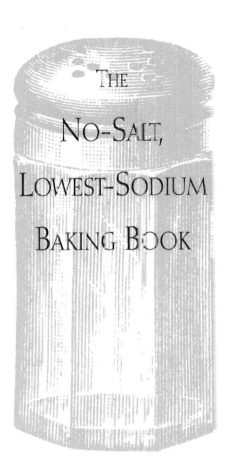

The
No-Salt,
Lowest-Sodium
Baking Book

THE IMPORTANCE OF DIETARY FIBER FOR A HEALTHIER YOU

❖ ❖ ❖ ❖ ❖ ❖ ❖ ❖

BY JEANNIE GAZZANIGA MOLOO, PH.D. R.D.

The biggest shortfall in the American diet isn't vitamins or minerals. It is dietary fiber. Health experts say adults should eat between 20 and 30 grams of dietary fiber a day for general health and cancer prevention. Most Americans consume only 12 grams of fiber a day.

Dietary fiber is the portion of plant cell walls that cannot be digested and absorbed to produce energy. Yet, fiber is essential to good health. It is credited with helping to fight serious conditions such as high blood cholesterol, heart disease, stroke, cancer, gastrointestinal disease, and diabetes. In the category of less scary, but quite uncomfortable conditions, fiber relieves constipation and can help avoid hemorrhoid flare-ups.

Dietary fiber is found in all plant-based foods, with most whole foods containing a combination of the two types of fiber—soluble and insoluble. As it travels through the body, soluble fiber combines with water and forms a gel. This process serves to slow the emptying of the stomach and the absorption of starch and sugars from the small intestines after eating. The result is a significant reduction in blood cholesterol level over time, which may help prevent heart disease and stroke. Intake of soluble fiber may also improve glucose tolerance in people with diabetes. Insoluble fiber, which is not easily broken down during the digestive process, is a natural laxative. It gives stool its bulk, helping it move more quickly through the gastrointestinal tract. This may help prevent colorectal cancer.

The best way to increase dietary fiber is to eat foods high in fiber. However, when following a low-sodium diet, sometimes it is not easy to just eat more fiber-rich foods. Here are a few ideas to help boost the fiber content of your diet without adding more sodium. Emphasize fresh fruits and vegetables, preferably in their raw form, and avoid peeling produce. Add beans or other lentils (no-salt-added) whenever possible to side and main dishes (see the recipe for Beef and Bean Stew in *The No-Salt, Lowest-Sodium Cookbook*, for cooking low-sodium beans). When you eat pasta or rice, choose the whole wheat or brown variety, for added fiber.

Emphasizing whole grain breads and cereals in your diet is key to increasing fiber intake. However, the traditionally high-sodium content of many whole grain products, including breads and other baked goods, can be difficult to fit into a low-sodium diet. An answer to this challenge is *The No-Salt, Lowest-Sodium Baking Book*, which is filled with creative low-sodium recipes for breads, muffins, cookies, and cakes.

More good news: If you have access to *The No-Salt, Lowest-Sodium Cookbook*, you will notice that in The Sample Four-Week Menu Planner each menu is designed to provide between 20 and 30 grams of dietary fiber a day. In general, each bread, muffin, cookie, or cake recipe in this cookbook can be easily substituted for its like in The Sample Four-Week Menu Planner. You can also try experimenting with whole grains in some of the recipes and don't limit yourself to just whole wheat. For example, try adding oat bran to cookies and muffins, or be creative with millet, buckwheat, flax, barley, bulgur, and triticale in bread.

As with any change in your health regimen, please check with your health care professional before increasing the fiber content of your current diet. Eating more dietary fiber requires drinking more fluids. Rare cases of intestinal obstruction have occurred in people with preexisting gastrointestinal problems and in individuals consuming high amounts of fiber supplements in a dry, unhydrated form. If you have been advised to limit your fluid intake or are on diuretics, be sure to consult with your physician regarding increasing the fiber content of your diet.

What about taking a fiber supplement instead of eating fiber-rich foods? Unless recommended by your physician, it is generally healthier to eat fiber in foods than take a pill. Keep in mind that fiber supplements may reduce the body's ability to absorb digoxin, a medication used to regulate heart function. Therefore, you should not take fiber supplements at the same time as this medication. While fiber supplements may help to regulate blood sugar levels, they may also interfere with the absorption of your antidiabetic medications, specifically glyburide and metformin. Therefore, you should not take fiber supplements at the same time as your antidiabetic medications. If you must take a fiber supplement, please consult with your physician for the best timing to take the supplement.

Remember, moderation is key when adding fiber to your diet. It's better to eat a wide variety of foods than just to add a single high-fiber food, such as oat bran. Eating a wide variety of foods will furnish far better nutrition, since different kinds of dietary fiber provide different benefits.

BREAD MACHINES AND BREAD BAKING

❖ ❖ ❖ ❖ ❖ ❖ ❖ ❖

When I worked in Hollywood the phrase "Trust me on this one" was really a signal that the listener was about to get hoodwinked. But I mean it honestly when I say "Trust me on this one." *The bread machine has made bread making a whole lot easier, and surprisingly, it has helped make the bread much better*

Bread machines can do it all:

- Mix the ingredients
- Knead the dough
- "Rise" the dough
- Bake the dough . . . or you can use it to do just part of the job— remove the dough after it has been mixed and kneaded (and, if desired, risen) and form your own breads by hand, from baguettes to cinnamon rolls to bagels, pizza bases, or bread loaves.

In my opinion, both methods of baking bread—machine and hand baking—have something to be said for them but for the heart patient, there is a huge plus in using the machine for kneading. Most of the recipes in this book call for kneading in the machine, although my recipes can be made by hand as well. The main reason I use the bread machine for kneading is that this book was designed for those with heart disease. Although the term "heart disease" can mean different things to different patients, it almost always involves a loss of enduring physical strength. Some patients even only have the use of one arm or one hand and some must rely on the help of others. For a heart patient, there is a huge plus in using the machine for kneading.

Since most of the sodium in regular bread comes directly from the salt used in the mixture (2,350 mg sodium per level teaspoon), no-salt bread might seem to present a problem, and adjustments do have to be made. Salt, which is the principal flavor in ordinary bread, actually slows the fermentation of the yeast. The recipes are designed with that in mind.

Do not use "salt substitutes" in baking bread by either method. They won't work. Salt inhibits yeast, so most regular bread recipes have more yeast in them than we need. Our salt-free recipes have been tested for the amount of yeast listed. Any more and the bread may "explode" on you and collapse. When we remove the salt from bread recipes, we need to reduce the amount of yeast. Sometimes, if your bread doesn't rise properly or if it collapses, change to the "rapid bake" cycle to keep the fast-rising yeast from overworking.

One advantage of the bread machine is that you don't have to "proof" the yeast, as you do using the old method. Just set the warmed liquid ingredient(s) into the pan first, follow with the flour and other dry ingredients, and set the yeast in a dry spot on the top. Voilà!

The machine's consistently better rise is because the bread machine provides a draft-free environment that never gets too hot or too cold. Another plus is that dough comes out better when we use the bread machine knead cycle than when we hand-knead it. This is because the machine is even-handed and ensures that all ingredients are mixed well. It also provides a controlled temperature for the first rise.

Bread machines are quite easy to operate. Just follow our recipes. Begin with the ingredients: put them into the pan of your machine, liquids first, then flour, and yeast on the top. Insert the pan into the machine, close the lid, set the machine for whatever setting the recipe calls for, and press START.

Most machines take about 1½ hours to knead and perform the first rise. If you've set the machine just to mix and knead the dough, remove it after the kneading and press down the dough (never "punch" down dough). Shape it into loaves, buns, rolls, or whatever other baked foods you are making. Cover it with a light cloth or waxed paper and let rise again outside the machine, covered, for about 45 minutes. Bake in your oven at the suggested temperature.

If you plan to do the whole process from mixing through to baking in the bread machine, simply put in the ingredients, turn the machine on, and wait the usual three-plus hours. Remove the baked bread from the pan when the whole job is done. Of course, smaller foods like buns and rolls must be shaped by hand.

Each machine is a bit different. Some will take longer to knead;

some will take longer to bake. Baking temperatures also vary. During the kneading period feel free to open the lid and make sure there is enough liquid for the ball to form. (But never open the machine after the baking cycle starts.) If it's too sticky (unless it is a sweet bread, which is sticky by nature), add a little bit of flour, enough for the bread to become pliable without the stickiness.

Many of the recipes in this book call for 5 cups flour (my bread machine will make up to 6 cups). That quantity of flour bakes into a 2- to 2½-pound loaf. My recipes often use all this amount because it allows you to make enough bread for a week or so at one session, freezing most of it and taking out just what is needed at any one time. That's better than spending 3½ hours a couple of times a week just to make a 16-slice single loaf. With a machine, it takes no more time to make a large recipe than a small one. And bread, as you know, freezes well and easily.

The best way to make sure each of our recipes produces good results is to check the dough after the mixing cycle has begun, adding water or flour as seem to be needed.

Our recipes were designed using a Breadman TR810, a machine that I have personally come to like and trust over all others. It's the most reliable machine I've used and the easiest. (I have also used the Panasonic/National, Oster, West Bend, Welbilt, Williams Sonoma, and Zojirushi, and others.) The price for a double-paddle Breadman machine at this writing ranges from $99 to $149, depending upon where you find it and whether or not it's on sale. Generally around Christmastime these machines are advertised with a sale price. The factory backs up their machines within the warranty period with no questions asked. There are other good machines, but the inexpensive ones are not very good ones, even though they may come from a reputable manufacturer. In this case, you do get what you pay for. Whatever brand you decide to buy, I highly recommend a double-paddle type.

Everyone to whom I've recommended a machine has thanked me and told me it was worth every dollar spent.

Converting from Bread Machine to Making Bread by Hand

The only change in converting a bread machine recipe to a hand-knead recipe is the way you handle the yeast. To use a bread machine recipe to make handmade bread, just dissolve the yeast in warm (not hot) water with a pinch or so of sugar (not too much sugar, since too much will slow the yeast down, or even kill it; it makes the bread hard and thicker). (If you have trouble with your loaves collapsing, some manuals might tell you just the opposite. But they have it backwards.) Mix in the liquid, then knead. Bake the loaf in a bread pan in a preheated oven at 350°F. for up to 30 minutes. A 3-cup recipe makes a 1-pound loaf of bread—use an 8.5 × 4.5-inch loaf pan. If you are making one of our recipes calling for 5 or 6 cups of flour, use two of the pans that size.

To make a yeast "ball," or "foam," I usually use whatever liquid is in the recipe—water, orange juice, or whatever I've chosen. Never use tap water unless your water comes from a well. City water is loaded with chlorine and chlorine can kill yeast. (It will also nullify a sourdough starter.) Use ¼ to ½ cup of the liquid. Heat it to 110°F. either in your microwave or on top of the stove. It doesn't take much heating since it's probably already at room temperature. Stir in the yeast and a pinch or more of sugar to get the yeast started.

You can also add dry active yeast into the flour without doing the above. If you do, raise the temperature of the liquid about 10 to 15 degrees.

Always use the amount of yeast the recipe calls for. But if you want to make a double recipe, don't double the yeast; use 1½ times the amount. Conversely, in cutting a recipe in half, remember that in these recipes without salt the less yeast, the better the rise. If a recipe calls for 1 tablespoon yeast (which is 3 teaspoons) and you want to cut the recipe in half, use 2 teaspoons yeast.

CONVERTING FROM HANDMADE TO BREAD MACHINE BAKING

To convert the other way, use bread machine yeast and place it dry on top of the flour in the machine.

RISING THE DOUGH

After you form the dough into the shape of whatever you are baking, you'll want to put it to rise in an area that is about 75°F. to 90°F. Not much warmer and not much cooler. If you have a cold house, heat your oven slightly. Or, if you have an old-fashioned gas oven with a pilot light, you can rise the bread in it. The pilot will give you the right warmth. (Many of today's gas ovens, however, use electronic starters and have no pilot light.)

I like to heat my oven slightly, turn off the heat (about 90°F.), and let my dough rise in there. To effectively use your oven for rising time, cover each recipe lightly with oil spray, waxed paper, or a very light cloth (not oiled). If your house isn't warm, then turn on your oven at its "lowest" temperature setting for a minute or two (don't exceed 100°F.), turn it off, and set the dough inside. The temperature in the oven should be between 80°F. and 90°F. If for some reason your oven gets too hot, open the door and let it cool down for a few minutes. Then place dough in oven and close the door. Let it rise for about 45 minutes.

(Or you could do what my mother used to do. She had an old heating pad she used for her back pains. She would just set the bread in its pan or on its baking sheet onto the heating pad, plug it in, and in 1 hour she had a perfect rise.)

Another option is to refrigerate the dough in a large lightly greased mixing bowl, covered, for 12 to 24 hours on the top shelf of the refrigerator, where it's warmest. The dough will rise to a perfect height. Bring it out, press it down (never "punch" dough down), and let it rise again at room temperature. Perfect. (Room temperature is always figured at 65°F. to 75°F.)

Your dough is ready when it has doubled in size in the baking pan. Bake according to the instructions. In most cases, when the bread is done, remove it from the pan and set it on a cooling rack. Not doing this will cause the bread to turn into a "wet log."

INGREDIENTS

AUTHOR'S NOTE

Many of the ingredients called for in this book's recipes are available at your local supermarket. In addition, you can find a wealth of information about low-sodium cooking on our Web site, www.megaheart.com, including the question-and-answer section and by clicking on "chef" at that address. We welcome your letters.

FLOUR

Your choice of flour will determine your success with each recipe you select. You'll want a high-quality unbleached, unbromated flour that has at least 12 grams of protein per cup. In most of my recipes I use a "best for bread" flour or flour with a notation on the package that it is good for bread machine baking. These flours are milled with bread machine baking in mind and often contain more protein, about 20 grams per cup, and more gluten than the approximately 12 grams of protein per cup of all-purpose flour.

Wheat is the most common flour used in bread baking. It includes all-purpose flour, bread flour, whole wheat flour, and whole wheat pastry flour. It is generally rich in gluten, a protein that gives dough its elasticity and strength. When yeast and flour are mixed with liquid, and then kneaded or beaten, the gluten traps the carbon dioxide bubbles produced by the yeast.

Whole wheat flour has less gluten and makes denser loaves, which is why we often increase the gluten by adding some all-purpose or white unbleached bread flour for lighter, taller loaves. It's also why cookies, cakes, and other recipes using only whole wheat or whole wheat pastry flour must also contain baking powder or baking soda.

To make a good whole wheat bread, add bread machine white unbleached flour to the whole wheat flour. Also add 1 level tablespoon vital wheat gluten for each cup of whole wheat flour you use. Whole wheat flour has bran in it, and bran cuts the gluten strands during the rise, neutralizing them. The neutralized gluten fails to trap the carbon dioxide generated by the yeast. That is why it is difficult to make a successful bread that is 100 percent whole wheat. Without the added gluten, you'll probably get a loaf solid enough to play football with.

Whole wheat flour designed for bread machines is available in much of the West (Stone Buhr Flour), but doesn't at this writing seem to be available elsewhere. A great whole wheat flour for bread machines, though, can be found at www.bobsredmill.com or at www.truefoodsmarket.com. Purchase their standard whole wheat flour. Locally, your market carries national brands such as Pillsbury, Gold Medal, and possibly King Arthur Whole Wheat flour.

Substituting 1 cup white flour for 1 cup whole wheat flour helps to cut this effect. I use a 1:2 ratio. In a 3-cup recipe, that would be 2 cups white bread machine flour and 1 cup whole wheat flour. To that I will add only 2 teaspoons vital wheat gluten, since the white flour I use has enough in it to compensate.

A flour that is relatively new, but now widely available, is whole wheat pastry flour. This flour has a rich flavor, is higher in fiber (4 grams per ¼ cup), and rises beautifully when used with recipes calling for baking powder or baking soda. You can replace white flour in any of my muffin, waffle, cookie, pie crust, or pastry recipes with this whole wheat pastry flour. I use whole wheat pastry flour from Bob's Red Mill, out of Oregon, but you can find this pastry flour most anywhere, from Pillsbury to other brands. Often they use the phrase "specialty flour."

For the bulk of my bread recipes I use a Montana white bread flour (Stone Buhr is one), or a flour from Bob's Red Mill in Oregon. Wheat, of course, is not the only grain from which we can produce flour. Corn, rice, rye, oats, and more are used in baking. If one is used in a recipe here, the recipe will let you know whether anything different from wheat flour is necessary.

"Risers"

Yeast

Yeast breads need just the right amount of yeast. This can be tricky. If your bread machine loaf collapses, for instance, your recipe will need an adjustment, and in most cases it's to cut the yeast measurement down. Try ½ less teaspoon the next time.

There may be another reason. During the kneading process, reach into the machine a bit and just touch the dough. If it's not slightly sticky, it's probably too dry. You may want to add 1 tablespoon liquid. If it's too wet, then this loaf may also collapse during the rise. Part of the balancing act is that we don't want dough too dry, nor do we want it too wet. If your dough is too wet, after a few minutes of kneading, slowly add more flour.

Always use bread machine yeast for recipes in this book. Do not use rapid-rise yeast. Bread machine yeast is a highly active instant yeast especially suited to breads made in bread machines. However, it also is equally effective for baking when a bread machine is not used. For instance, 2¼ teaspoons bread machine yeast is equivalent to 1 envelope dry yeast. Introduce it into bread machines in a dry state, and put it on top of dry ingredients, such as flour. I use Fleischmann's Bread Machine Yeast exclusively. I have tried all others, but Fleischmann's has been the most consistent.

BAKING POWDERS AND BAKING SODA

Some of the recipes in this book call for baking powder or baking soda rather than yeast as the rising material. For those, Featherweight Baking Powder and Ener-G Baking Soda are suggested. (Ener-G Baking Powder will not work for the recipes in this book, with the exception of cookies and muffins; use only Featherweight.) Both are low in sodium, compared to the ordinary baking powder and baking soda.

Featherweight uses potassium bicarbonate as its base. Because potassium bicarbonate produces less gas than regular baking powder, we have to use at least twice the amount and sometimes three times. If there is anything you may not like about this product, it might be the baking-powder "flavor," especially notable in white flour batter.

Ener-G Baking Soda is a calcium carbonate product. The trick is to double the amount of Ener-G over what you would normally use, and get the batter into the hot oven quickly. For your information, ½ teaspoon regular baking soda contains 629.3 mg sodium; Ener-G contains 0 mg.

And then there are some particularly tasty recipes that just won't rise enough without double-action baking powder—the baking powder most cooks think of as "regular" baking powder. Calumet or Clabber Girl double-acting baking powder will work with any recipe in this book that uses Featherweight Baking Powder. The general rule for low-sodium diets is to use a quarter of the amount of Featherweight listed. That is, if the recipe says *1 tablespoon* Featherweight, use only ¾ *teaspoon* Calumet or other double-acting baking powder. (*Note*: There are three teaspoons in a tablespoon.) Using the higher-sodium regular baking powder is up to you. If you can handle the sodium levels, then do it. It's no secret that it will make the recipe work better, but you will have to calculate the added sodium into each serving: ½ teaspoon of double-acting baking powder contains 243.8 mg; divide by the number of servings to find how much sodium it adds to each serving. And if you have a muffin you love that doesn't rise enough, try adding ¼ teaspoon (122 mg) double-action baking powder to the recipe to help give it that extra kick.

LIQUIDS

Liquid is the most critical ingredient in a bread recipe because it does two important things: it dissolves and activates the yeast, and it blends with the flour to create a sticky and elastic dough.

I use fresh or unsweetened not-from-concentrate orange juice with calcium (the kind in milk containers from Tropicana or Florida), unsweetened apple juice, prune juice, water, milk, buttermilk, and sometimes cranberry juice. Milk, buttermilk, cream, or juice may be used exclusively or together to enhance the flavor or texture. A crisper crust is made when you use water instead of milk as the liquid. (Reducing the amount of oil or unsalted butter in the recipe will also give you crusty bread.)

Nearly always add at least 1 teaspoon vital wheat gluten when the recipe has orange juice. In most of those recipes you'll find a recommendation to use gluten, or it will be in the ingredients. If you are allergic to gluten, you may leave it out and still get a great bread.

If you are converting a recipe from a book or your family secrets to a salt-free bread made in your machine or even hand-kneaded, always add 1 tablespoon apple cider vinegar and at least 1 teaspoon vital wheat gluten. If you use orange juice as your liquid, the combination of vital wheat gluten and vinegar will guarantee you a high-rise bread.

You will note that I recommend higher than room temperatures for liquids in my recipes. The reason is that only warm liquids should be added to dry ingredients in a bread machine pan; a too-cool liquid will slow or stop yeast action. I heat it up because it it is follwed by flour in the bread machine, and the flour quickly absorbs most of the heat. But caution prevails here: A too-hot liquid will destroy the yeast and prevent it from rising.

Ideal liquid temperature ranges for recipes in this book are 110°F. to 120°F. when undissolved yeast is added to dry ingredients. (For buttermilk and nonfat milk it should not be above 90°F.) In most bread machine recipes you add the yeast last, on top of dry ingredients. Temperatures for dissolving yeast directly in water range from 70°F. to 80°F. (usually you will do this when you hand knead your bread).

FLAVORINGS

Use any fresh fruits or vegetables compatible with what you are making. I use a lot of fresh diced or minced garlic, green onions with the first quarter of the green stem, shallots, red onions, green peppers, chili peppers, cinnamon, cloves, almond extract, vanilla extract. You may also add onions to any white bread recipe in this book for more flavor (¼ diced fresh onion for every 1½ cups flour).

EGGS

In my book *The No-Salt, Lowest-Sodium Cookbook*, I indicate that eggs raise the sodium and cholesterol counts. They do. Egg whites contain sodium; yolks contain cholesterol. However, new research suggests that eggs do not raise our body's cholesterol count unless you eat them by the dozen every day. Nutrients n eggs are good for us too. With their protein (11 g), energy, and flavor, why should we now exclude them from otherwise great recipes? You can find more information about eggs at www.megaheart.com.

Available in some health food stores and at Healthy Heart Market is Ener-G Baking Soda, which can be used in some bread recipes to replace real eggs. We don't advise it for waffles, aebelskivers, or pancakes, however.

FATS AND OILS

I have included in the recipes some grain breads that contain a high level of fiber and a low level of fat. However, the total fat in most of my otherwise nonfat breads is not generally high in saturated fat. I use olive oil, which contains 9.95 g of monounsaturated fats among its 14 grams of total fat per tablespoon; as a comparison, unsalted butter contains nearly 8 g of saturated fat. The triglycerides of olive oil are at a very much lower level than those of butter and especially those of margarine. You can add more oil to your bread recipes (up to 1 or 2 tablespoons only) if you want a softer bread, but if you do, decrease the primary liquid by the same amount, and add the fat content in your calculations as well. (You may also replace oil in some baked goods with flaxseed meal, which is ground flaxseed. Just use twice as much flaxseed meal as the recipe lists for oil, and add up to 4 tablespoons water.) The sodium in olive and canola oil is negligible.

SWEETENERS FOR BREAD

Sugar adds flavor and color to a bread's crust. It also helps the yeast to rise when dissolved in water. Brown sugar, honey, molasses, jams, and dried fresh fruits also serve as sweeteners in some recipes.

There is a great addition to the list of dietary ingredients called Splenda Sugar Substitute. It replaces sugar without an aftertaste, and is measure for measure otherwise exactly like sugar when cooking. Splenda is not Aspartame, as some sugar substitutes like Sugar Twin are. Used in the recipes in this book to replace sugar, it will give the same results. Nutrient values of Splenda are listed per single teaspoon by the manufacturer as follows: Calories: 0, Total Fat: 0, Sodium: 0, Total Carbohydrates: 1 g, Protein: 0, Sugars: 0.

Unique Ingredients
Necessary for Many No-Salt Bread
Recipes

Buttermilk
Reduced Fat, Cultured, Reduced Sodium

The following brands supply buttermilk with 130 mg to 150 mg per cup or less. Standard buttermilks range from 260 mg to 290 mg per cup. These can generally be found at your local supermarket. The USDA lists a buttermilk with only 6 mg of sodium, but we've never found it.

Figures are based on 1 cup of skim, nonfat, or reduced fat, cultured buttermilk:

Knudsen (130 mg)
A & P (125 mg)
Borden (130 mg)
Borden Skim-Line (150 mg)
Crowley (130 mg)
Darigold Trim (130 mg)
Weight Watchers (140 mg)

One of our visitors to www.megaheart.com (LeeAnn Sutherland) brought a great low-sodium buttermilk to our attention. It's Bob's Red Mill Dry Buttermilk Powder. A cup of reconstituted buttermilk contains 85 mg of sodium if you use distilled bottled water, and only 1 gram total fat (compared to about 4.9 grams fat in regular 1% buttermilk). For more updates of ingredients including this product, visit www.megaheart.com. If you can't find Bob's Red Mill Buttermilk Powder locally, visit www.healthyheartmarket.com or www.bobsredmill.com.

If you need to, you may replace buttermilk with distilled water or nonfat milk in these recipes—just add a tablespoon of lemon juice and Don's Bread Dough Enhancer, or a commercial enhancer if you prefer. If you are allergic to eggs, then leave the egg out and add 3 tablespoons of water per egg to the mix, or use Ener-G's Egg Replacer, following package instructions.

The following items are obtainable via the Internet or by telephone. They are available locally in some cases, but generally they are, at this writing, more difficult to locate locally than by simply calling Healthy Heart Market at 1-888-685-5988. Or visit www. healthyheartmarket.com.

ENER-G BAKING SODA
NECESSARY ITEM (AVAILABLE FROM HEALTHY HEART MARKET)

Ener-G Baking Soda is a calcium carbonate product. To understand the way it works I had to test it over and over. In the end I figured out we had to double the amount of Ener-G over what we would normally use, and we had to get the batter into the hot oven quickly. ½ teaspoon of regular baking soda contains 629.3 mg.

FEATHERWEIGHT BAKING POWDER
NECESSARY ITEM (AVAILABLE FROM HEALTHY HEART MARKET) SEE Q&A FOR USE OF REGULAR BAKING POWDER IN MUFFINS, CAKES AND COOKIES

Featherweight uses potassium bicarbonate as its base. Because potassium bicarbonate produces less gas than regular baking powder, we have to use at least twice the amount and sometimes three times. If there is anything you may not like about this, it might be the "flavor," especially noted in white flour batter/dough.

FLAXSEED MEAL

Flaxseed Meal is amazingly high in fiber with only ¼ cup providing 6 grams of fiber. It's also been credited with fighting colon and breast cancer tumors and lowers the bad cholesterol (LDL). Flaxseed Meal with a small measure of water can replace oil, butter, or margarine. Flaxseed Meal will also add a nuttier flavor to your breads. It's great with waffles, pancakes, muffins, and quick breads, and with whole wheat or other grain breads. It's also great to mix in with your cold cereal. A formula for replacing oils or shortening is a 3-to-1 ratio. For instance, replace ½ cup of butter, oil, or other shortening with 1½ cups flaxseed meal. Add about ¼ to ½ cup liquid when you make this exchange. When substituting flaxseed for shortening, the baked good may brown more rapidly.

ENER-G EGG REPLACER

Available in some health food stores and from the Web site www. healthyheartmarket.com, this product can be used in some bread recipes to replace real eggs. Not advised for waffles, aebleskivers, or pancakes.

FLOUR AND GRAIN

For the bulk of my bread recipes, I use a Montana White Bread Flour or a flour from Bob's Red Mill in Oregon. This book also uses the following specialty items from Bob's Red Mill. Each of these is available from www.healthyheartmarket.com.

White flour, organic
Oat flour
Whole wheat pastry flour
Whole wheat flour
7-grain cereal
10-grain cereal
Oats rolled, regular old fashioned
Oats rolled, quick cooking

SOURDOUGH STARTER

Probably one of the most misunderstood ingredients, sourdough can be both a great pleasure to work with and a frustrating one. You can learn how to make Sourdough Starter in this book. See page 57.

COMMERCIAL BREAD DOUGH ENHANCER

First brought to my attention by www.megaheart.com member Jon Vena, a journalist who resides in New Jersey, this commercial product improves the rise, taste, texture, color crumb, and shelf life of whole grain breads. Natural ingredients include vital wheat gluten, diastatic malt, and ascorbic acid. The wheat gluten strengthens and conditions the dough and is especially important when baking with whole wheat, rye, buckwheat, barley, and other whole grain flours that do not contain as much gluten as white flour does. The ascorbic acid (Vitamin C) and diastatic malt act as yeast activators that insure your yeast yields the maximum rise. Comes in an attractive 10 oz can with instructions and recipes included. Obtainable on the web at http://www.armchair.com/store/gourmet/bal.html. The bread enhancer has a trace of sodium.

SPICES, FLAVORS, AND THINGS

I like to use some of the spice mixes from a company called Oregon Flavors Rack, out of Eugene, Oregon. You can find their products at www.spiceman.com. Their Garlic Lovers Garlic and Italian Herbs Mix are great for breads. They also have Sensational Onion & Herbs and a great Lemon & Herb mix that works well.

Other flavors to add to breads include caraway seeds, poppy seeds, sesame seeds, cinnamon, rosemary, diced onions, cranberries (cooked or raisins), and citrus fruits.

FOR BREAD MAKING EQUIPMENT I RECOMMEND:

Breadman TR-810 double paddle bread machine
Braun 550 Hand Mixer, food processor, puree machine (all in one)
Either Sunbeam or Kitchen Aid double blade beater
Wooden spoons
Plastic scraper
Set of mixing bowls
Muffin tins
Bread pans
Baguette pans
Cookie sheets, heavy duty
Bread board

SOURCE OF NUTRIENT DATA USED IN THIS BOOK

The nutrient and sodium values in this cookbook are based on the most recent data supplied by the Food and Drug Administration (FDA), by the United States Department of Agriculture (USDA), and by manufacturers of many of the food products we use. We used a USDA-based software program called Foodworks, from The Nutrition Company, to list calories and all other nutrients.

Please see *The No-Salt, Lowest-Sodium Cookbook* for more explanations concerning FDA and USDA listings and FDA food labels.

OVENS

PREHEATING TIME

Many ovens take upwards of 20 minutes to come to cooking/baking temperature. If you put a recipe into your oven and it doesn't bake properly, you may well have not waited long enough for it to heat, or your oven's temperature may not match your digital or analog gauge. Some manufacturers have set their digital gauges to come to temperature before their ovens do. Use an oven thermometer to test yours and learn how long it really takes. Bread recipes work best when put into an oven that is at the recommended temperature. Also, ovens aren't constant They don't arrive at 350°F., for instance, and stay there They can rise as high as 450°F., then drop to 250°F., then rise again. All this is planned for in the recipe's suggested baking temperature, but you still should be aware of it If you try the thermometer, you'll know to put the dough in when the desired temperature is reached.

CONVECTION OVENS

Convection ovens use different temperatures and different cooking times. The formula is unique and available in your oven's manual. In a few recipes in this book I suggest convection oven times, but not in many. That's because I tested the recipe in both types of ovens and in some cases it made no difference.

THE EFFECT OF WEATHER ON BREAD BAKING

❖ ❖ ❖ ❖ ❖ ❖ ❖ ❖

If the weather is changing and a low pressure area is coming in, your bread will probably not rise as much as on a day when the pressure is high or climbing. (A barometer will let you know if weather is changing, and how.) The effect of a weather change on breadmaking will be a surprise to you, especially if you've not made your own bread before.

Weather can beat up the dough in your bread machine, too. The great thing about making bread by hand is that we can feel if the "sponge," the ball of dough, is too wet or too dry. Remember to open up your bread machine three or four times during the first 10 minutes of kneading to see what's going on and whether or not your dough needs help (Yes, you may open your machine, in spite of what your manufacturer might have written in the manual.) Flour sucks up liquid quickly, some flours more than others. If your weather is dry or humid, it will have a major affect on your sponge. If the dough turns out too dry, add more liquid (1 tablespoon at a time); if it's too wet, add more flour.

BAKING AT HIGH ALTITUDES

This is for those of you who live 3,000 feet above mean sea level or higher.

I was a pilot for many years, flying at high altitudes with proper oxygen equipment but no pressurization. I didn't do any baking up there, but I could feel the difference because of the changes in my breathing. Those changes affect our baking also.

High-Altitude Baking Adjustments

Ingredient	*3,000 feet*	*5,000 feet*	*6,500 feet*
Yeast	½ teaspoon less less for every tablespoon or ⅓ teaspoon less for each 2¼-teaspoon package	Same as 3,000 feet	Same as 3,000 feet
Liquid	1 tablespoon more per cup	2 to 3 tablespoons more per cup	3 to 4 tablespoons more per cup
Sugar	1 tablespoon less per cup	2 tablespoons less per cup	3 tablespoons less per cup
Flour	1 tablespoon more per cup	2 tablespoons more per cup	3 tablespoons more per cup
Ener-G Baking Soda	¼ teaspoon less per teaspoon	½ of what recipe calls for	½ of what recipe calls for
Featherweight Baking Powder	¼ teaspoon less per teaspoon	½ of what recipe calls for	½ of what recipe calls for
Oven	25° more for all elevations above 3,000 feet, including convection ovens		

High-altitude cooking demands a need for experimenting through trial and error.

It's impossible for me to explain how to adapt each recipe for every altitude, so here are some general points to begin with.

Most bread machine manufacturers detail how to handle high altitude problems and challenges. But to allow for your dough springing up in the oven right away, put the shaped, risen dough in the oven just *before* your bread or rolls double in size. Test your recipes by using the amount of yeast the recipe lists without adjusting that amount. Then, if putting the risen dough into the oven before it doubles doesn't work (that is, if it still rises quickly and then collapses), try cutting the yeast back by 15 to 20 percent.

For recipes calling for whipped egg whites, whip the egg whites until they are just stiff and fold in nicely. The egg whites will help form air bubbles.

I have not yet learned a rule for Featherweight Baking Powder and Ener-G Baking Soda at high altitude. Regular baking powder and baking soda that high would be reduced by as much as 60 percent, depending upon your distance above sea level. If you live in Leadville, Colorado, for instance, you might even reduce it more. When you finally get the correct formula, write it down in your cookbook. You'll be happy you did.

The table on page 26 will help you if you live at 3,000 feet above sea level or higher. These figures are based or a no-salt baking routine.

TROUBLESHOOTING THE INEVITABLE FAILURES

❖ ❖ ❖ ❖ ❖ ❖ ❖ ❖

Nobody ever fails, we just learn a lot." That's a quote from my father. He sure was right on the money when i comes to making bread. You can expect collapsed loaves, hard loaves, inedible loaves and buns, but once you figure out your flour's capabilities, you'll have nearly 100 percent successes. You may even be lucky and bat 1.000 right from the get-go. If not, here are some tips for what may happen to your bread. These tips work for either a bread machine or handmade bread. They are listed from the most popular "failures to the least."

BREAD IS FLAT

The dough was not kneaded enough or the yeast may have not dissolved properly. Also, not enough flour will cause this problem.

HOLES IN THE BREAD

This is nearly always restricted to handmade bread. It's because hand kneading isn't as perfect an art as machine kneading. When kneading, all of the air was not completely pressed out of the dough while the loaves or buns were being shaped. It's also caused by dough rising too long before the baking period.

Dry, Coarse Grain

Another hand-kneading problem. Too much flour was added and the dough was not kneaded enough. Again, the rising time may have been too long or the oven temperature too low.

Bread Is Doughy and Wet Inside

For hand kneading, it's probably because of insufficient rising time. For bread machines, it may be for the same reason or it may be caused by either too much sugar or not enough yeast.

Bread Is Wet on the Bottom

Wet or doughy bottoms are generally caused by not being removed from the pans quickly and then allowed to cool on a rack.

Bread Doesn't Brown Evenly

In oven baking, which we also recommend even though your machine kneads the dough, this can be caused by a bright pan like an aluminum pan, which reflects the heat away from the sides and top. It can also be due to uneven heat in your oven from poor placement of the pan or from overcrowding, with too many pans in the same oven.

Bread Collapses or Falls

Too much rise in the dough or too much leavening action—when this happens it gets too light and falls back into itself. Fix it by one of the following methods: Decrease the liquid or cut the sugar in half. You can also try cutting the yeast (but not all these things at the same time). Adding 1 tablespoon olive oil may also help.

Dough Doesn't Rise

There are too many reasons to list them all, but the main one is often that the yeast is too old. Second in line is cold water or water not warm enough to activate the yeast, or it may be too hot and kill the yeast. The third biggest reason is the location for the rise was too cool (or too hot). The fourth is usually a hand-knead problem: the dough is just too stiff or has too much flour; it must remain elastic at all times. Solution: Test the yeast. If it's "dead," then redo recipe with fresh yeast.

Thick Crust

This is generally caused by too much flour but may also be caused by insufficient rising time or a too-low baking temperature. This may also happen in a bread machine if the right settings aren't made. The solution is to cut the flour by ¼ cup at the next attempt.

Bread Cracks or Breaks on Top

Generally, this is a handmade bread problem, meaning the dough was not mixed well or that it was too stiff. Also, bread will crack if cooled too quickly or left in an open draft to cool.

Dense Bread

This is my favorite problem. It's because when I develop new recipes this happens a lot. It's usually caused by too much flour, not a long enough rising time, or by flours that aren't designed for standard recipes, like rye flour, rice flour, whole wheat flour, and others. All-purpose unbleached flour can also do this. Stick with the bread flours. Solve this problem by adding some vital wheat gluten (about 1 teaspoon or 1½ teaspoons if it's a grain bread). Substitute some grain or whole wheat flour for the white bread flour.

Bread Is Too Small

Check your ingredient quantities. You may need to add more high gluten flour, yeast, sugar or water. Is your yeast and flour fresh? Also check the water and room temperatures. If either is too cold, your bread might not rise as high.

LOW-SODIUM
SUBSTITUTES

◈ ◈ ◈ ◈ ◈ ◈ ◈ ◈

Salt substitutes that will help bread or other baked goods do not exist at this writing. But there are substitutes for baking powder and baking soda.

For other substitutions I recommend each one that's available in each recipe where I feel there might be a need for it. However, as a review I list those here, too. Many of these that are not readily available at our local grocery store are available at www.healthyheartmarket.com (1-888-685-5988).

Acidity ingredient (sometimes referred to as "bread enhancer")—cider vinegar; lemon juice; buttermilk

Baking powder—Featherweight Baking Powder

Baking soda—Ener-G Baking Soda

Black seedless raisins—Golden seedless raisins; dried cranberries; currants; date bits, SunMaid Baking raisins

Bread improver/bread enhancer—Replaces salt in bread as a leavening agent and provides for a higher rise that brings about a better texture. Use when gluten is very low in the flour. I also recommend using when bread recipes with added fruits and nuts use water instead of orange juice. See Don's Own Bread Dough Enhancer (page 100).

Brown sugar—Twin Sugar Substitute (brown) Splenda Sugar Substitute.

Butter—Unsalted butter; olive oil; applesauce; cranberry sauce; flaxseed meal (two times the recipe amount with some added water.)

Buttermilk—You can use buttermilk powder if you want to set a bread machine timer overnight to make a bread requiring buttermilk. When doing so, follow the buttermilk powder instructions on the package for making the correct amount of liquid your recipe calls for. Set the dry powder on top of the dry flour when waiting overnight. We prefer buttermilk powder from Bob's Red Mill, available at www.bobsredmill.com.

Cereal/grains—Use commercially packaged grains from the various companies. Read the labels to make sure they haven't added salt. We use Bob's Red Mill products, out of Oregon. Go to www.bobsredmill.com

Cheeses—An excellent low-sodium cheddar (10 mg per ounce), can be found at www.heluvagood.com. Low sodium Gouda, Muenster, and Monterey can be found at http://www.koshercheese.com/pg-3.htm.

Diabetic recipes—Each recipe we converted for use for diabetics has a listing at the top whether or not it's adaptable. When considering using sugars or not, also consider that bread dough enhancers that have diastatic malt in them are converting starch to sugar.

Dry milk solids—I recommend not using dried milk unless you add the increased sodium levels and can afford them. Dried milk powder is often used in bread machine recipes when you want to set the overnight timer for early-morning baking. It is not recommended that you use regular milk or buttermilk and let it sit overnight. However, when using orange juice, or even water, dried milk is not necessary.

Eggs—Ener-G Egg Replacer is usable in the recipes in this book, but it is not nutritionally the same. It lowers the sodium appreciably, but it also cuts out protein, which is needed. It's used for baking purposes only. It cannot be used to make scrambled eggs and it cannot be whipped. Available at www.healthyheartmarket.com.

Ketchup for burgers, sandwiches, etc.—Hunt's No Salt Added; Heinz No Salt Added at your market; Enrico's Low Sodium (available at www.healthyheartmarket.com).

Liquid for bread recipes—Water; milk; unsweetened orange juice fortified with calcium; low-sodium buttermilk; unsweetened apple juice (pure).

Maple syrup—Use natural 100% maple syrup only, none of the imitations.

Molasses—Brown sugar, Twin Sugar substitute (brown).

Mustard—For burgers, sandwiches, etc., use East Shore; Mendocino; or other brands found in stores with low sodium ratings. Grey Poupon has a low-sodium mustard.

Oil—Extra virgin olive oil (but not "light olive oil" since this oil has little body and an absence of flavor); applesauce; unsalted butter; cranberry sauce; flaxseed meal; fresh shredded carrots. Never use margarine because of its very high triglycerides.

Raisins—Fresh shredded carrots, crushed pineapple in its own juice.

Salt—apple cider vinegar (for extended shelf life); yeast combined with sugar, vital wheat gluten, and apple cider vinegar in recipe ingredients (for leavening).

Sourdough—See our Sourdough Starter recipe (page 57).

White granulated sugar Splenda Sugar Substitute.

When new substitutes come to market, they will be posted at www.megaheart.com.

BREAD MAKING FOR PEOPLE WITH DIABETES

❖ ❖ ❖ ❖ ❖ ❖ ❖ ❖

If you have questions about diabetes and your diet, you should consult a Registered Dietitian (R.D.). Bring along *The No-Salt, Lowest-Sodium Cookbook* and this cookbook, and your dietitian will be able to help tailor your daily diet to your tastes and lifestyle.

Diabetes is a disease that affects the way the body turns food into energy. Normally the body changes carbohydrates, or sugars and starches, and other foods eaten into blood glucose (sugar), which is then used by the body as fuel for energy. Insulin, a hormone produced by the pancreas, helps glucose enter the body's cells. Once inside cells, glucose is changed into energy and used immediately or stored for later use.

In diabetes, something interferes with this process—either the body does not make enough insulin or the body cannot use the insulin correctly. When glucose is not able to enter the cells, it builds up in the bloodstream. If left untreated, high levels of blood sugar may cause heart disease, stroke, blindness, kidney failure, or loss of circulation to the feet and legs, leading to amputation.

If you have diabetes and must restrict or monitor your carbohydrate intake then you will find the recipes in his book usable where listed as "Adaptable for Diabetics." You know your optimal carbohydrate intake, so we have developed recipes where you may exchange high-sugar foods (such as raisins) with other non-sugar foods or leave them out altogether. (See suggested the bread recipe substitutions for diabetics in the following section.)

Some of the recipes are marked "Not Adaptable for Diabetics." Usually these recipes did not fare well when we tested them with a sugar substitute. Omitting the sugar-containing ingredients destroyed the integrity and flavor of the recipe. *The recipes with no reference to diabetes are those that you can experiment with; the substitution may or may not work for you. I did not want to be the judge in these cases.*

Every recipe in this book that says it is "Adaptable for Diabetics" has been baked with the sugar substitute Splenda and the final product was found to be just as good as when it was made with regular sugar.

In general, when a recipe uses sugar (white or brown), you may replace the white sugar with Splenda and in some cases Splenda can replace brown sugar as well. Where Splenda does not work in place of brown sugar, I have listed Twin Sugar Brown (however, this product can leave a bitter aftertaste). *Note*: I have found replacing brown sugar with Splenda and a drop or two of maple syrup to be successful in some recipes but not all.

Yeast will also work with Splenda. I've tested it over and over and never had a failure. Use the same amount of Splenda in each recipe that it lists for sugar.

Carbohydrates, or more specifically sugar content, are listed with each recipe. None of these listings should be confused with FDA figures on packages. For instance, raisin packages will list 29 grams sugars per ¼ cup. However, the actual sugar content is 26.3 grams per ¼ cup. This type of discrepancy can be found with most packaged foods or ingredients.

We also learned that you can find "soft" nutrient numbers for fruits and vegetables much closer than you may have thought. In fact, the information is at your local supermarket. All supermarkets are required under the FDA Labeling Act to have nutrition information available for all produce. It may be on a sign, on a wall chart, or in a notebook, but it is required. You can look up anything the store carries. Remember, these are "soft" (food label accuracy) numbers. They reflect nothing about the origin or ripeness of the fruit, which has a strong influence on sugar content, but they may be better than nothing when considering your nutritional needs.

Aside from our raisin effort, we caution you to read all package food labels carefully. Check the serving size when reading the nutrient values.

Suggested Substitutions
to Modify Recipes in this Book
for Diabetes

Measurements are based on per cup *sugar* level. To get the sugar count for 1 tablespoon, divide the cup amount by 16.

Sugar, white, granulated (198 g)—Splenda (0 mg)

Orange juice with calcium (24.9 g)—Low-sodium buttermilk (9 g), no-sodium bottled water (trace).

Blueberries, frozen, unsweetened (18.9 g carbohydrates). (No replacement suggested. USDA has not released the sugars count.)

Raisins, seedless, golden or black, not packed (105.2 g)—Substitute: Raisins are an optional use, possibly replace them with chopped nuts for flavoring. Use unsalted walnuts, pecans, or almonds. Also, you may substitute an equal amount of fresh shredded carrots for the raisins and get the added benefit of beta carotene from the carrots.

Oranges (8.5 g per cup) Nothing replaces an orange.

Orange peel or zest (1.5 g carbohydrates per tablespoon)—Orange peel's sugar depends on how it has been treated. If it has been zested right off a fresh orange, the sugar content is probably very low or negligible in a 100 g portion (FDA standard for establishing nutrient values for all foods and ingredients). On the other hand, if it has been candied for use in baking, it is probably almost entirely sugar. There are no hard sugar numbers for orange peel.

Buttermilk (9 g sugars, 10 g carbohydrates)—Substitute same amount of no-sodium water or 2 teaspoons Ener-G Baking Soda.

Apples (sauce, sliced, or eating)—One medium apple equals 17.5 grams total sugars; 1 cup sliced apples equals 14.5 grams total sugars. Apples are difficult to replace or substitute. Flaxseed meal may be used to replace oil, butter, or applesauce. When doing so, replace by using twice the amount of flaxseed meal, which has zero sugars.

Dates—1 cup chopped dates has 124.6 grams total sugar and 130.8 grams carbohydrates. There really are no replacements or substitutes for dates that will work with recipes in this book.

Prunes—No substitute. 1 cup prunes has 124.6 grams total sugar.

Lemons—Substitute like amounts of apple cider vinegar. Lemons have 3.78 grams total sugar for 1 lemon.

BAKING AT HOME

W hen you are preparing any meals or baking any breads, cakes, muffins, or cookies, always remember we are doing it now for our efforts to regain or manage our health. Healthy people, who eat for their health, are doing so to stay healthy. We now know, even more than many of our healthy friends might know, just what we must do to achieve a known goal from a position of threatened health. Many of us who lived "healthy" lifestyles before our diagnosis found it confusing when trying to grasp what happened. Denial may have been your first reaction, since you did live according to the "rules." But the rules have changed for us, and now we have to do nearly everything differently—including accepting different flavors in some cases, and different textures in others. In the end, however, we have perfected what we need in order to live a healthier lifestyle, and that's important.

The upside is, it can be done. If we stick to our balanced eating plan and low sodium in combination with our medications, and exercise each day, we will improve our chances for a longer, healthier life.

In all cases, however, whatever your target goal for sodium a day is, whether it's 500 mg or 2500 mg, it's important to consult with your registered dietitian (R.D.) or your cardiologist beforehand.

I hope that I've been helpful in providing you enough material to help you along on that trail to improved health. If ever you have questions about this book, or the recipes in this book, or any of your own recipes, please don't hesitate to e-mail me at chef@ megaheart.com. Best of bread baking to you. Enjoy!

THE RECIPES

BREAD

❖ ❖ ❖ ❖ ❖ ❖ ❖ ❖

NOTE: Many of the recipes in the Bread section can also be adapted for muffins or buns. See recipe descriptions for details.

❖ FRENCH BREAD AND BAGUETTES ❖

WITHOUT SOURDOUGH
BREAD MACHINE KNEAD—HAND SHAPE—OVEN BAKE
ADAPTABLE FOR DIABETICS

Baguettes were my favorite before my heart decided they weren't. French bread, too, had been high on my list. Unfortunately, both baguettes and French bread normally have more salt that other breads—nearly twice as much. So much so that if after just a few months on a no-salt diet you bit into a piece, you'd probably spit it out. It tastes that salty. I tried for three years to make the "perfect" clone, but until I arrived at this recipe, I just couldn't get it right. This is as close as we can come to making a sweet French bread without the salt, and as requested by some www.megaheart.com visitors, without the sourdough. Yet the texture, crust, and flavors are very similar. For a sourdough baguette, see our Sourdough Baguette recipe.

MAKES 2 FRENCH BREAD LOAVES   MAKES 3 TO 4 BAGUETTES
MAKES 40 1-INCH SLICES   SODIUM PER RECIPE: 126.7 MG
SODIUM PER SLICE: 3.167 MG

  1 cup (70°F. to 80°F.) bottled water (trace)* at room temperature
¼ cup white granulated sugar (.5 mg)
  1 tablespoon apple cider vinegar (.15 mg)
  2 large eggs (109.5 mg), whites only

*May exchange 1% reduced fat cultured buttermilk or orange juice for the cup of water. See the "Unique Ingredients" section (page 17) for a brand available in your area. Sodium will increase by 130 mg for whole recipe.

¼ **cup extra virgin olive oil (trace)**
1 **tablespoon grated orange or lemon zest, grated (.36 mg)**
4 **cups bread machine flour (10 mg)**
2 **teaspoons vital wheat gluten (1.5 mg)**
1 **tablespoon bread machine yeast (6 mg)**
1 **tablespoon cornmeal (.258 mg)**

If you have a baguette or French loaf pan, please use that. Otherwise, you'll shape your logs and let them rise on a baking sheet.

Place all ingredients except the cornmeal into your bread machine basket. Set the machine on Dough cycle, and after it has kneaded, roll it out onto a lightly floured bread board. Form into a large ball and place this into a large mixing bowl, lightly greased with olive oil spray. Roll the ball around in the bowl to make sure all of it picks up some of the olive oil. Cover with wax paper or a very light cloth and set in a warm place for about 2 to 2½ hours.

When the dough has risen, press it down gently as far as you can, then let it rise again for about 1 hour.

When it's ready, remove it from the bowl gently, press down, cut into two pieces if making French bread, three or four if making baguettes. Shape each French bread piece into a "log" about 16 inches long and set them into French bread pans (or the narrower baguette pans if you have them), or on a cornmeal-dusted baking sheet about 5 inches apart. Cover lightly with plastic wrap and let rise for about 30 minutes. To form baguettes, roll the dough into either two or more very long 1-inch-diameter logs and let rise. They will rise to double or triple in size. Cover and let rise in a warm area for 1 hour.

Preheat your oven to 425°F. about 15 minutes before baking.

Just before baking, make a cut with a very sharp knife lengthwise down each loaf.

Bake French bread at 425°F. for about 15 minutes, reduce heat to 375°F., and bake for another 20 minutes, or until golden brown. Serve hot, warm, cold, or reheated.

Bake the baguettes at 425°F. for about 15 minutes, reduce heat to 375°F., and bake for another 12 to 15 minutes, or until golden brown. Serve hot, warm, cold, or reheated.

Nutrient Values per 1-inch Slice Calories: 64.8 Protein: 1.6 g. Carbohydrate: 11.1 g. Dietary Fiber: .416 g. Total Sugars: 1.237 g. Total Fat: 1.49 g. Saturated Fat: .204 g. Monounsaturated Fat: 1.014 g. Polyunsaturated Fat: .167 g. Cholesterol: 0 mg. Calcium: 57.2 mg. Potassium: 22.5 mg. Sodium: 3.167 mg. Vitamin K: .662 mcg. Folate: 26.7 mcg.

FLEISCHMANN'S FRENCH BREAD
❖ (MODIFIED) ❖

HAND KNEAD OR MACHINE KNEAD—OVEN BAKE
GREAT FOR GARLIC TOAST
ADAPTABLE FOR DIABETICS

*This recipe was offered to us by Fleischmann's, the people
who bring us Fleischmann's Bread Machine yeast. This is
a "hand knead" recipe we have adapted for your bread
machine to knead and perform the first rise. You may
add caraway seeds to this recipe to flavor it up, or sautéed
onions or any other "improver" you like. Serve it hot. It's
very good and worth a try. Don't miss the Garlic Toast
variation below.*

MAKES 2 LOAVES   MAKES 32 SLICES
SODIUM PER RECIPE: 74.5 MG   SODIUM PER SLICE: 2.238 MG

1 **cup bottled water (trace), at 80°F. to 90°F.**
1 **tablespoon apple cider vinegar (.15 mg)**
6 **cups best for bread flour (15 mg)**
1 **tablespoon white granulated sugar (.126 mg)**
2 **teaspoons vital wheat gluten (1.5 mg)**
1 **level tablespoon fresh lemon peel, grated (.12 mg)**
1 **tablespoon Fleischmann's active dry yeast or bread machine
    yeast (6 mg)**

OPTIONAL GLAZE
1 **egg white (54.8 mg)**
  plus
1 **tablespoon cold water (trace)**

Place all ingredients except for the glaze in your large bread machine pan
and set for Dough cycle. Be prepared to remove the dough before it
begins to push against the lid of your machine.

When the dough is ready, roll it out onto a lightly floured bread board
and cut into two pieces. Roll each up into a log and place on a lightly
greased and cornmeal-dusted French bread pan or baking sheet. (A
French bread pan helps to control the shape and form a great French
bread loaf.)

Slice the dough with a sharp knife diagonally in three places. Place a
light cloth over it, let it rise in a warm place for up to 1 hour, or until it has
doubled in size.

Preheat your oven to 425°F. for a convection, 450°F. for a standard one.

Bake on the lower third rack for 20 minutes. In a standard oven, reach in and turn bread around after 10 minutes of baking.

When the bread has turned a nice golden brown, remove and set the loaves on cooling racks. Serve warm.

GARLIC TOAST VARIATION: You can make garlic toast with this bread that competes with any restaurant. Simply slice your loaf into 1-inch-wide pieces diagonally. Stir together 1 tablespoon olive oil (trace sodium) and 1 teaspoon Oregon Flavor Rack's Garlic Lover's Garlic (trace sodium) and spread on your bread slice. Then toast in your flat toaster until browned. Yum!

Nutrient Values per Slice Calories: 88.4 Protein: 2.675 g. Carbohydrate: 18.4 g. Dietary Fiber: .699 g. Total Sugars: .39 g. Total Fat: .253 g. Saturated Fat: .038 g. Monounsaturated Fat: .026 g. Polyunsaturated Fat: .097 g. Cholesterol: 0 mg. Calcium: 3.973 mg. Potassium: 31.3 mg. Sodium: 2.328 mg. Vitamin K: 0 mcg. Folate: 41.3 mcg.

❖ FRENCH ONION BREAD ❖

WITH RAW GARLIC
ADAPTABLE FOR DIABETICS

While working in Paris, I often ate at a great Basque restaurant. Great because it was local, and rustic, and by all appearances had been there longer than the U.S. has been a country. I learned to speak French in that restaurant as well as in other Paris locales. The funny thing was that by the time I moved operations to southern France, the locals were telling me I had a Paris accent. Magnifique, I thought. At least I'm speaking their language.

I consumed more of this French Onion Bread than the ubiquitous baguettes. This recipe is a favorable version of the fabulous original made in that restaurant. Bake this in your Farberware or other French bread pan. Slice the loaf diagonally and serve with pasta, or thinly slice and crisply toast for party crunchies with a dab of garlic paste or other favorite dip for your guests.

MAKES 2 LOAVES   MAKES 36 1-INCH SLICES
SODIUM PER RECIPE: 132.6 MG   SODIUM PER SLICE: 3.684 MG

  1 **cup bottled water (trace), at room temperature (70°F. to 80°F.)**
 ¼ **cup extra virgin olive oil (trace)**
  1 **tablespoon apple cider vinegar (.15 mg)**
  1 **egg white (54.8 mg)**
4¼ **cups white unbleached or best for bread flour (10.6 mg)**
  1 **teaspoon vital wheat gluten (.72 mg)**

2 teaspoons grated lemon or orange zest (.12 mg)
2 tablespoons white granulated sugar (.252 mg)
1 tablespoon bread machine yeast (6 mg)

At the sound of the raisin buzzer, add:
3 cloves garlic, raw, diced (1.53 mg)*
1 medium to large onion, chopped (4.5 mg)

THE GLAZE
1 egg white (54.8 mg)

Place the first 9 ingredients in the bread pan in the order listed. Set your bread machine for the Dough cycle. Five minutes before your raisin buzzer is supposed to sound, add the garlic and onion. When Dough cycle is completed, transfer the dough ball to a lightly oiled deep bowl and cover with plastic wrap. Let rise for 2 hours in a warm environment (75°F. to 95°F.). When it has risen, roll it out onto lightly floured bread board and cut in half. Roll each half into logs about the length of your French bread pan (average size is 15 inches). Lay into bread troughs, make 6 quick diagonal slashes with a very sharp knife evenly spaced along the length, and cover with wax paper coated with a light spritz of olive oil spray. Let rise for about 1 hour.

Preheat your oven to 375°F. 15 minutes before you are ready to bake.

For the glaze, beat the egg white until foamy.

When the dough is ready, lightly brush half the egg white across the 2 loaves. (Be careful not to knock down the risen dough; you may also brush the bread before the rise, if you prefer.) Bake the bread at 375°F. for about 20 minutes. Brush the remainder of the egg white on the bread and bake for another 10 to 12 minutes at 375°F. or until golden brown.

You may serve this bread hot out of the oven, or warmed later. It will stay fresh in sealed zipper-type bags for up to 6 days. You may freeze finished loaves and thaw later.

Nutrient Values per Slice Calories: 73.6 Protein: 1.911 g. Carbohydrate: 12.6 g. Dietary Fiber: .549 g. Total Sugars: .688 g. Total Fat: 1.668 g. Saturated Fat: .229 g. Monounsaturated Fat: 1.128 g. Polyunsaturated Fat: .19 g. Cholesterol: 0 mg. Calcium: 3.856 mg. Iron: .763 mg. Potassium: 33.1 mg. Sodium: 3.684 mg. Vitamin K: .819 mcg. Folate: 31.4 mcg.

*Optional. Provides needed calcium, and some kick to the bread dough.

❖ PANETTONE ❖

BREAD MACHINE PREPARATION—OVEN BAKE
LOW SODIUM, LOWERED FAT
FOR A SPECIAL PANETTONE, SEE OUR HOLIDAY PANETTONE RECIPE

A classic Italian bread you can find in most of Italy around Christmastime. It was a regular at our house during my childhood years. With salt it's a light bread and heavily laden with butter and dried fruit, very nearly matching a German Stolen. I've re-created this bread for our no-salt, low-sodium, and lowered-fat diets.

MAKES 1 BREAD   MAKES 16 SLICES
SODIUM PER RECIPE: 160.2 MG   SODIUM PER SLICE: 10 MG

½ cup unsweetened orange juice with pulp (1.244 mg), at room temperature (70°F. to 80°F.)
2 medium eggs (110.9 mg)
3½ cups unbleached white bread flour (8.75 mg)
1 teaspoon vital wheat gluten (.75 mg)
2 teaspoons white granulated sugar (trace)
2½ teaspoons bread machine yeast (4.5 mg)

At the raisin buzzer add:
⅔ cup grated orange zest (peel) (1.8 mg)
½ cup (not packed) golden seedless raisins (8.7 mg)
½ cup currants (5.76 mg)

Before the second rise add:
⅓ cup unsalted butter, softened (8.24 mg)
2 medium egg yolks (14.3 mg), beaten
1 teaspoon melted unsalted butter for brushing top of loaf (.156 mg)

Using oven paper, line and "butter" a loaf pan, soufflé dish, or cake pan. When lining, make sure to build a "wall" of paper above the dish or pan where the panettone will rise and shape itself. Set pans aside. If you don't have paper, use a pan that's a bit higher than normal, and lightly grease and flour the pan.

Warm the bread pan with hot water before using. Warm the orange juice to about 115°F. Place the juice, eggs, flour, gluten, sugar, and yeast into the bread machine.

At the sound of the raisin buzzer, add the orange zest, raisins, and currants. Set the machine on the Dough cycle, and after the dough is ready (rises in machine), place it on a lightly floured bread board.

Roll the dough in the softened unsalted butter and egg yolks, and knead for about 5 minutes. Transfer the dough into a lightly buttered or olive oil–greased cake pan, soufflé pan, or loaf pan. Cover with a light cloth and let rise for about 45 minutes. I place this into an oven that's been heated to about 90°F. to 100°F. and close the door. If you have a double oven, preheat the other oven to 375°F. about 1 to 15 minutes before the second rise is complete. (If you don't have a second oven, let the dough rise, remove carefully, and set covered in a warm area. Then heat the oven to 375°F.) Brush the risen dough with a light coating of unsalted butter. Using a sharp knife, scar the top of the loaf with an X or cross.

Bake for 20 minutes, then reduce the heat to 350°F. Brush the top of the loaf when you do this with a bit more unsalted butter and bake for another 18 to 30 minutes, or until golden brown. (I've had them finish baking in 18 minutes and sometimes the full 30, because I've baked them in different ovens in different locations.)

Cool in the pan for up to 10 minutes before removing the panettone. Place on a wire rack to cool. Remove paper. Serve warm, hot, or reheated.

Nutrient Values per Slice Calories: 161.7 Protein: 4.744 g. Carbohydrate: 31 g. Dietary Fiber: 1.79 g. Total Sugars: .52 g. Total Fat: 2.259 g. Saturated Fat: .873 g. Monounsaturated Fat: .705 g. Polyunsaturated Fat: .319 g. Cholesterol: 51.9 mg. Calcium: 32.3 mg. Iron: 1.799 mg. Potassium: 151.4 mg. Sodium: 10 mg. Vitamin K: .042 mcg. Folate 66.9 mcg.

❖ HOLIDAY PANETTONE ❖

BREAD MACHINE KNEAD—HAND SHAPE
NOT ADAPTABLE FOR DIABETICS

My mother's original recipe for this wonderful sweet bread has been altered for our low-sodium, lower-fat diets. Each slice of this holiday treat has fewer grams of fat and sodium than her original. Since we exchanged some of the saturated fats with mono and polyunsaturated ones, we feel a bit better about enjoying this treat— of course, in moderation. You can hand-knead this if you like, after floating the yeast in a ¼ cup of room temperature (70°F. to 80°F.) water or milk, but I recommend letting the bread machine do the kneading, or your Kitchen Aid with its paddle. I've tested two of these methods and my Breadman bread machine does a terrific job. Otherwise, hand kneading takes about 10 to 12 minutes. Most panettone bread is made in a round loaf. I like to split the dough in half and make one round and one standard loaf, offering guests their choice of sliced bread or pie-shape wedges. (Your guests will love this bread.)

MAKES 1 BREAD   MAKES 32 SLICES
SODIUM PER RECIPE: 234.3 MG
SODIUM PER SLICE (BASED ON 32 SLICES): 7.322 MG

THE DOUGH

1¼ cup orange juice not from concentrate, fortified with calcium
    (3.109 mg), at room temperature (70°F. to 80°F.)
4 tablespoons unsalted butter (6.248 mg)
4 tablespoons extra virgin olive oil (trace)
1 tablespoon apple cider vinegar (.15 mg)
2 teaspoons pure vanilla extract (.756 mg)
3 medium to large eggs (189 mg)
2 oranges, lemons, or mandarins, grated zest only (.72 mg)
5 cups best for bread white flour (12.5 mg)
2 teaspoons vital wheat gluten (1.5 mg)
¼ cup white granulated sugar (.5 mg)
1 tablespoon plus ½ teaspoon bread machine yeast or active dry
    yeast (7.98 mg)

Warm the orange juice and place into the bread machine basket. Add the butter, olive oil, vinegar, vanilla, eggs, citrus zest, flour, gluten, sugar, and yeast in the order listed.

Prepare the following while the dough is in the machine:

FRUIT MIX

⅓ cup golden seedless raisins, packed (6.534 mg)
⅓ cup diced or sliced pitted dates (1.762 mg)
½ teaspoon ground anise (.326 mg)
⅔ cup glazed cherry/pineapple mix, juice/liquid drained*
    (125 mg)
3 tablespoons slivered or sliced unsalted almonds (3.4 mg)
1 tablespoon white unbleached flour (.156 mg)

Mix the fruits and nuts together using the flour to help keep the fruit separated. You may add a bit more flour if needed.

Prepare two 9 × 5-inch loaf pans by very lightly greasing them. If doing as I do (that is, making one round loaf and one standard loaf), then lightly grease one round 8-inch or 9-inch cake pan and one loaf pan.

Set the machine on Dough cycle and when the dough is ready, turn it onto a lightly floured bread board. Slice it into two halves.† You can also make "the monster," a term used around here for a single loaf. Press down each piece until it becomes about ½-inch thick. Spread fruit mix on half of each piece and fold over. Then hand-knead about three or four times

---

*If a glazed cherry/pineapple mix isn't available in your area, use the fruit mix.
†You can also make "the monster," a term used around here for a single loaf. If making the single large loaf you'll need a panettone bread form you can purchase at most kitchen stores or at www.surlatable.com. Bake the single large round loaf at 350° F for about 40 minutes (or a bit longer if necessary).

until the fruit is evenly dispersed within the dough. Shape each ball for a round or loaf. (This dough will grow in the oven while baking. It becomes a very finely textured, almost croissant-like dough.)

Cover the dough with a light cloth or loose plastic wrap spritzed with olive oil spray, and set in a warm place (70°F. to 90°F. for rising). This will take about 1 hour.

About 15 minutes before you are ready to bake, preheat your oven to 350°F. Set the baking rack in the lower third of the oven, or, if using a convection oven, where your oven manufacturer recommends it for bread baking (not near the top however).

When bread is ready for baking, use a *very sharp* knife to slice a cross X on the top of the round loaves, or a series of two diagonal cuts or one lengthwise slice on the standard bread loaf.

Spread the top of your chosen loaves with Homemade Almond Paste mix (page 205).

Bake the two single loaves or the two standard bread loaves in the preheated oven for about 30 to 32 minutes.

Nutrient Values per Slice Calories: 239.9 Protein: 5.227 g. Carbohydrate: 35.5 g Dietary Fiber: 2.252 g. Total Sugars: 12 7 g. Total Fat: 9.186 g. Saturated Fat: 1.75 g. Monounsaturated Fat: 5.272 g. Polyunsaturated Fat: 1.662 g. Cholesterol: 23.8 mg. Calcium: 47.1 mg. Potassium: 159.9 mg. Sodium: 11.4 mg. Vitamin E: 827 mcg. Folate 53.3 mcg.

❂ ITALIAN GARLIC TOAST ❂

BREAD MACHINE RECIPE
ADAPTABLE FOR DIABETICS

Panettone is generally what we regard as "Italian bread." (See our Panettone bread recipe on page 50 for the best unsalted version.) This garlic toast recipe attempts to replicate an Italian bread often found in long rolls or loaves but always kneaded by hand and baked on bread stones in a very hot oven. This bread is best served toasted with a mix of unsalted butter and Sensational Garlic & Herb Seasoning from Oregon Flavor Rack, available from www.healthyheartmarket.com or www.spiceman.com. Makes terrific French toast also. You may freeze this bread and thaw it on the countertop or in the microwave.

MAKES 1 BREAD   MAKES 16 SLICES
SODIUM PER RECIPE 175.8 MG   SODIUM PER SLICE: 11 MG

¾ **cup plus 2 tablespoons 1% milk with calcium (107.2 mg),
   warmed to about 100°F.**
1 **tablespoon apple cider vinegar (.15 mg)**
2 **tablespoons olive oil (trace)**

1 tablespoon lemon juice (.15 mg)
1 large egg white (54.8 mg)
3 cups white unbleached bread flour (7.5 mg)
1½ teaspoons vital wheat gluten (1.2 mg)
3 cloves garlic (1.53 mg), minced
2 tablespoons white granulated sugar (.252 mg)
1 teaspoon Oregon Flavor Rack Italian Herb Blend (trace)
1 tablespoon bread machine yeast (6 mg)

ALTERNATE GARLIC MIX PER PIECE OF TOAST
1 teaspoon unsalted butter (.515 mg), melted
⅛ teaspoon Oregon Flavor Rack Garlic Lovers Garlic* (trace)

Place the ingredients into your bread machine per your manufacturer's recommendations. Otherwise combine in the order listed.

Set your machine to "Rapid White" or its equivalent, with a Medium Crust setting for a lighter crust or a Heavy Crust setting for a thick, crunchy crust. Start the machine and when bread is baked, remove and cool on rack. Slice, spread with Oregon Flavor Rack Sensational Garlic & Herb Seasoning and unsalted butter mix and toast lightly.†

Nutrient Values per Slice Calories: 115 Protein: 3.406 g. Carbohydrate: 20.6 g. Dietary Fiber: .74 g. Total Sugars: 1.559 g. Total Fat: 1.989 g. Saturated Fat: .282 g. Monounsaturated Fat: 1.281 g. Polyunsaturated Fat: .241 g. Cholesterol: .234 mg. Calcium: 21.1 mg. Potassium: 62.8 mg. Sodium: 11 mg. Vitamin K: .83 mcg. Folate: 47.2 mcg.

❄ FOCACCIA A LA GARLIC CHEESE ❄

BREAD MACHINE PREPARATION—OVEN BAKE
GREAT CHOICE FOR DIABETICS
REQUIRES 2 9- OR 10-INCH CAKE PANS, 1 MEDIUM BOWL,
2 LARGE BOWLS

Focaccia is Italian. It's a great flatbread that you can play with by changing its flavors. Simply add fresh basil or rosemary or oregano to the dough or sprinkle them on top before baking. Minced or thinly sliced and diced raw garlic sprinkled on top is a must before baking. A standard focaccia can have upwards of 6,000 mg sodium. Naturally the "real thing" tastes very, very salty. Don't worry, you'll love these, too. Add the cheese and herbs and more if you like.

*www.healthyheartmarket.com or www.spiceman.com
†Another way is to toast first and then spread the unsalted butter/garlic mix.

FOR THE BREAD MACHINE PAN
1½ cups plus 2 tablespoons unsweetened orange juice with calcium (4.04 mg). at (70°F. to 80°F.) room temperature
 3 cups white unbleached bread flour (12.5 mg)
 1 teaspoon white granulated sugar (trace)
 2 teaspoons vital wheat gluten (1.5 mg)
 1 tablespoon extra virgin olive oil (trace)
 4 garlic cloves (2.04 mg), finely diced
 1 tablespoon bread machine yeast (6 mg)

Heat the orange juice to about 80°F to 90°F. Place the ingredients in your bread machine in the order listed. Set the machine on Dough cycle and start.

FOR HAND KNEADING DOUGH AT FIRST RISE IN BREAD MACHINE
 6 oz Heluvagood low sodium cheddar cheese (60 mg)
 2 tablespoons extra virgin olive oil (trace)
 6 garlic cloves (3.06 mg), finely chopped
 2 tablespoons freshly chopped basil (or ½ teaspoon dried) (.212 mg)

Lightly oil the cake pans with 1 tablespoon of olive oil, dust with flour, and set aside.

When the first rising is completed in the machine, move dough to a lightly floured board and gently knead in ½ the grated cheese, olive oil, ½ garlic, and basil. Make sure to distribute the cheese throughout the bread and do the same with the basil. Break dough in half and form into 2 balls you can roll out with your pin. Spread each ball a bit with your hands to form a circle that matches your 9- to-10-inch cake pan. Place the dough circles in the cake pans and let rise again, covered with lightly oiled wax paper or plastic wrap, for about ½ hour.

Now comes the fun part. Take the covering wrap off and poke holes with your fingers all around the dough about 1 inch apart. Poke your fingers all the way down to the pan. Evenly sprinkle remaining ½ garlic and remaining ½ grated cheese into the holes. You may also sprinkle some on top. Cover with wax paper or a very light cloth and let rise until double in size.

Preheat your oven to 400°F. and bake for about 20 to 22 minutes, or until the loaves turn golden brown. Remove, cool or rack, and serve warm. Loaves may be reheated later. Store loaves in zipper-type bags in your refrigerator for up to 1 week.

Nutrient Values per Serving: Calories: 194.6 Protein: 7.195 g. Carbohydrate: 27 g. Dietary Fiber: 1.054 g. Total Sugars: .208 g. Total Fat: 6.205 g. Saturated Fat: .237 g. Monounsaturated Fat: 1.04 g. Polyunsaturated Fat: .25 g. Cholesterol: 12.5 mg. Calcium: 137.7 mg. Iron: 1.619 mg. Potassium: 103.1 mg. Sodium: 6.504 mg. Vitamin K: .662 mcg. Folate: 71.1 mcg.

❖ IRISH SODA BREAD ❖

HANDMADE
ADAPTABLE FOR DIABETICS

When St. Patrick's Day comes around, my Irish wife insists upon her Irish soda bread. Well, we've made it each year for the past 40 years, but now we bake this no salt, no baking soda, no baking powder version. We use Ener-G Baking Soda and Featherweight Baking Powder instead of the "real stuff," and you'll not notice the difference. Your guests won't either. We added caraway seeds and lush currants to tip the flavor our way, and the seedless golden raisins top it off with an Irish Soda Bread sweetness you'll love. Give it a try, you'll enjoy it. (Diabetics: a good exchange here for raisins might be chopped unsalted walnuts or unsalted pecans.)

MAKES 1 LOAF   MAKES 16 SLICES
SODIUM PER RECIPE: 366.8 MG   SODIUM PER SLICE: 22.9 MG

3 cups white unbleached bread or all-purpose flour (7.5 mg)
1 tablespoon Ener-G Baking Soda (0 mg)
1 tablespoon Featherweight Baking Powder (13.5 mg)
5 tablespoons white granulated sugar (.63 mg)
1 medium to large egg, beaten slightly (63 mg)
2 cups reduced-fat buttermilk with sodium levels at or near 130 mg a cup* (260 mg)
¼ cup unsalted butter (6.248 mg), softened or melted
½ cup Zante currants (5.76 mg)
½ cup seedless golden raisins, not packed (8.7 mg)
1 tablespoon caraway seeds (1.139 mg)

Preheat your oven to 325°F.
Lightly grease and flour a 5×9-inch loaf pan.

*Choose Knudsen's or other reduced-fat, lowest-sodium buttermilk in your local store or use Bob's Red Mill Buttermilk Powder obtainable at www.bobsredmill.com (1-888-685-5988).

Combine the flour, baking soda, baking powder, and sugar in a large bowl.

In a medium size bowl, lightly beat the egg and add the buttermilk. Stir until mixed. Pour this into the flour mixture and stir until well blended. Stir in the melted butter. Add the currants, raisins, and caraway seeds and mix lightly. The dough will be thick and sticky.

Pour this into the prepared loaf pan.

Bake at 325°F. for 60 minutes on the middle rack of your oven, or until a toothpick stuck into the center pulls out dry.

Cool on a rack. If serving immediately, you'll find it wonderful. If you need to store it overnight, wrap in either a zipper-type bag or aluminum foil. Leave on countertop or store in refrigerator.

Nutrient Values per Slice Calories: 165 Protein: 4.388 g. Carbohydrate: 30.7 g. Dietary Fiber: 1.3 g. Total Sugars: 5.023 g. Total Fat: 4.145 g. Saturated Fat: 2.312 g. Monounsaturated Fat: 1.004 g. Polyunsaturated Fat: .275 g. Cholesterol: 24.2 mg. Calcium: 297.9 mg. Potassium: 204.1 mg. Sodium: 22.9 mg. Vitamin K: 0 mcg. Folate: 28.3 mcg.

❖ SOURDOUGH STARTER ❖

Sourdough is made by using yeast and flour. Some packaged sourdough starters claim to use wild yeast, but any yeast works well if you have the right climate for sourdough. That's where the real challenge is when attempting to make bread like my San Francisco Sourdough Loaf in The No-Salt, Lowest-Sodium Cookbook. Sourdough is the result of yeast, water, and flour working together with the yeast's natural action of living organisms eating the sugars in the grain (flour). It's important to understand that weather plays a big role in the success or failure of sourdough breads. The best climate for sourdough is in fact San Francisco, California. To make your own sourdough, just follow the recipe below. When mixed, let it sit on your kitchen sink for about a week, unrefrigerated (best in spring, fall, and winter months). If you live along the western coast, especially in the San Francisco Bay Area, let it sit in front of an open window during this period. Once the week is up, you'll have a starter that can be kept on hand to make sourdough bread anytime. You'll store your starter in your refrigerator, covered. Note: Sourdough may not work in areas of high humidity.

If your starter becomes too "wet" you may have to cut back on the water or add more flour. If it's too dry, you may have to add 1 tablespoon or more water. Once you have succeeded making a sourdough recipe, you'll know more about your particular starter and what to modify, if necessary, in all other sourdough recipes.

*   **Remember:** Use bottled water. Most tap water has cholorine in it. Chlorine in any amount can harm or kill the yeast and thereby stop sourdough action. It's wise to use bottled water for all recipes requiring water.*

*   Care and Maintenance: You'll "feed" your starter every 2 weeks if not used. Take the starter out of the refrigerator, drain the water, stir, discard about ½ of the total, and replace with equal amounts of 50/50 mix (flour and water).*

*   It's best to use your sourdough regularly. If you use a ½ cup in a recipe, replace the ½ cup with ½ cup flour and ½ cup water mixed until it's like a heavy pancake batter. Stir together and return to storage. Maintain as suggested above. If the sourdough becomes too watery, add ½ cup flour only, and ½ teaspoon yeast and let it sit on your countertop for a few days more. It will bubble up again.*

*   **NOTE:** Do not let your sourdough starter get warmer than 90°F. Heat will "kill" your starter.*

*   Prep Time: Take your sourdough starter out of the refrigerator about 8 to 12 hours before making a sourdough recipe. (The longer the better the sour flavor.) Let it sit covered only by wax paper in a warm (about 70°F. to 80°F.) area. It will bubble, which is what you want it to do. After using your recipe's measurement, then replace the water/flour as explained above and let it rest again in the refrigerator.*

MAKES 2 CUPS SOURDOUGH STARTER
SODIUM PER RECIPE: 6.98 MG   SODIUM PER CUP: 3.49

2 cups white unbleached flour (5 mg)
2 cups bottled water (trace), at room temperature (70°F. to 80°F.)
1 teaspoon active dry yeast (1.98 mg)

Stir the ingredients together, let sit out of the refrigerator for 1 week as described in the narrative above. When ready to use, bring out of the refrigerator and cover it only with wax paper and let it sit out overnight or at least for 12 hours. After using and refreshing, refrigerate the starter again, covered.

    NOTE: If you have trouble with this recipe for various reasons, you can find a good sourdough starter at http://www.armchair.com/store/gourmet/

starter1.html. You can also find a sourdough enhancer at this site to give your breads that sourdough flavor.

Nutrient Values for 1 Cup Calories: 460.8 Protein: 13.7 g. Carbohydrate: 96.1 g. Dietary Fiber: 3.791 g. Total Sugars: 0 g. Total Fat: 1.316 g. Saturated Fat: .206 g. Monounsaturated Fat: .159 g. Polyunsaturated Fat: .516 g. Cholesterol: 0 mg. Calcium: 20 mg. Potassium: 173.4 mg. Sodium: 3.49 mg. Vitamin K: 0 mcg. Folate: 238.8 mcg.

❈ SOURDOUGH BAGUETTES ❈

BREAD MACHINE PREPARATION—OVEN BAKE
ADAPTABLE FOR DIABETICS

Baguettes vary from one bakery to another. But while working in France in the seventies for a while, I discovered their baguettes were fairly consistent—very, very salty, darkly cooked, and crispy. They delivered them to anyone who wanted them every morning. They were served in the morning, at noon and dinner time, and they were carried around as snacks. Later, while working in Tahiti, a French "protectorate," I discovered the same baguettes and the same tradition of every morning delivery. We can't use the salt, but we can make tasty baguettes. If you like the smaller-in-diameter loaf and want it crispier yet, just make six 18-inch loaves out of this recipe instead of three large loaves. The recipe remains the same, as do the nutrient values per serving. The vinegar helps keep the baguettes fresh a few days longer without freezing.

NOTE: *If you have a French bread or baguette loaf pan, use it with this recipe for better results.*

MAKES 3 LONG BAGUETTES   SODIUM PER RECIPE: 24.6 MG
SODIUM PER SLICE (BASED ON 1-INCH SLICES): .512 MG

1½ cups bottled water or orange juice (3.731 mg), heated (110°F to 120°F)
½ cup homemade Sourdough Starter* (1.754 mg)
1 tablespoon cider vinegar (.15 mg)
1 teaspoon white granulated sugar (trace)
2 tablespoons extra virgin olive oil (trace)
6 cups white best for bread flour (15 mg)
2 level tablespoons vital wheat gluten (4.5 mg)
1 tablespoon bread machine yeast (6 mg)
4 tablespoons Albers, Quaker, or other cornmeal for dusting (trace)

*See page 57 for Sourdough Starter.

Heat the liquid, add in the rest of the ingredients in the order given (sourdough starter first), holding out the cornmeal. Set your machine on the Dough cycle. When done, transfer the dough to lightly floured bread board. Cut into 3 equal sections. Roll each section on a lightly floured board into logs about 18 inches in length. These will be about 1½ inches diameter (a line drawn through the roll).

Very lightly spritz your baking pan(s) with olive oil and then sprinkle with cornmeal.

Place the logs on the prepared baking pans. Make 4 diagonal slices along the top of each and then cover with lightly oil-spritzed wax paper or a light cloth and let rise in a warm place for up to 1 hour.

About 10 minutes before the rising is completed, preheat your oven to 350°F.

After rising, bake on your center rack for 22 to 25 minutes, or until golden brown. Remove, cool on racks, and serve hot. You may cut the baguettes in half and store in zipper-type bags for a few days or freeze. To reheat, place in a microwave and reheat for just about 10 seconds. Without salt, too much reheating in a microwave can turn bread into a "rock." Serve with plain pasta, lasagna, or any meat or chicken dish.

Nutrient Values per Slice or Piece Calories: 70.5 Protein: 2.125 g. Carbohydrate: 13.5 g. Dietary Fiber: .547 g. Total Sugars: .087 g. Total Fat: .754 g. Saturated Fat: .104 g. Monounsaturated Fat: .436 g. Polyunsaturated Fat: .117 g. Cholesterol: 0 mg. Calcium: 2.732 mg. Iron: .901 mg. Potassium: 23.8 mg. Sodium: .572 mg. Vitamin K: .276 mcg. Folate: 32.4 mcg.

❖ OLD-FASHIONED ITALIAN SOURDOUGH ❖

WITH RAISINS OR CARAWAY SEEDS
BREAD MACHINE PREPARATION — OVEN BAKE
ADAPTABLE FOR DIABETICS

Golden brown, crispy. You can make small rounds with this recipe, freeze some or share them with neighbors and friends. They are best served the day you make them. (That's even true with the sourdough you buy in a bakery.) I've added raisins here, but you can exchange caraway seeds for those and get a very nice flavor.

MAKES 4 SMALL ROUNDS OR 2 LARGE LOAVES   MAKES 32 SLICES
SODIUM PER RECIPE: 48.4
SODIUM PER ROUND (BASED ON 4 ROUNDS): 12.1 MG
SODIUM PER SLICE (BASED ON 32 SLICES): 1.508 MG

1½ **cups apple juice or orange juice fortified with calcium (3.731 mg), at room temperature (80°F)**
2 **tablespoons white granulated sugar (.252 mg)**

¾ **cup homemade Sourdough Starter* (2.617 mg)**
6 **tablespoons extra virgin olive oil (.039 mg)**
1½ **tablespoons apple cider vinegar (.225 mg)**
1 **cup best for bread white flour (12.5 mg)**
1 **tablespoon vital wheat gluten (2.25 mg)**
1 **tablespoon bread machine yeast (6 mg)**

Add at the raisin buzzer:
1 **package Sun Maid Baking Raisins (approximately 1.25 cups) (19.8 mg)**

For dusting the pan:
¼ **cup Albers, Quaker, or other cornmeal (1.052 mg)**

Heat the liquid, pour into the bread machine, then add in the rest of ingredients, except for the ¼ cup cornmeal. Set your machine on the Dough cycle. Add the raisins at "raisin buzzer." Lightly spray your bread machine's basket with olive oil halfway through the kneading process. This is a sticky dough and might be difficult to remove from the basket otherwise. When done, transfer dough to lightly floured bread board. If baking in 2 loaf pans, lightly oil each pan on all sides, dust with the cornmeal, and place each loaf into its pan, rolling it once inside the pan. Set aside, covered with a light cloth, and let rise for about ½ hour to 45 minutes, or until double in size. If making 4 rounds, shape and set them on baking sheets or in French bread pans (you can also make baguettes with this recipe). To make 2 or 3 baguettes, roll dough on a floured board and place pieces into baguette baking tins.

About 10 minutes before the rising is completed, preheat your oven to 350°F.

After rising, bake the rounds for about 22 to 24 minutes, or until golden brown. If baking loaves, bake for 25 to 30 minutes. Remove, cool on racks, and serve hot. You may store these breads in zipper-type bags for a few days or freeze them. To reheat, place in the microwave and reheat for 20 seconds. To thaw, cover with wax paper and defrost in the microwave for 1½ minutes on the Defrost setting. Makes a great breakfast toast.

Nutrient Values per Slice or Piece Calories: 141.1 Protein: 3.001 g. Carbohydrate: 26 g. Dietary Fiber: 1.164 g. Total Sugars: 5.685 g. Total Fat: 2.855 g. Saturated Fat: .395 g. Monounsaturated Fat: 1.911 g. Polyunsaturated Fat: .337 g. Cholesterol: 0 mg. Calcium: 20.5 mg. Potassium: 99.3 mg. Sodium: 1.508 mg. Vitamin K: 1.24 mg. Folate: 55.8 mcg.

*See page 57.

❋ PUMPERNICKEL RAISIN RYE ❋

This is a moist "heavy" bread with a fruity flavor. It will not rise like a standard loaf of bread, but it will be soft, delicious, and popular with even those who like saltier breads. To check for doneness with this bread, use an instant-read thermometer and test the temperature in the center or at the bottom. You should get a reading of 200°F. This bread is what I refer to as a "tough cooker," in that it takes longer than most other bread recipes. (See page 33 for more about added fruits and improvers.)

**MAKES 1 LOAF MAKES 16 SLICES   SODIUM PER RECIPE: 59.9 MG
SODIUM PER SLICE: 3.741 MG**

1⅓ cups less 1 tablespoon orange juice (3.308 mg), at room
   temperature (70°F. to 80°F.)
 1 tablespoon cider vinegar (.15 mg)
 2 cups best for bread white unbleached flour (5 mg)
 2 cups dark rye flour (2.56)
 1 level tablespoon vital wheat gluten (2.25 mg)
 1 teaspoon white granulated sugar (trace)
 2 tablespoons (unpacked) brown sugar (7.02 mg)
1½ tablespoons caraway seeds (1.708 mg)
 1 teaspoon Don's Sweet Chocolate Mix (see page 207) (.291 mg)
 1 tablespoon bread machine yeast (6 mg)
1½ cups unpacked seedless raisins* (26.1 mg)

Place all the ingredients except the raisins in your bread pan in the order listed. Make sure everything, including the bread machine pan, is at least room temperature. Set your machine on Dough cycle. Add the raisins at the raisin buzzer.

When the Dough cycle finishes, transfer the dough to a slightly floured board (whole wheat flour) and using your hands roll up to loaf size. Place into a lightly greased and flour-dusted 9-inch loaf pan. Bake in a preheated standard oven at 350°F, or a convection oven at 325°F, for between 35 and 40 minutes. Use a knife to test for doneness, or an instant-read thermometer. Place the thermometer tip into center or just below center; when it reaches 200°F, this loaf is done.

You may apply ¼ cup confectioners' sugar (trace) mixed with 1 or 2 teaspoons orange juice (trace) as a glaze when hot out of the oven, if desired.

*You may replace the raisins with chopped unsalted pecans or walnuts.

Serve this bread hot. Refrigerate the remaining bread to preserve freshness. It may be toasted, or served warm, or at room temperature.

Nutrient Values per Slice Calories: 184.2 Protein: 5.354 g. Carbohydrate: 39.9 g. Dietary Fiber: 5.214 g. Total Sugars: 1.482 g. Total Fat: 1.621 g. Saturated Fat: .593 g. Monounsaturated Fat: .411 g. Polyunsaturated Fat: .325 g. Cholesterol: 0 mg. Calcium: 49.9 mg. Iron: 2.449 mg. Potassium: 319 mg. Sodium: 3.741 mg. Vitamin K: 0 mcg. Folate: 60.8 mcg.

❧ QUICK AND EASY PUMPERNICKEL ❧

WITH CARAWAY SEEDS AND RAISINS
ADAPTABLE FOR DIABETICS
MAKES 1 LOAF   MAKES 16 SLICES
SODIUM PER RECIPE: 45.5 MG   SODIUM PER SLICE: 2.841 MG

1 cup bottled water (trace), at room temperature (70°F. to 80°F.)
1 tablespoon apple cider vinegar (.15 mg)
2 cups less 2 tablespoons white unbleached best for bread flour (4.725 mg)
1 cup dark rye flour (1.28 mg)
2 teaspoons vital wheat gluten (1.5 mg)
2 teaspoons grated orange zest (.12 mg)
1¼ tablespoons caraway seeds (1.424 mg)
1½ tablespoons dark brown sugar (5.85 mg)
1 tablespoon extra virgin olive oil (trace)
⅔ cup homemade sourdough starter (.075 mg)
2½ teaspoons bread machine yeast (4.5 mg)
1½ cups unpacked seedless raisins (26.1 mg)

Place first 11 ingredients into your bread machine pan (preferably a Breadman TR810) and set machine at White Bread, 1.5-pound loaf, Medium Crust. At the raisin buzzer, add in the raisins.

When the bread is done, cool before slicing.

Nutrient Values Calories: 129.3 Protein: 3.664 g. Carbohydrate: 27.1 g. Dietary Fiber: 3.073 g. Total Sugars: .909 g. Total Fat: .532 g. Saturated Fat: .075 g. Monounsaturated Fat: .093 g. Polyunsaturated Fat: .193 g. Cholesterol: 0 mg. Calcium: 13.1 mg. Iron: 2.201 mg. Potassium: 198.1 mg. Sodium: 2.841 mg. Vitamin K: 0 mcg. Folate: 41.5 mcg.

❧ Raisin Rye ❧

BREAD MACHINE KNEAD — OVEN BAKE
ADAPTABLE FOR DIABETICS*

A standard loaf of rye bread will have about 3,000 mg sodium and some may be even higher. Divide that by 16 slices or so and you're way off the scale. This rye bread tastes just as good and it's low in fat, sugar, and has almost no sodium. You can lower the fat to nearly zero by leaving out the oil.

**MAKES 1 LOAF   MAKES 16 SLICES   SODIUM PER RECIPE: 26.1 MG
SODIUM PER SLICE: 1.632 MG**

1¼ cups plus 2 tablespoons unsweetened apple juice† (10.4 mg)
 2 cups best for bread white flour (5 mg)
 1 cup light rye flour (2.04)
 ½ teaspoon white granulated sugar (.021 mg)
 1 teaspoon vital wheat gluten (.72 mg)
 1 tablespoon caraway seeds (1.139 mg)
 1 tablespoon olive oil (trace)
 2 teaspoons apple cider vinegar (trace)
 1 tablespoon honey (.84 mg)
2½ teaspoons bread machine yeast (5.04 mg)

   Add at the raisin buzzer:
 ½ **cup seedless black raisins (8.7 mg)**

Heat your bread pan with hot water. Heat the apple juice to 120°F. Put juice into pan, then the flour, followed by all the remaining ingredients except the raisins. When the buzzer for adding raisins sounds, add the raisins. Set the machine on the Dough cycle, and after it has risen, transfer the dough to a bread board and then place it in a 9-inch loaf pan. Cover with a light cloth, and let rise in a warm place or an oven heated to between 80°F. and 90°F. with the door closed for about 45 minutes.

If you have a double oven, preheat the other oven to 375°F. Bake for about 30 minutes but no longer than 35 minutes. The loaf should turn a golden brown.

Nutrient Values per Slice Orange Juice Version: Calories: 118.3 Protein: 2.76 g. Carbohydrate: 24.5 g. Dietary Fiber: 1.868 g. Total Sugars: 6.488 g. Total Fat: 1.207 g. Saturated

*Diabetics may change the flavor of this bread by using water instead of apple juice or orange juice, and exchanging raisins for a favorite chopped unsalted nut. To replace the honey, use 1½ tablespoons Splenda. In any case, you'll still have the rye flavor and texture.
†You may use orange juice instead.

Fat: .162 g. Monounsaturated Fat: .694 g. Polyunsaturated Fat: .194 g. Cholesterol: 0 mg. Calcium: 33.8 mg. Potassium: 123.6 mg. Sodium: 1.632 mg. Vitamin K: .413 mcg. Folate: 49.3 mcg.

Nutrient Values per Slice Apple Juice Version: Calories: 117.9 Protein: 2.649 g. Carbohydrate: 24.5 g. Dietary Fiber: 1.847 g. Total Sugars: 4.465 g. Total Fat: 1.213 g. Saturated Fat: .164 g. Monounsaturated Fat: .692 g. Polyunsaturated Fat: .197 g. Cholesterol: 0 mg. Calcium: 10.4 mg. Potassium: 108.7 mg. Sodium: 2.737 mg. Vitamin K: .413 mcg. Folate: 40.5 mcg.

Nutrient Values per Slice Diabetic Version: (No juice, using Splenda; if adding nuts, add in sodium levels) Calories: 91.1 g. Protein: 2.473 g. Carbohydrate: 17.5 g. Dietary Fiber: 1.644 g. Total Sugars: 0 g. Total Fat: 1.174 g. Saturated Fat: .154 g. Monounsaturated Fat: .691 g. Polyunsaturated Fat: .185 g. Cholesterol: 0 mg. Calcium: .01 mg. Potassium: 50.4 mg. Sodium: .833 mg Vitamin K: .413 mcg. Folate: 40.2 mcg.

❖ TEN-GRAIN BREAD WITH WALNUTS ❖

BREAD MACHINE RECIPE
ADAPTABLE FOR DIABETICS

This is one of my favorite grain bread recipes.
MAKES 1 LOAF   MAKES 16 SLICES
SODIUM PER RECIPE: 90.4 MG   SODIUM PER SLICE: 5.652 MG

1½ cups plus 2 tablespoons orange juice with calcium (3.746 mg), at room temperature (70°F. to 80°F.)
  1 tablespoon cider vinegar (.15 mg)
  3 tablespoons Homemade Applesauce (see page 206) (.097 mg), at room temperature (70°F. to 80°F.)
  2 tablespoons olive oil (trace), at room temperature
  2 cups unbleached white flour (5 mg)
  2 cups whole wheat flour (12 mg)
  1 level tablespoon vital wheat gluten* (2.25 mg)
  ¾ cup 10-grain mix† (7.5 mg)
  ½ cup light brown sugar, packed (42.9 mg)
2½ teaspoons bread machine yeast (4.8 mg)
  ¾ cup chopped walnuts (9 mg)

Place the room temperature orange juice in your bread machine. Add all the ingredients except the walnuts to the machine in the order listed. Set the machine for White Bread with a Medium Crust. I recommend the Breadman TR810 machine for this recipe. If you are using the Breadman,

---

*I use Bob's Red Mill from Oregon. If you cannot find it in your supermarket, order through www.bobsredmill.com.
†For a coarser bread, leave out the gluten.

set it for White Bread for a 2-pound loaf. If your machine chooses bake time by loaf size or weight, choose the 2-pound size or a 3-hour-20-minute cycle. When the beeper sounds for adding raisins, add in the walnuts (about 30 to 33 minutes for the Breadman).

Serve this bread with dinner, for sandwiches, or as a crispy toast in the morning, topped with your favorite jam.

Nutrient Values per Slice Calories: 243.6 Protein: 6.799 g. Carbohydrate: 41.7 g. Dietary Fiber: 3.962 g. Total Sugars: 7.125 g. Total Fat: 6.305 g. Saturated Fat: .728 g. Monounsaturated Fat: 1.918 g. Polyunsaturated Fat: 3.183 g. Cholesterol: 0 mg. Calcium: 49.5 mg. Iron: 2.24 mg. Potassium: 230.5 mg. Sodium: 5.652 mg. Vitamin K: .911 mcg. Folate: 98.2 mcg.

SEVEN-GRAIN BREAD
❖ WITH ORANGE ZEST ❖

BREAD MACHINE RECIPE
ADAPTABLE FOR DIABETICS

Years ago I was taught to eat "all the orange." This lesson came from my parents who had survived with some difficulty, like others, the dark days of the Depression. You just didn't throw anything away. My mother would grate the orange peel into a zest. We would eat the white pulp along with the zest when she mixed it into many of her recipes. Back then ground meat was "extended" with bread, onions, anything she could find, and once in a while they'd taste a bit orangey. Our quarter-pounders were probably one ounce beef and three ounces vegetables and leftovers. I learned to cook from her (but I don't throw the whole kitchen into each recipe). You will find orange zest a great source of Vitamin C and bioflavonoids and I use it in many of my bread recipes. It's especially flavorful in this high-fiber bread. Bread/Dough enhancers are not needed for this recipe.

MAKES 1 LOAF   MAKES 16 SLICES
SODIUM PER RECIPE: 81.4 MG   SODIUM PER SLICE: 5.088 MG

1½ **cups plus 2 tablespoons unsweetened orange juice with calcium (3.746 mg), at room temperature (about 70°F. to 80°F.)**
3 **tablespoons Homemade Applesauce (see page 206) (.097 mg), at room temperature (70°F. to 80°F.)**
1 **tablespoon apple cider vinegar (.15 mg)**
1 **tablespoon olive oil (trace), at room temperature**
2 **cups best for bread white flour (5 mg)**

2 cups best for bread whole wheat flour (12 mg)
¾ cup 7-grain mix* (7.5 mg)
2 level teaspoons vital wheat gluten† (1.44 mg)
½ cup (packed) light brown sugar (42.9 mg)
2½ teaspoons bread machine or dry active yeast (4.8 mg)
   Grated zest of 1 orange (.72 mg)
½ cup chopped fresh unsalted walnuts (.55 mg), optional

Place the orange juice in your bread machine. Add the remaining ingredients to the machine in the order listed, except for the nuts. Set machine for White Bread and a Medium Crust. I recommend the Breadman TR-810 machine for this recipe. For the Breadman, use the Rapid Whole Wheat setting for a 2-pound loaf. If your machine chooses bake time by loaf size or weight, choose the 2-pound size or a 3-hour-30-minute cycle

Serve this bread with dinner, for sandwiches, or as a crispy toast in the morning topped with your favorite jam.

Nutrient Values per Slice Calories: 202.7 Protein: 6.325 g. Calories: 109 Protein: 5.836 g. Carbohydrate: 41 g. Dietary Fiber: 3.477 g. Total Sugars: 6.978 g. Total Fat: 1.746 g. Saturated Fat: .262 g. Monounsaturated Fat: .761 g. Polyunsaturated Fat: 459 g. Cholesterol: 0 mg. Calcium: 45.5 mg. Iron: 1.373 mg. Potassium: 183.3 mg. Sodium: 5.088 mg. Vitamin K: .498 mcg. Folate: 63.3 mcg.

❖ Standard Cinnamon Raisin Bread ❖

Bread Machine or By Hand
Not Adaptable for Diabetics

This recipe is based on the standard rolled cinnamon loaf. When you slice it, the circles of cinnamon will stand out. When you toast it, it will crunch wonderfully in your mouth. It's really very good.

Makes 1 loaf   Makes 16 Slices
Sodium per Recipe: 33.6 mg   Sodium per Slice: 2.098 mg

DOUGH
1⅓ cups plus 1 tablespoon orange juice with calcium (3.483 mg),
   heated (105°F. to 115°F.)
1 tablespoon extra virgin olive oil (trace)
1 tablespoon apple cider vinegar (.15)
3½ cups white unbleached best for bread flour (3.75 mg)
1 level tablespoon white granulated sugar (.120 mg)

*I use Bob's Red Mill from Oregon. If you cannot find it in your market, order through www.bobsredmill.com For a coarser bread, leave out the gluten.
†Optional.

½ **level teaspoon ground cinnamon (.303 mg)**
1 **teaspoon vital wheat gluten (.72 mg)**
2½ **teaspoons Fleischmann's bread machine yeast (4.8 mg)**

FILLING (Add at buzzer)
¾ **cup (packed) golden or black seedless raisins (14.8 mg)**
1 **tablespoon ground cinnamon (1.791 mg)**
2 **tablespoons white granulated sugar (.252 mg)**

OPTIONAL TOPPING
6 **level tablespoons confectioners' sugar (.48 mg)**
1 **tablespoon orange juice (plus extra drops if needed to mix) (.155 mg)**

IF BAKING IN BREAD MACHINE: Place the dough ingredients only into your bread machine pan in the order listed. Add the filling ingredients at the sound of the raisin buzzer. Choose the White Bread setting, Medium Crust, 1½-pound loaf and bake.

Spread the topping on the loaf after it cools on rack for 5 minutes.

IF MAKING BY MACHINE AND THEN HAND: Place the dough ingredients into your bread machine in the order listed, or in the order your manufacturer suggests. Set the machine on the Dough cycle and let the dough rise to the end of the cycle.

Transfer the dough to a very lightly floured bread board and press it down. (Never punch down bread dough.) Make a 7-inch-wide by about 12-inch-long shape. Sprinkle the filling mix generously over the entire surface. Roll up from end to end to make a loaf shape.

Place the dough in a 7- or 9-inch loaf pan lightly greased with olive oil. Cover with wax paper and let sit in warm place for about 45 minutes to rise.

Preheat your oven to 450°F.

Bake for 8 minutes in the preheated 450°F. oven, then turn the heat down to 350°F. and bake for another 21 to 26 minutes.

Cool on rack. Serve this bread hot, warm, or as toast.

Nutrient Values per Slice Calories: 158 Protein: 3.428 g. Carbohydrate: 33.9 g. Dietary Fiber: 1.455 g. Total Sugars: 3.75 g. Total Fat: 1.2 g. Saturated Fat: .176 g. Monounsaturated Fat: .664 g. Polyunsaturated Fat: .201 g. Cholesterol: 0 mg. Calcium: 42.2 mg. Iron: 1.703 mg. Potassium: 142.4 mg. Sodium: 2.098 mg. Vitamin K: .413 mcg. Folate: 62.7 mcg.

CINNAMON RAISIN BREAD
❖ WITH CRANBERRY RAISINS ❖

BREAD MACHINE RECIPE
ADAPTABLE FOR DIABETICS

This sweet bread that can also be made with Splenda sugar substitute. Use either Ocean Spray Craisins, generally available in most supermarkets, or cranberry raisins, found at Trader Joe's and other specialty stores.

MAKES 1 LOAF   MAKES 16 SLICES
SODIUM PER RECIPE: 177.5 MG   SODIUM PER SLICE: 11.1 MG

 1 **cup reduced-fat cultured buttermilk (Knudson's or other local brand) (See unique ingredients section for the brand in your area)* (130 mg)**
 2 **tablespoons light sour cream (15 mg)**
 1 **tablespoon apple cider vinegar (.15 mg)**
 1 **tablespoon grated orange or lemon zest (.12 mg)**
1½ **teaspoons vital wheat gluten (1.22 mg)**
2½ **cups white unbleached best for bread flour (6.25 mg)**
 ½ **cup whole wheat best for bread flour (3 mg)**
2½ **teaspoons ground cinnamon (.908 mg)**
 2 **tablespoons white granulated sugar (.252 mg)**
 1 **tablespoon extra virgin olive oil (trace)**
2¼ **teaspoons Fleischmann's bread machine yeast (4.5 mg)**
 ½ **cup (not packed) black seedless raisins (8.7 mg)**
 ½ **cup (not packed) cranberry raisins† (3.99 mg)**

Warm buttermilk and sour cream together to about 100°F. Place the ingredients into your bread machine in the order listed or in the order your bread machine manufacturer suggests (except for the raisins). (We use the Breadman 810 series.) Set on White Bread, 1.5-pound loaf, Light to Medium Crust.

Add the raisins at the sound of the raisin buzzer.

Cool on a rack when done. It makes great toast in the morning.

Nutrient Values per Slice Calories: 136.4 Protein: 4.723 g. Carbohydrate: 27 g. Dietary Fiber: 1.555 g. Total Sugars: 7.984 g. Total Fat: 2.054 g. Saturated Fat: .55 g. Monounsaturated Fat: .751 g. Polyunsaturated Fat: .2 g. Cholesterol: 2.229 mg. Calcium: 29.3 mg. Potassium: 83.3 mg. Sodium: 11.1 mg. Vitamin K: .428 mcg. Folate: 42.4 mcg.

*Most buttermilk has over 275 mg sodium per cup. Use a brand that has only 130 to 150 mg per cup. If Knudsen's is not available in your area, then check for a brand you can find locally.
†If cranberry raisins are not available, use ½ cup golden or black raisins (8.7 mg).

❧ HEARTY CINNAMON BREAD ❧

BREAD MACHINE PREPARTION—OVEN BAKE
ADAPTABLE FOR DIABETICS

Cinnamon bread for real! Toasted with more cinnamon and sugar on top. That's the way it was when I was a kid, and we longed for it. We even got some with melted butter added in. Not today. Not with hypertension, CHF, Menière's, and other maladies requiring lowered sodium. So what do we do? We make this version. It has all those old flavors, but at the right levels for a healthier heart. The hearty *in this recipe means this is one solid toastable piece of great-tasting bread with all the right nutrients in it. Not like the usual commercial cinnamon bread, this one hunkers down as heart-healthy because of the lowered fat and sugar, and higher fiber content. It's also packed with calcium and potassium.*

Easy to prepare, this bread makes a great toast.

MAKES 2 LOAVES   MAKES 32 SLICES
SODIUM PER RECIPE: 55.8 MG   SODIUM PER SLICE: 1.744 MG

1¾* cups orange juice fortified with calcium (4.353 mg), at room
      temperature (70°F. to 80°F.)
   4 cups white unbleached bread flour (10 mg)
   1 cup whole wheat bread flour (6 mg)
   1 tablespoon bread machine yeast (6 mg), at room temperature
      (70°F. to 80°F.
   3 tablespoons white granulated sugar (.378 mg)
1½ tablespoons olive oil (trace)
   1 level tablespoon vital wheat gluten (2.25 mg)
   1 orange zest (grate the zest from the whole orange) (.72 mg)
   1 tablespoon ground cinnamon (1.791 mg)
1½ cups (not packed) seedless raisins (26.1 mg)

Prepare the ingredients in the order listed. Heat the orange juice to about 90°F. before putting into the bread machine pan. Place the yeast on the dry flour and finishing adding the ingredients, except for the cinnamon and raisins. Set the machine on the Dough cycle. Check the bread machine in about 10 minutes to make sure the dough is balling. If it appears dry, add 1 tablespoon warm water or orange juice. If it still doesn't ball up

*For a lighter cinnamon bread, substitute 3/4 cup nonfat or reduced-fat, cultured lowered-sodium buttermilk, or buttermilk made from Bob's Red Mill Buttermilk Powder (85 mg per cup), for 3/4 cup of the orange juice. You can find it at www.bobsredmill.com or at your local grocer's health food section.

after a few more minutes add only 1 additional tablespoon of warm water or orange juice. At the 30-minute mark (or when your machine's raisin buzzer sounds), add the cinnamon and raisins.

When the dough is about ready, warm your oven to about 90°F. and turn it off. Leave the door closed.

Prepare two 9-inch loaf pans by lightly greasing the sides. Dust with whole wheat flour. When the dough is ready, cut the ball in half and roll it up into a loaf shape with your hands once, then place it into a loaf pan. Repeat with the other half. Cover with light cloth and let rise in the warmed oven with the door closed (it should have dropped to about 80°F. or 90°F.). Let the dough rise for 45 minutes. At the 30-minute mark, if you have a double oven, preheat the other to 450°F. If you have only one oven, remove the loaves very carefully at the 45-minute time and turn on the oven. When it's at 450°F. (in about 10 to 15 minutes), bake both loaves. Place them on the center of the middle shelf with about 4 or 5 inches between them. Bake at 450°F. for 10 minutes. Reduce the heat to 350°F. and bake for another 20 to 30 minutes. Cool on rack.

Nutrient Values per Slice Calories: 107.2 Protein: 2.774 g. Carbohydrate 23 g. Dietary Fiber: 1.337 g. Total Sugars: 1.169 g. Total Fat: .707 g. Saturated Fat: .107 g. Monounsaturated Fat: .346 g. Polyunsaturated Fat: .14 g. Cholesterol: 0 mg. Calcium: 24.9 mg. Iron: 1.096 mg. Potassium: 117.9 mg. Sodium: 1.744 mg. Vitamin K: .201 mcg. Folate: 40.9 mcg.

❖ APPLESAUCE BREAD ❖

WITH FRESHLY SHREDDED CARROTS
BREAD MACHINE RECIPE
ADAPTABLE FOR DIABETICS

For more than thirty years I grew apples—not one tree or two, but a small family orchard. We lived in the country and I had the luxury of land to grow them. I would harvest the apples and can them as applesauce, or for apple pies during the winter. They were the Golden Delicious variety from Stark Nurseries in Missouri. Juicy, golden/green, and perfect for pies, applesauce, and this recipe. This recipe is healthy with apples and carrots. It makes a great luncheon bread or early morning toast. To make applesauce, apples may be green or ripe. If you decide to make an apple bread with just slices of apples, then make sure those apples are ripe, nearly soft. This is a very good recipe for using apples that "got away from you" and became overripe while waiting for you to eat them.

MAKES 1 LOAF   MAKES 16 SLICES
SODIUM PER RECIPE: 192.9 MG   SODIUM PER SLICE: 12.1 MG

1 **cup* low-fat cultured buttermilk (Knudsen's)† (130 mg), at**
   room temperature (70°F. to 80°F.)
2 **tablespoons extra virgin olive oil (trace)**
2 **ripe medium apples (trace), unpeeled, diced**
1 **cup best for bread whole wheat flour (12 mg)**
3 **cups best for bread unbleached white flour (5 mg)**
1 **medium farm-fresh carrot (21.4 mg), grated**
3 **tablespoons white granulated sugar or Splenda Sugar**
   Substitute (trace)
1 **teaspoon ground cinnamon (.606 mg)**
2 **teaspoons vital wheat gluten (1.5 mg)**
1 **tablespoon bread machine yeast (6 mg)**
½ **cup seedless golden raisins (8.7 mg)**

Place all the ingredients except the raisins into your bread machine pan in the order listed or in the order your manufacturer suggests. Bake on White Bread setting, Medium Crust, 2½-pound loaf. Add the raisins at the sound of the raisin buzzer.

Remove from the pan and cool on rack. Slice and serve warm or cold, best toasted.

Nutrient Values per Slice Calories: 159.6 Protein: 5.109 g. Carbohydrate: 31.6 g. Dietary Fiber: 3.249 g. Total Sugars: 1.654 g. Total Fat: 2.571 g. Saturated Fat: .511 g. Monounsaturated Fat: 1.316 g. Polyunsaturated Fat: .351 g. Cholesterol: 1.563 mg. Calcium: 33.3 mg. Iron: 3.788 mg. Potassium: 163 mg. Sodium: 12.1 mg. Vitamin K: 1.018 mcg. Folate: 49.5 mcg.

◈ APPLESAUCE CINNAMON RAISIN BREAD ◈

BREAD MACHINE PREPARATION — OVEN BAKE
WITH FLAXSEED MEAL
ADAPTABLE FOR DIABETICS

This dough is great for making holiday breads. You can add whatever you like, and even change the water to orange juice or apple juice if you like. When I want a sweet bread, this is the one I make. Splenda works so well with it that I usually substitute it for the sugar.

MAKES 2 LOAVES   MAKES 32 SLICES
SODIUM PER RECIPE: 39.8 MG   SODIUM PER SERVING: 1.243 MG

*Watch the mix when it begins to knead. If after 10 minutes the mix doesn't ball up, add more buttermilk 1 tablespoon at a time. Let it work in for 1 minute. When it begins to ball up, then close the bread machine and let it do its work
†If Knudsen's or another low-sodium brand isn't available where you live, then use standard low-fat cultured buttermilk (192.8 mg) and add 5.96 mg sodium per slice to the current total.

1¾ cups bottled water (trace) heated to about 120°F.
  1 tablespoon olive oil (trace)
  5 tablespoons sugar or Splenda substitute (.63 mg)
  1 tablespoon apple cider vinegar (.15 mg)
  1 tablespoon vanilla extract (1.17 mg)
  5 cups best for bread white flour (12.5 mg)
  3 tablespoons flaxseed meal (trace)
  1 heaping tablespoon bread machine yeast (6 mg), at room
      temperature

  At the sound of the raisin buzzer add:
  1 cup seedless raisins, black or golden (17.4 mg)
  ⅓ cup Homemade Applesauce (see page 206) (.125 mg)
  1 heaping tablespoon ground cinnamon (1.791 mg)

Place the dough ingredients in the bread machine pan in the order listed. Add the raisins, applesauce, and cinnamon at sound of raisin buzzer. Set the machine on the Dough cycle.

When the dough is ready, transfer it to a lightly floured bread board. If the dough is sticky, add flour while rolling it over. Slice the dough in half, roll up each half, and place them into lightly greased 7- or 9-inch bread loaf pans. Let rise covered with wax paper or a very light cloth in a warm place for about 45 minutes to 1 hour.*

Preheat your oven to 350°F. for a standard oven, 325°F. for a convection oven.

Bake on the middle or lower middle rack for 25 to 30 minutes. Test with a sharp knife to make sure the loaves are done. [May bake both loaves at same time.]

You can add a topping or nothing at all. If for a party or holiday, add a mix of confectioners' sugar with a dollop of unsalted butter and a touch of orange juice. Or, if you favor maple, heat and stir together ¼ cup brown sugar (21.5 mg), 1 tablespoon maple syrup (18 mg), 1 teaspoon maple extract (.378 mg), and 1 tablespoon unsalted butter (1.562 mg). Spread on top when bread is pulled out of the oven.

Total Sodium per Serving for Glaze: .787 mg

Nutrient Values per Slice Calories: 100.9 Protein: 2.461 g. Carbohydrate: 21.5 g. Dietary Fiber: 1.156 g. Total Sugars: 5.38 g. Total Fat: .878 g. Saturated Fat: .099 g. Monounsaturated Fat: .34 g. Polyunsaturated Fat: .126 g. Cholesterol: 0 mg. Calcium: 8.351 mg. Potassium: 67.3 mg. Sodium: 1.243 mg. Vitamin K: .297 mcg. Folate: 39.1 mcg.

*You may also use this dough to make dinner rolls, hamburger buns, or slice each half into three pieces, roll out each piece into a long log, braid, and set on lightly greased baking sheet. Bake at same temperatures listed above.

❖ WALNUT RAISIN BREAD ❖

BREAD MACHINE RECIPE
ADAPTABLE FOR DIABETICS*

I find bread like this one while traveling. I always wonder why our local bakeries don't have the same breads that "tourist trap" areas do. This is a terrific flavor for a bread. Diabetics will have to leave out the raisins if the sugar count is too high.

Baker's Note: *Some bread recipes using whole wheat and fruit might "collapse" on the top after baking. The bread will still be good. To fix the problem next time, assuming you use the same brand of flour, cut the yeast about ¼ teaspoon.*

MAKES 1 LOAF   MAKES 16 SLICES   SODIUM PER RECIPE: 56.9 MG
SODIUM PER SLICE: 3.556 MG

1½ **cups plus 1 tablespoon orange juice with calcium (4.023 mg), at room temperature (about 80°F.)**
 1 **tablespoon apple cider vinegar (.15 mg)**
 2 **cups white unbleached bread machine flour (5 mg)**
 2 **cups whole wheat flour (12 mg)**
 1 **level tablespoon vital wheat gluten (2.25 mg)**
 ½ **ripe medium-size banana (.59 mg), sliced**
 1 **tablespoon olive oil (trace), at room temperature**
 2 **tablespoons white granulated sugar or Splenda Sugar Substitute* (.252 mg)**
 1 **tablespoon bread machine or dry active yeast (6 mg)**
 ¾ **cup SunMaid Baking Raisins (1.6 ounce package)**
 ¼ **cup golden seedless raisins (4.95 mg)**
 ½ **cup unsalted walnuts (.8 mg), chopped in processor**

Place the orange juice in your bread machine. Add the remaining ingredients into machine in the order listed, except the raisins and walnuts. Set the machine for White Bread, 2-pound loaf or Medium Crust. I recommend the Breadman TR810 machine for this recipe. If your machine chooses bake time by loaf size or weight, choose the 2-pound size or a 3-hour-30-minute cycle. Add the raisins and walnuts at the raisin buzzer.

*If you want to cut sugars to zero, exchange orange juice for no-sodium bottled water, use Splenda instead of sugar, and leave out the raisins. Add another ¼ cup unsalted chopped walnuts and maybe some caraway seeds to flavor this if you do.

Serve this bread with dinner, for sandwiches, or as a crispy toast in the morning, topped with your favorite jam.

Nutrient Values per Slice Calories: 285.9 Protein: 7.647 g. Carbohydrate: 54.3 g. Dietary Fiber: 3.728 g. Total Sugars: 1.624 g. Total Fat: 4.944 g. Saturated Fat: .631 g. Monounsaturated Fat: 2.183 g. Polyunsaturated Fat: 1.689 g. Cholesterol: 0 mg. Calcium: 51.8 mg. Iron: 2.834 mg. Potassium: 266.1 mg. Sodium: 3.556 mg. Vitamin K: 1.259 mcg. Folate: 99.7 mcg.

❖ MAPLE WALNUT BREAD ❖

BREAD MACHINE KNEAD — OVEN BAKE
ADAPTABLE FOR DIABETICS

This is a great flavored bread to serve guests at breakfast as toast, or as rolls for a salad with a rib or chicken barbecue.

MAKES 2 LOAVES   MAKES 32 SLICES
ALSO CAN MAKE 24 TO 36 DINNER ROLLS
SODIUM PER RECIPE: 51.8 MG   SODIUM PER SLICE: 1.546 MG
SODIUM PER DINNER ROLL (24) 2.157 MG
SODIUM PER DINNER ROLL (36): 1.438 MG

1¼ cups plus 2 tablespoons unsweetened orange juice with calcium (3.358 mg), at room temperature (70°F. to 80°F.)
½ cup natural maple syrup (14.2 mg), at room temperature (70°F. to 80°F.)
1 tablespoon extra virgin olive oil (trace)
1 cup whole wheat flour (6 mg)
1 teaspoon white granulated sugar or Splenda (trace)
4 cups unbleached white bread flour (10 mg)
1 level tablespoon vital wheat gluten (2.25 mg)
1 tablespoon bread machine yeast (6 mg)
1 cup chopped walnuts (1.25 mg)
½ cup (unpacked) black seedless raisins (8.7 mg)

Place all the ingredients except the walnuts and raisins in your bread machine in the order listed, but heat the orange juice and maple syrup to about 115°F. to 120°F. first. Place the yeast on a dry spot on top of the flour. Set the machine to the Dough cycle and turn on. At the sound of the raisin buzzer, add the walnuts and raisins.

When the Dough cycle ends, transfer the dough to a lightly floured bread board and cut in half. If making 2 loaves, roll evenly into lightly greased 9- or 10-inch bread pans and place a dry light cloth over each. Set in a warm place to rise for about 45 minutes. (If your house is cold, heat your oven to about 80°F. to 100°F. and turn it off; set the dough on the middle rack and close the door and allow to rise.)

If making dinner rolls instead of loaves, form groups of 3 walnut-sized balls and place them into muffin cups or lightly greased muffin tins. Another option is to form triangles and roll the long side to a point for crescent-shaped rolls. Cover with light cloth and let rise as you would the loaves.

For baking loaves, set the oven to 350°F. and bake for 45 minutes on the middle rack.

For baking dinner rolls, set oven at 425°F. and bake for 7 to 9 minutes, checking at 7 minutes to make sure they aren't "burning."

When your bread is done, take it out and lightly drizzle a few drops of melted unsalted butter on the tops of the rolls or loaves while they are hot. Let them cool on a rack. Serve sliced or toasted for breakfast.

Note for Diabetics: To adapt this recipe, use 1¾ cups orange juice or water. Replace the maple syrup with 1 tablespoon maple extract. This also reduces the total recipe sodium by 10 mg. You can leave the raisins out if you need to. Sugars without maple syrup and raisins total 1.643 g. Carbohydrates total 18.2 g.

Nutrient Values per Slice Calories: 106.9 Protein: 3.153 g. Carbohydrate: 19.3 g. Dietary Fiber: 1.125 g. Total Sugars: 2.902 g. Total Fat: 2.205 g. Saturated Fat: .165 g. Monounsaturated Fat: .474 g. Polyunsaturated Fat: 1.393 g. Cholesterol: 0 mg. Calcium: 20.7 mg. Iron: 1.04 mg. Potassium: 95 mg. Sodium: 1.438 mg. Vitamin K: 0 mcg. Folate: 37.1 mcg.

❈ BANANA BREAD ❈

LOAF PAN, BATTER BREAD
ADAPTABLE FOR DIABETICS

We figure you may already have a version of banana bread in your repertoire. It seems to be one of the most popular nonyeast breads in America. But here's one we've developed to help lower the sodium.

MAKES 1 LOAF   MAKES 16 SLICES
SODIUM PER RECIPE: 174.5 MG   SODIUM PER SLICE: 10.9 MG

1½ **cups unbleached best for bread flour (3.75 mg)**
 2 **teaspoons Featherweight Baking Powder (9 mg)**
 ⅓ **cup white granulated sugar (.66 mg)**
 2 **tablespoons extra virgin olive oil (trace)**
 ¼ **cup honey (3.39 mg)**
 1 **cup ripe mashed bananas (about 2 to 3 medium ripe bananas) (3.54 mg)**
 2 **teaspoons lemon juice (trace)**
 1 **teaspoon apple cider vinegar (trace)**
 ⅓ **cup nonfat milk (41.6 mg)**

2 medium eggs (110.9 mg), beaten
½ cup chopped unsalted walnuts (5 mg)
2 tablespoons walnuts (1.5 mg), partially chopped (for top layer)

Lightly grease a 9-inch loaf pan. Dust it with white flour. Sift together the flour and baking powder and set aside. In a large bowl cream the sugar and oil with your hand-held mixer or another mixer. Add the rest of ingredients except for the walnuts. Purée with your hand-held mixer or other processor. Once blended well, stir in the nuts and pour the mixture into the prepared pan. Sprinkle with partially chopped nuts.

If you have a convection oven, bake at 325°F on the lower rack for about 35 minutes, or until a toothpick or knife inserted pulls out dry. If using a standard oven, bake for about 30 to 35 minutes on the middle rack at 350°F. The time may vary because of your altitude. Cool on rack. Serve warm or roasted. Store in a zipper-type bag for up to 1 week.

Nutrient Values per Slice Calories: 151.4 Protein: 3.03 g. Carbohydrate: 23.9 g. Dietary Fiber: 1.188 g. Total Sugars: 8.444 g. Total Fat: 5.528 g. Saturated Fat .751 g. Monounsaturated Fat: 1.894 g. Polyunsaturated Fat: 2.457 g. Cholesterol: 23.5 mg. Calcium: 44.4 mg. Potassium: 202.9 mg. Sodium: 10.9 mg. Vitamin K: .939 mcg. Folate: 29.9 mcg.

❖ BANANA OATMEAL BREAD ❖

WITH ORANGE ZEST
BREAD MACHINE RECIPE
ADAPTABLE FOR DIABETICS
MAKES 1 LOAF   MAKES 16 SLICES
SODIUM PER RECIPE: 38.7 MG   SODIUM PER SLICE: 2.279 MG

1½ cups orange juice with calcium (3.731 mg), heated to between 115°F and 120°F
1 medium-size ripe banana (1.18 mg), mashed
2 tablespoons brown sugar (7.02 mg)
1½ cups white unbleached best for bread flour (3.75 mg)
1½ cups best for bread whole wheat flour (9 mg)
1½ cups quick oats (unsalted) (4.86 mg)
2 level teaspoons vital wheat gluten (1.5 mg)
1 medium orange zest (grated peel of whole orange) (.54 mg)
1 tablespoon olive oil (trace)
1 teaspoon vanilla extract (.378 mg)
1 tablespoon bread machine yeast (6 mg)

Place all the ingredients in your bread pan in the order listed. We bake this one in a Breadman TR-810 (double paddle) on White Bread setting, 2-

pound loaf, Medium Crust. If you use another machine, bake on White Bread setting. Remove from the pan when done. Cool on rack. Serve fresh, warmed, or toasted.

Nutrient Values per Slice Calories: 144.9 Protein: 4.865 g. Carbohydrate: 28.2 g. Dietary Fiber: 2.994 g. Total Sugars: 1.091 g. Total Fat: 1.742 g. Saturated Fat: .273 g. Monounsaturated Fat: .833 g. Polyunsaturated Fat: .391 g. Cholesterol: 0 mg. Calcium: 41.5 mg. Iron: 1.504 mg. Potassium: 179.9 mg. Sodium: 2.419 mg. Vitamin K: .45 mcg. Folate: 54.9 mcg.

❖ OATS, DATES, AND PRUNE BREAD ❖

BREAD MACHINE OR OVEN BAKE
DIABETICS MAY SUBSTITUTE SPLENDA FOR THE SUGAR

This bread is great for high-fiber diets. Remember, the higher the fiber content in your diet, the less chance of eating too much fat. Oats also help fight LDL cholesterol. Diabetics may either leave out the sugar or replace it with Splenda substitute. If the prunes and dates have too much sugar, then you can replace them with equal amounts of chopped unsalted walnuts for a nutty flavor.

MAKES 12 BUNS IN YOUR OVEN
MAKES 1 LOAF WITH 16 SLICES IN YOUR BREAD MACHINE
SODIUM PER RECIPE: 164.1 MG   SODIUM PER BUN: 13.7 MG
SODIUM PER SLICE: 10.3 MG

1 **cup reduced-fat, cultured, and lowered-sodium buttermilk* (130 mg), warmed to 80°F.**
¾ **cup unsweetened orange juice fortified with calcium (1.866 mg), heated to 115°F. to 125°F.**
2 **cups oat bran or Quaker Quick Oats (7.52 mg), ground in your processor**
1 **cup whole wheat flour (6 mg)**
1¾ **cups unbleached white flour (4.375 mg)**
1 **level tablespoon vital wheat gluten (2.25 mg)**
1 **tablespoon extra virgin olive oil (trace)**
1 **teaspoon white granulated sugar (trace)**
1 **tablespoon bread machine yeast (6 mg), at room temperature**

Add just before the raisin buzzer:
½ **cup dried SunSweet or other pitted prunes† (3.4 mg), sliced**

*You may substitute 1 cup unsweetened orange juice or water if you don't want to use buttermilk.
†Flour-covered date bits are available at Trader Joe's and other specialty stores. You may substitute chopped unsalted walnuts or pecans for the dates.

½ **cup chopped or flour-covered chopped date bits***
   (2.67 mg)

TO MAKE A BREAD MACHINE LOAF: Heat the buttermilk to about 80°F. and the orange juice to 80°F to 90°F. Chop or cut up the dates and prunes and set them aside. Place the 9 dough ingredients into your bread machine pan in the order listed.

Add the dates and prunes after 20 minutes—usually just before the raisin buzzer. Set your machine to the Dough cycle if you're going to make buns or set to White Bread for a 2-pound loaf. The Breadman 810 series machines are great for this recipe. After about 10 minutes, check to make sure your dough is balling up. If not, add 1 tablespoon warm orange juice or water every 3 minutes but no more than 3 tablespoons. (The quality of the oats and whole wheat flour will determine this amount.)

TO MAKE BUNS IN THE OVEN: This can be an especially good recipe for dinner rolls or buns. After the dough is formed, roll it out on a slightly floured board. Press down gently until dough is about ½ inch thick. Cut out 12 round buns or shape dinner rolls. Set on two lightly greased baking sheets, cover with a light towel, and set in a warm place to rise. You may use your oven, heating it to about 90°F.) After about 45 minutes, or when the dough has doubled in size, bake at 425°F for 6 to 8 minutes. (You can also roll up 1-inch balls and set three into lightly greased muffin cups for great dinner rolls.) Cool on rack. Slice and serve warm. Toast for breakfast. Spread with strawberry jam or eat plain.

Nutrient Values per Slice Calories: 152.7 Protein: 6.009 g. Carbohydrate: 33.6 g Dietary Fiber: 4.069 g. Total Sugars: .822 g. Total Fat: 2.358 g. Saturated Fat: .521 g. Monounsaturated Fat: .977 g. Polyunsaturated Fat: .52 g. Cholesterol: 1.563 mg. Calcium: 48.5 mg. Iron: 4.039 mg. Potassium: 224.5 mg. Sodium: 10.3 mg. Vitamin K: 413 mcg. Folate: 54.1 mcg.

Nutrient Values per Bun (12) Calories: 203.6 Protein: 8.012 g. Carbohydrate: 44.8 g. Dietary Fiber: 5.425 g. Total Sugars: 1.097 g. Total Fat: 3.145 g. Saturated Fat: .694 g. Monounsaturated Fat: 1.303 g Polyunsaturated Fat: .693 g. Cholesterol: 2.083 mg. Calcium: 64.7 mg. Iron: 5.386 mg. Potassium: 299.3 mg. Sodium: 13.7 mg. Vitamin K: .551 mcg. Folate: 72.1 mcg.

*Use Knudsen low-sodium buttermilk or another low-sodium brand. See page 17 for brand name. Or, you can use Bob's Red Mill Powder Buttermilk (www. bobsredmill.com). Some local markets carry Bob's Red Mill products. Reconstitute to meet recipe requirements

❧ NUTTY DATE BREAD ❧

BREAD MACHINE RECIPE
ADAPTABLE FOR DIABETICS

The "nutty" refers to bulgur, a cracked wheat. The flavor with this bread is great; try it in the morning as a toast. You can make this in your machine and set the timer for your arrival at breakfast.* Mmmmm, good.

MAKES 1 LOAF   MAKES 16 ½-INCH SLICES
SODIUM PER RECIPE: 42 MG   SODIUM PER SLICE: 2.62 MG

1¾ **cups orange juice fortified with calcium (4.353 mg), at room temperature (70°F to 80°F.)**
2 **tablespoons extra virgin olive oil (trace)**
2 **tablespoons honey or sugar (.252 mg)**
2 **cups best for bread machine whole wheat flour (12 mg)**
2 **cups white best for bread machine flour (2.5 mg)**
1 **level tablespoon vital gluten (2.25 mg)**
½ **cup dates (some are with oat flour coating) (2.67 mg), whole, chopped, or pieces**
½ **cup bulgur (11.9 mg)**
1 **package or 2½ teaspoons bread machine or active dry yeast (3.5 mg)**

Warm the orange juice to about 115°F. in your microwave. Place all ingredients into your bread machine in the order given. Set for White Bread, 2-pound loaf, Medium Crust. (That will be about 3 hours 20 minutes of kneading, rising, and cooking).

Remove when done and set on a cooling rack. You can cut this loaf into slices with a sharp serrated bread knife right away. Serve hot or toasted.

Nutrient Values per Slice Calories: 173 Protein: 4.711 g. Carbohydrate: 34.9 g. Dietary Fiber: 3.617 g. Total Sugars: 1.559 g. Total Fat: 2.247 g. Saturated Fat: .327 g. Monounsaturated Fat: 1.324 g. Polyunsaturated Fat: .354 g. Cholesterol: .026 mg. Calcium: 44 mg. Potassium: 192.2 mg. Sodium: 2.627 mg. Vitamin K: .827 mcg. Folate: 54.7 mcg.

*Bulgur can be tooth-breaking tough. Use the package instructions to soften or soak for about 1 hour in water or overnight. Drain the water before using in mixture.

✦ BRAIDED ORANGE CINNAMON TWIST ✦

BREAD MACHINE KNEAD—HAND SHAPE—OVEN BAKE
ADAPTABLE FOR DIABETICS

Whoops! Another successful recipe created while baby-sitting. Our granddaughter asked if I knew how to braid. Of course she meant her hair, but instead I suggested learning how to do it with bread dough. Here it is, and it's absolutely delicious.

MAKES 2 TWIST LOAVES   MAKES 32 SLICES
SODIUM PER RECIPE: 90.5 MG   SODIUM PER SERVING: 2.827 MG

¾ **cups plus 2 tablespoons orange juice (1.866 mg), at room temperature (70°F. to 80°F.)**
1 **egg (63 mg), beaten**
2 **tablespoons olive oil (trace)**
2½ **cups white unbleached best for bread machine flour (6.25 mg)**
¼ **cup best for bread whole wheat flour (1.5 mg)**
2 **teaspoons white granulated sugar (trace)**
1 **teaspoon vital wheat gluten (.81 mg)**
2 **teaspoons bread machine yeast (3.96 mg)**
1½ **teaspoons ground cinnamon (.908 mg)**
⅔ **cup raisins (11.5 mg)**
Zest from ½ orange (.36 mg), grated
1 **tablespoon cornmeal for dusting baking sheet (.258 mg)**

Place all the ingredients except the raisins, zest, and cornmeal at room temperature into the bread machine pan and prepare under the Dough cycle. Add the raisins and zest at the sound of the raisin buzzer.

When the dough is ready, transfer it to a floured bread board and roll out (or flatten with your hands) until it's about 6 inches wide and 12 inches long. Cut lengthwise to make three lengths of dough. Roll each one lengthwise to make a rolled stick. Braid these three and place on a baking sheet dusted with cornmeal as the base (instead of grease). If you need more cornmeal, go ahead and add it; the sodium level is negligible.

Let the dough rise in a warm place (I use my oven heated to 100°F. and then turned off, with the door closed), for about 45 minutes, or until double in size. Bake at 375°F. for 13 to 15 minutes. Cool on rack. Slice and serve warm. You may store it in zipper-type bags in the freezer for up to 1 month or in the refrigerator for up to 1 week. Reheat slowly or toast. You can slice it for French toast.

Nutrient Values per Slice Calories: 63.8 Protein: 1.66 g. Carbohydrate: 11.9 g. Dietary Fiber: .679 g. Total Sugars: .26 g. Total Fat: 1.152 g. Saturated Fat: .188 g. Monounsaturated Fat: .701 g. Polyunsaturated Fat: .147 g. Cholesterol: 6.641 mg. Calcium: 13.2 mg. Iron: .671 mg. Potassium: 56.4 mg. Sodium: 2.827 mg. Vitamin K: .413 mcg. Folate: 24.5 mcg.

❧ DON'S SECRET BREAD RECIPE ❧

WITH BUTTERMILK AND ORANGE
BREAD MACHINE KNEAD—HAND SHAPE—OVEN BAKE
BREAD DOUGH IS ADAPTABLE FOR DIABETICS
TOPPING IS NOT ADAPTABLE FOR DIABETICS

Now and then it's perfectly all right to have a treat. If you don't use these as hamburger buns, sandwich buns, or even dinner rolls, then top them when hot out of the oven with the glaze mix below and turn them into donut-like buttermilk bars. (You can even roll these up on the board, shape them into balls, flatten them a bit like donuts, cut a large hole out of center, and let them rise; then add sugar glaze after baking.) These are a special breakfast treat— just like the real things used to be for our family years ago.

MAKES 18 BUNS OR BARS

SODIUM PER RECIPE—UNGLAZED: 363.5 MG
SODIUM PER RECIPE—GLAZED: 428.4 MG
SODIUM PER BUN/BAR—UNGLAZED: 20.2 MG
SODIUM PER BUN/BAR—GLAZED: 23.8 MG

BREAD DOUGH

1¾ cups Knudsen or other lower-sodium buttermilk (227.5 mg), at room temperature (70°F. to 80°F.)
5 cups unbleached white bread flour (12.5 mg)
1 heaping teaspoon Ener-G Baking Soda (trace)
2 teaspoons white granulated sugar (trace mg)
2 tablespoons olive oil (trace)
2 medium to large egg whites (109.6 mg)
1 egg yolk (7.138 mg)
 Zest of 1 medium orange, grated through white pulp (.54 mg)
1 teaspoon vital wheat gluten (.72 mg)
1 tablespoon bread machine or active dry yeast (6 mg)

OPTIONAL GLAZE FOR BUTTERMILK BARS

1 egg white (54.8 mg), beaten until foamy

GLAZE AFTER BAKING*

2 cups unsifted confectioners' sugar (2.4 mg)
2 to 4 tablespoons pure maple syrup (7.2 mg)
1 teaspoon vanilla or maple extract (.378 mg)

*This is not adaptable for diabetics.

Place the dough ingredients in your bread machine in the order listed. Set the machine for the Dough cycle.

When the dough is ready, turn it out onto a lightly floured bread board. Cut it in half. Press down with your hands until the dough is about ½ inch thick, or slightly more. (You may also use a rolling pin gently to do this.) Slice or cut the dough into bar shapes for either buns or bars. (Or roll into balls for glazed donuts.) Make long slashes with a very sharp knife down the length of each bun or bar. If making bars, brush each bun with egg glaze.

Set buns or bars on lightly greased baking sheets (use olive oil spray). Cover with a very light cloth or wax paper and set in a warm place. (Preheat your oven to about 100°F., turn off the heat, and let dough rise in there.) Let the dough rise for about 45 minutes. Set aside and raise the oven temperature to 425° F. Bake for about 6 to 8 minutes, or until golden brown.

When done, if the buns are to be used for sandwiches, set them on a rack to cool.

If they are to be used for donut-type buttermilk bars, combine the confectioners' sugar, maple syrup, and extract to make a glaze. Use this to glaze each bar hot out of the oven. Set aside to cool.

Nutrient Values with Glaze and Topping per Bar Calories: 218.4 Protein: 5.282 g. Carbohydrate: 44.9 g. Dietary Fiber: 1.219 g. Total Sugars: 17.4 g. Total Fat. 2.667 g. Saturated Fat: .644 g. Monounsaturated Fat: 1.269 g. Polyunsaturated Fat: .72 g. Cholesterol: 14.2 mg. Calcium: 40.4 mg. Iron: 5.167 mg. Potassium: 69.2 mg. Sodium: 20.7 mg. Vitamin K: .754 mcg. Folate: 70.9 mcg.

Nutrient Values with No Glaze or Topping per Bar Calories: 154.2 Protein: 5.282 g. Carbohydrate: 28.6 g. Dietary Fiber: 1.219 g. Total Sugars: 1.337 g. Total Fat: 2.644 g. Saturated Fat: .64 g. Monounsaturated Fat: 1.262 g. Polyunsaturated Fat: .309 g. Cholesterol: 14.2 mg. Calcium: 37.3 mg. Iron: 5.105 mg. Potassium: 59.5 mg. Sodium: 20.2 mg. Vitamin K: .754 mcg. Folate: 70.9 mcg.

❂ ENGLISH MUFFIN BREAD ❂

BREAD MACHINE KNEAD—OVEN BAKE
ADAPTABLE FOR DIABETICS

Slice and toast this one for great breakfast bread.
**MAKES 1 LOAF   MAKES 24 SLICES   SODIUM PER RECIPE: 29.3 MG
SODIUM PER SLICE: 1.222 MG**

1¼ cup plus 3 tablespoons orange juice with calcium (3.483 mg), heated to 115°F. to 125°F.
  1 teaspoon apple cider vinegar (.05 mg)
  2 cups white best for bread flour (5 mg)
1½ cups whole wheat best for bread flour (9 mg)
  1 teaspoon vital wheat gluten (.72 mg)

1½ **teaspoons white granulated sugar or Splenda Sugar Substitute (.063 mg)**
1 **teaspoon Featherweight Baking Powder (6.75 mg)**
1 **tablespoon bread machine yeast (6 mg)**
4 **tablespoons cornmeal (1.032 mg)**

Place all the ingredients except the cornmeal in the bread machine pan in the order listed. Set your machine to the Dough cycle.

While the dough is kneading, prepare two 9 × 5-inch loaf pans with light coating of olive oil spray. Dust each pan with 1 tablespoon cornmeal. Evenly spread the remaining 2 tablespoons cornmeal on a breadboard.

When dough is ready, roll it across the cornmeal. Cut the dough ball in half and shape or place into loaf pans and cover with a light towel.

Set in an oven that has been preheated to 100°F. Close the oven door and let rise for about 45 minutes. The dough should double in size. If you have a double oven, preheat the other oven to 400°F. about 10 minutes before the dough is ready.

Bake for about 15 minutes at 400°F. Test for doneness with knife or long toothpick. Serve toasted.

Nutrient Values per Slice Calories: 77.9 Protein: 2.515 g. Carbohydrate: 16.6 g. Dietary Fiber: 1.441 g. Total Sugars: .26 g. Total Fat: .299 g. Saturated Fat: .048 g. Monounsaturated Fat: .047 g. Polyunsaturated Fat: .114 g. Cholesterol: 0 mg. Calcium: 31.1 mg. Potassium: 105.2 mg. Sodium: 1.222 mg. Vitamin K: 0 mcg. Folate: 38.1 mcg.

❖ FLAXSEED BUNS, ROLLS, AND BREAD ❖

ADAPTABLE FOR DIABETICS

You can replace shortening (oil, butter, and other) almost always with Flaxseed Meal (ground). Simply triple the amount of flaxseed meal called for in bread, muffin, and cookie recipes. This recipe was created especially for flaxseed meal and was designed for use by diabetics. Leave out the raisins and the sugars/carbohydrates drop to the levels seen in the nutrient data at the end of this recipe. Buttermilk in this recipe accounts for 17.5 grams of carbohydrate (sugars) for the entire recipe. If you need to, you may replace the buttermilk with water. If you are allergic to eggs, then leave the egg out and add 3 tablespoons of water to the mix or use Ener-G's egg replacer.

MAKES 1 LOAF (32 SLICES)   MAKES 12 BUNS   MAKES 24 ROLLS
SODIUM PER RECIPE: 338.8 MG   SODIUM PER BUN (12): 28.2 MG
SODIUM PER ROLL (24): 14.1 MG)
SODIUM PER BREAD LOAF SLICE (32): 10.6 MG

1¾ cups low-sodium buttermilk (227.5 mg), warmed (80°F.)
3 tablespoons bottled water (trace)
1 tablespoon cider vinegar (.15 mg)
1 medium to large egg, whole (63 mg)
4½ cups white unbleached bread flour (11.2 mg)
½ cup ground flaxseed meal (13.2 mg)
2 teaspoons vital wheat gluten (1.5 mg)
2 teaspoons white granulated sugar or Splenda Sugar Substitute (trace)
1 tablespoon Fleischmann's bread machine yeast (6 mg)

At the raisin buzzer add:
1 cup Bakers Raisins (17.4 mg)

Place the dough ingredients into your bread machine in the order listed or in the order your manufacturer suggests.

When the dough is ready, roll it out on a flour dusted-bread board, then slice in half. You can make a loaf of bread or buns or cinnamon buns or dinner rolls. For instructions on cinnamon buns, see the Egg Bread Cinnamon Buns recipe (page 200). The cooking time is the same.

Once your choice of bread is selected, place the dough in a warm area for rising. Let it rise for about 45 minutes

Bake buns in a preheated 425°F. oven for 6 minutes.

Bake cinnamon rolls in a preheated 350°F. oven for about 20 minutes.

Bake the bread loaf in a preheated 350°F oven, in a lightly greased roll pan on the middle rack for 20 to 25 minutes When it turns golden brown, it should be done.

Note: Leave out the raisins if sugars are a problem, and replace the buttermilk (17.5 grams carbohydrates) with water.

Nutrient Values per Bun (12) Calories: 240.9 Protein: 8.092 g. Carbohydrate: 48.9 g. Dietary Fiber: 2.886 g. Total Sugars: 10.1 g. Total Fat: 2.808 g. Saturated Fat: .767 g. Monounsaturated Fat: .45 g. Polyunsaturated Fat: .992 g. Cholesterol 21.4 mg. Calcium: 64.7 mg. Potassium: 189.4 mg. Sodium: 28.2 mg Vitamin K: 0 mcg. Folate: 106.9 mcg.

Nutrient Values per Roll (24) Calories: 120.4 Protein: 4.046 g. Carbohydrate: 24.5 g. Dietary Fiber: 1.443 g. Total Sugars: 5.036 g. Total Fat: 1.404 g. Saturated Fat: .384 g. Monounsaturated Fat: .225 g. Polyunsaturated Fat: .496 g. Cholesterol 10.7 mg. Calcium: 32.4 mg. Potassium: 94.7 mg. Sodium: 14.1 mg. Vitamin K: 0 mcg. Folate: 53.5 mcg.

Nutrient Values per Slice (32) Calories: 90.3 Protein: 3.034 g. Carbohydrate: 18.4 g. Dietary Fiber: 1.082 g. Total Sugars: 3.777 g. Total Fat: 1.053 g. Saturated Fat: .288 g. Monounsaturated Fat: .169 g. Polyunsaturated Fat: .372 g. Cholesterol: 8.008 mg. Calcium: 24.3 mg. Potassium: 71 mg. Sodium: 10.6 mg. Vitamin K: 0 mcg. Folate: 40.1 mcg.

High-Grain, Low-Fat, Low-Sugar
◆ Sandwich Bread ◆

BREAD MACHINE RECIPE
ADAPTABLE FOR DIABETICS

I love this recipe. It's crunchy, flavorful, satisfying, and full of nutrients. It makes terrific toast to serve with your own homemade strawberry jam. This bread will work with many diets and it's good for diabetics, too.

**MAKES 1 LOAF   MAKES 16 SLICES   SODIUM PER RECIPE: 81.1 MG
SODIUM PER SLICE: 5.067 MG**

1½ cups bottled water less 1 tablespoon (trace), at room
      temperature (about 70°F. to 80°F.)
  1 tablespoon orange or lemon juice (.155 mg)
  1 tablespoon apple cider vinegar (.15 mg)
  3 tablespoons fresh Homemade Applesauce (see page 206)
      (trace)
  1 large egg white (54.8 mg)
  2 cups best for bread or unbleached white flour (5 mg)
2¼ cups best for bread whole wheat flour (12 mg)
  ¾ cup 10-grain mix* (15 mg)
  1 level tablespoon vital wheat gluten (2.25 mg)
  1 teaspoon white granulated sugar (trace)
  1 tablespoon bread machine yeast (6 mg)

Place the water in your bread machine, then add the rest of the ingredients in the order listed. Set the machine for White Bread and a Medium Crust. (I recommend using the Breadman TR-810 machine for this recipe. For the Breadman use the White Bread setting for a 2-pound loaf.) If your machine chooses bake time by loaf size or weight, choose the 2-pound size or a 3-hour-20-minute cycle. Check 10 minutes into the kneading to make sure your recipe has enough liquid. If it needs more, add water 1 tablespoon at a time, and continue until it balls up.

When done, remove from the loaf from the bread machine and cool on a rack.

Use for sandwiches, as toast for breakfast, as a snack, or with dinner.

Nutrient Values per Slice Calories: 123.7 Protein: 4.746 g. Carbohydrate: 25.7 g. Dietary Fiber: 2.546 g. Total Sugars: .437 g. Total Fat: .505 g. Saturated Fat: .082 g. Monounsaturated Fat: .07 g. Polyunsaturated Fat: .192 g. Cholesterol: 0 mg. Calcium: 8.778 mg. Iron: 1.559 mg. Potassium: 103 mg. Sodium: 5.067 mg Vitamin K: 0 mcg. Folate: 51.5 mcg.

*I use Bob's Red Mill from Oregon; it's available at www.healthyheartmarket.com (1-888 685-5988) or www.bobsredmill.com.

❧ MUSKETEERS BREAD ❧

BREAD MACHINE KNEAD — OVEN BAKE
BAKE IN OVEN
BREAD ADAPTABLE FOR DIABETICS;
TOPPING NOT ADAPTABLE

A few nights ago I baby-sat with two of our grandchildren. At this time, one of the children is five and the other is three. They wanted to make bread. Actually, they said they wanted to "create" new bread. So, we pulled the bread machine out and put together the Musketeers Bread. That's what we call ourselves when we are together. (Thanks to their mother's three sisters and one brother, we now have ten grandchildren members in our "Musketeer Club.")

When we finished with the bread, their mommy came home and she dove into it with gusto. Her finicky taste-buds proved that the recipe is good—and it's child safe.

MAKES 12 MINIATURE LOAVES   SODIUM PER RECIPE: 190.9 MG
SODIUM PER MINIATURE LOAF: 15.9 MG

THE DOUGH
1 cup plus 2 tablespoons cultured, reduced-fat buttermilk (146.3 mg), at room temperature (70°F. to 80°F.)
1 tablespoon pure maple syrup (1.8 mg)
1 tablespoon cider vinegar (.15 mg)
2 cups best for bread white flour (5 mg)
1 cup whole wheat flour (6 mg)
2 teaspoons vital wheat gluten (1.5 mg)
1 tablespoon grated zest orange peel (.18 mg)
2 tablespoons white granulated sugar (.252 mg)
2 tablespoons extra virgin olive oil (trace)
1 teaspoon vanilla extract or flavoring (.378 mg)
2½ teaspoons active dry or bread machine yeast or 1 package (4.5 mg)

THE RAISIN MIX
1 cup seedless black raisins (not packed) (17.4 mg)
1 tablespoon white granulated sugar (.126 mg)
2 teaspoons ground cinnamon (1.211 mg)

THREE MUSKETEERS FROSTING (GLAZE)
1 cup unsifted confectioners' sugar (1.2 mg)
3 tablespoons pure maple syrup (5.4 mg) or ½ teaspoon maple extract (.189 mg)

1   **teaspoon vanilla extract or flavoring (.378 mg)**
1   **teaspoon almond extract (.378 mg)**

Place all the dough ingredients into your bread machine pan. Set the machine on the Dough cycle and turn on.

While the dough is rising, mix together the raisins, sugar, and cinnamon. Set aside.

If you have a miniature bread loaf pan (about 8 to 12 miniature bread loaves—often used for Christmas fruitcakes), then lightly grease it with a spritz of olive oil in each of the recessions. If you don't have miniature bread loaf pans, then cut the dough into 8 to 12 shapes and bake them instead on a lightly greased baking sheet.

When dough is ready, transfer it to a lightly floured bread board and flatten it gently with a rolling pin, rolling it out until it's about ½ inch thick. Sprinkle the raisins and sugar mixture on the dough, and then roll dough over and begin kneading in the raisin mixture. This takes about 3 minutes. (If you have your children or grandchildren helping, let them knead it, too. It is fun for them and exposes them to the joy of breadmaking.)

When the raisins, sugar, and cinnamon are well kneaded into the dough, then flatten it out again until it is about ¾ inch thick. The dough should be rectangular when you're done rolling it. Cut the dough into 3×1×¾-inch pieces and set each one in a section of the loaf pan. If you are using a baking sheet, set the pieces evenly on the sheet so that all 12 can be baked. The bread will rise and expand, so allow about 2 inches between the pieces.

Place the pan or sheet in a warm spot (the oven will do if it's heated to about 80°F.). Cover with wax paper and let rise for about 45 minutes to 1 hour.

While dough is rising, prepare the frosting/glaze. It should be very thick. If it's too loose, add more sugar; if it's too "thick," add a bit more maple syrup until it's smooth enough to manage but still thick.

Fifteen minutes prior to baking time, preheat a convection oven to 400°F or a standard oven to 425°F.

If using a convection oven, bake on the middle rack for about 8 minutes. Test for doneness. Some ovens might take another minute or two.

If using a standard oven, bake on the middle rack for about 7 minutes at 425°F.

When done, set the small loaves on a cooling rack and spoon on the glaze while the bread is hot. Delicious! The grandchildren loved them and you will too.

Serve hot, warm, or at room temperature. You may store these in zipper-type bags in the refrigerator. Can reheat in microwave for about 10 seconds.

Nutrient Values per Individual Loaf Calories 246.2 Protein: 5.312 g. Carbohydrate: 52 g. Dietary Fiber: 2.596 g. Total Sugars: 18.1 g. Total Fat: 3.235 g. Saturated Fat: .678 g. Monounsaturated Fat: 1.726 g. Polyunsaturated Fat: .383 g. Cholesterol: 2.344 mg. Calcium: 49.3 mg. Iron: 5.168 mg. Potassium: 183.8 mg. Sodium: 15.9 mg. Vitamin K: 1.103 mcg. Folate: 50.6 mcg.

❈ WHOLE WHEAT AND ORANGE ❈

BREAD MACHINE KNEAD—HAND SHAPE—OVEN BAKE
MAKES GREAT SLICED BREAD, BUNS, AND ROLLS
ADAPTABLE FOR DIABETICS
MAKES 12 TO 18 SANDWICH BUNS   MAKES 32 SLICES OF BREAD
SODIUM PER RECIPE: 33.9 MG
SODIUM PER SLICE (32): 1.059 MG
SODIUM PER BUN OR ROLL (12): 2.50 MG

1¾ cups orange juice with calcium (4.353 mg), heated to
    (110°F–115°F)
 1 medium to large orange peel (.54 mg) (3 tablespoons),
    grated
 2 cups best for bread whole wheat flour (12 mg)
 3 cups best for bread white flour (7.5 mg)
 1 level tablespoon vital wheat gluten (2.25 mg)
 2 tablespoons sugar or Splenda Sugar Substitute (.252 mg)
 2 tablespoons extra virgin olive oil (trace)
 1 tablespoon bread machine yeast (6 mg)

For rolls, buns, or loaves, place all the ingredients in your bread machine pan in the order listed or in the order suggested by your machine manufacturers. Set it on the Dough cycle and turn it on.

When dough is ready, transfer it to a lightly floured breadboard and cut it in half. If making loaves, roll each half into loaf shape and set into lightly greased (with olive oil spray) 5×9-inch loaf pans. Cover with a light cloth and set in a warm place for about 45 minutes to 1 hour, or until the loaves double in size.

Preheat your oven to 350°F. When ready, bake the loaves on the middle rack for 25 minutes, or until a long toothpick comes out dry.

To make buns or rolls, press down each half and, using a cutter, glass top, or other tool, cut each half into 6 or 9 buns or shape into dinner rolls. If making rolls, you can make more if you want them smaller. Place these on a large lightly greased cookie sheet (half on one cookie sheet, the other half on another). Cover with a light cloth and let sit at warm room temperature or in a preheated (80°F. to 90°F.) oven with the door closed. Let rise for about 45 minutes, or until doubled in size.

Preheat the oven to 425°F. When ready, bake the rolls or buns on the middle rack for 7 minutes.

Note: You can also make one loaf of bread and one batch of buns or rolls.

Cool on rack. Slice and serve warm or at room temperature. They will store in zipper-type bags for up to a week on your countertop or in your refrigerator and will freeze for up to a month.

Nutrient Values per Slice (32) Calories: 87.5 Protein: 2.686 g. Carbohydrate: 17 g. Dietary Fiber: 1.41 g. Total Sugars: .78 g. Total Fat: 1.132 g. Saturated Fat: .16 g. Monounsaturated Fat: .662 g. Polyunsaturated Fat: .18 g. Cholesterol: 0 mg. Calcium: 22 mg. Iron: .929 mg. Potassium: 78.7 mg. Sodium: 1.059 mg. Vitamin K: .413 mcg. Folate: 37.7 mcg.

Nutrient Values per Bun (12) Calories: 233.3 Protein: 7.163 g. Carbohydrate: 45.3 g. Dietary Fiber: 3.76 g. Total Sugars: 2.079 g. Total Fat: 3.019 g. Saturated Fat: .426 g. Monounsaturated Fat: 1.766 g. Polyunsaturated Fat: .479 g. Cholesterol: 0 mg. Calcium: 58.6 mg. Iron: 2.478 mg. Potassium: 209.9 mg. Sodium: 2.825 mg. Vitamin K: 1.103 mcg. Folate: 100.6 mcg.

❧ ORANGE ANISE BREAD ❧

BREAD MACHINE RECIPE
ADAPTABLE FOR DIABETICS

I first encountered this bread while in London directing a CBS magazine-format show back in the seventies and eighties. (Magazine-format shows back then were Real People, That's Incredible, *and* That's My Line, *to name a few.) It was a nice change from the standard tourist menu.*

**MAKES 1 LOAF   MAKES 16 SLICES   SODIUM PER RECIPE: 15.9 MG
SODIUM PER SLICE: .997 MG**

1¼ cups unsweetened orange juice with calcium and pulp (3.109 mg), at room temperature (70° F. to 80° F.)
  3 cups white unbleached best for bread flour (7.5 mg)
  1 tablespoon apple cider vinegar (.15 mg)
  2 tablespoons olive oil (trace)
1½ teaspoons vital wheat gluten (1.125 mg)
  1 teaspoon white granulated sugar (.378 mg)
  2 teaspoons anise seed (.652 mg)
2¼ teaspoons bread machine yeast (3.5 mg)

Warm the bread machine pan with hot water. Heat the orange juice to 115° F. Bring the yeast to room temperature if you have been storing it in the refrigerator. Either pull it out a few hours before using or use my double bowl method: place hot water in the larger bowl, yeast in a small bowl sitting in the hot water in the large bowl, and let sit for about 3 to 5 minutes. Stir the yeast once or twice with a dry spoon.

Place all the ingredients into the bread pan in the order listed or according to your bread machine's manufacturer. Bake on White Bread, Medium Crust, or a setting for a 3-hour-20-minute cycle. Remove from pan, cool on rack. Slice and serve warm or at room temperature. It will store in zipper-type bags for up to a week on your countertop or in your refrigerator and will freeze for up to a month.

Nutrient Values per Slice Calories: 113.1 Protein: 2.947 g. Carbohydrate: 20.6 g. Dietary Fiber: .802 g. Total Sugars: .26 g. Total Fat: 1.995 g. Saturated Fat: .27 g. Monounsaturated Fat: 1.303 g. Polyunsaturated Fat: .249 g. Cholesterol: 0 mg. Calcium: 29 mg. Iron: 1.283 mg. Potassium: 74.5 mg. Sodium: .997 mg. Vitamin K: .827 mcg. Folate: 54.9 mcg.

❖ ORANGE CURRANT BREAD ❖

WITH CARAWAY SEEDS
BREAD MACHINE PREPARATION—OVEN BAKE
ADAPTABLE FOR DIABETICS

The flavors of rye bread, the goodness of yeast bread and tasty currants make this an exciting bread to make and to serve. This is one of my favorites for flavor and for morning toast. It also makes quite a tasty hamburger bun.

MAKES 2 LOAVES   MAKES 16 BUNS
SODIUM PER RECIPE: 223.4 MG   SODIUM PER BUN: 14 MG
SODIUM PER SLICE: 6.98 MG

1 cup nonfat milk (126.2 mg), at room temperature (70°F. to 80°F.)
¾ cup orange juice with calcium (1. 866 mg), at room
    temperature (70° F. to 80° F.)
1 tablespoon apple cider vinegar (.15 mg)
1 tablespoon extra virgin olive oil (trace)
1 large egg (63 mg)
4 cups white unbleached flour (10 mg)
1 cup whole wheat flour (6 mg)
1 tablespoon grated orange peel (trace)
1 teaspoon white granulated sugar (trace)
1 level tablespoon vital wheat gluten (.72 mg)
1 tablespoon bread machine yeast (6 mg)

At the sound of the raisin buzzer add:
Zest of 1 orange (.54 mg), grated
½ cup Zante currants (5.76 mg)
1 teaspoon caraway seeds (.357 mg)

Spray the sides of your bread pan with a short spritz of olive oil (trace) and close the lid. (This is a sticky dough.)

Place all the dough ingredients in your bread pan in the order listed. When the raisin buzzer sounds, add the zest, currants, and caraway seeds.

When the dough is ready, turn it out onto a lightly floured breadboard and press down lightly. Slice in half and set one half aside.

If making loaves, roll each half once to form an elongated ball. Set into 9×5-inch lightly greased bread pan. Spritz the top of the dough with olive oil spray, lay wax paper over it, and let it stand in a warm place. (I turn my oven to about 100°F, turn it off, let it cool for a few moments, then put the bread in and close the door. The bread will rise perfectly in 30 to 45 minutes.) Do the same with the second half, or make buns.

To make buns, press down on the half you are working with and cut out seven to eight 3-inch buns. The last two may have to be hand shaped. Set on a lightly greased baking sheet, spritz the tops of the buns with a dash of olive oil, set wax paper on top of them, and place in a warm area.

For buns, preheat the oven to 425° F. Bake on the middle rack for 6 to 7 minutes.

For loaves, if you have a single oven, remove the rising bread dough from the oven and set it on the stovetop burners or countertop—very carefully, don't shake down the rise. Preheat the oven to 375° F and when ready bake for about 30 minutes on the middle or lower rack, but no longer than 35 minutes. The loaf should turn a golden brown. If you have a double oven, simply preheat the second oven and move dough from one oven to the next.

Serve hot, reheated, or thawed and reheated. This loaf makes great toast, too. You may freeze it in zipper-type bags.

Nutrient Values per Bun Calories: 181.4 Protein: 6.12 g. Carbohydrate: 35.7 g. Dietary Fiber: 2.415 g. Total Sugars: .26 g. Total Fat: 1.714 g. Saturated Fat: .309 g. Monounsaturated Fat: .825 g. Polyunsaturated Fat: .316 g. Cholesterol: 13.6 mg. Calcium: 48.8 mg. Iron: 2.114 mg. Potassium: 175.4 mg. Sodium: 14 mg. Vitamin K: .417 mcg. Folate: 77.1 mcg.

Nutrient Values per Slice Calories: 90.7 Protein: 3.06 g. Carbohydrate: 17.9 g. Dietary Fiber: 1.207 g. Total Sugars: .13 g. Total Fat: .857 g. Saturated Fat: .154 g. Monounsaturated Fat: .412 g. Polyunsaturated Fat: .158 g. Cholesterol: 6.794 mg Calcium: 24.4 mg. Iron: 1.057 mg. Potassium: 87.7 mg. Sodium: 6.98 mg. Vitamin K: .208 mcg. Folate: 38.6 mcg.

❖ THE IMPOSSIBLE BREAD ❖

BREAD MACHINE KNEAD—HAND SHAPE—OVEN BAKE DIABETICS—THIS ONE IS FOR YOU

I remember attempting many things in my life, and have learned with age that many of those attempts were driven by someone telling me it would be "impossible." I was often fed that warning while creating bread recipes, but since success demonstrates attitude better than words, I now hear the tempered phrase only occasionally. After this major "impossible" bread succeeds for you, you'll stop paying attention to those who warn you that the things you want to do are impossible. What's impossible about this one?

No sugar, no added fat, no salt.

They said it couldn't be done, but try this one and

jump with joy. It's great tasting, has great texture, and is perfect for those who can't consume sugar, fats, or salt. You can add options that you can enjoy, such as raisins, or nuts, or cinnamon, for example. (The fat in this recipe comes from the flour with a trace from the orange juice and yeast.)

MAKES 1 LOAF (16 SLICES)
PLUS 8 HAMBURGER OR SANDWICH BUNS
SODIUM PER RECIPE: 30.6 MG   SODIUM PER SLICE 16: 1.915 MG
SODIUM PER BUN 8: 3.83 MG

1¾ **cups orange juice with calcium (4.353 mg) (if water is substituted, the sugar level drops to 0 g), at room temperature (about 80°F.)**
4 **cups best for bread white flour (10 mg)**
1 **cup best for bread whole wheat flour (6 mg)**
1 **level tablespoon vital wheat gluten (2.25 mg)**
1 **tablespoon vanilla extract (1.17 mg)**
1 **tablespoon apple cider vinegar (.15 mg)**
1 **teaspoon Splenda Sugar Substitute (trace)**
   Zest from 1 large orange (.72 mg), grated
1 **tablespoon bread machine yeast (6 mg)**

Bring the yeast to room temperature (about 70°F. to 80°F.). Warm your bread pan with hot water. Heat the juice (you may substitute apple juice or bottled water if you prefer) to 110°F to 120°F. Pour the juice into the bread pan, next, add the flours, gluten, vanilla, vinegar, sugar substitute, then the orange zest followed by the yeast. Set bread machine on the Dough cycle. When it is done, transfer the dough to a floured board and roll once, cut in half, then put one half into a lightly olive-oil–spritzed (trace sodium) nonstick 9-inch loaf pan, and let it rise in a warm place, covered with a light cloth or lightly greased wax paper.

Roll out and press down the second dough half and cut out 8 hamburger-sized buns or shape dough into long sandwich buns. Place these on a cookie sheet dusted with cornmeal as the base (instead of grease). Cover it with a light cloth and let it rise in the same warm area.

This recipe is sufficient to make two 9-inch loaves, if you prefer.

After 45 minutes or after doubling in size, bake the loaf or loaves in a preheated 350°F. convection oven for 20 to 22 minutes, or in a standard 375°F. oven for 18 to 20 minutes. The bread should turn a golden brown. Test before removing it from the oven. If baking a single loaf, raise the oven temperature to 425°F. after it's done, and then bake the buns for 5 to 6 minutes. Cool on rack. Slice and serve warm or at room temperature. It will store in zipper-type bags for up to a week on your countertop or in your refrigerator and will freeze for up to a month.

Nutrient Values per Slice Calories: 79.7 Protein: 2.555 g. Carbohydrate: 16.6 g. Dietary Fiber: 1.065 g. Total Sugars: 0 g. Total Fat: .254 g. Saturated Fat: .04 g. Monounsaturated Fat: .034 g. Polyunsaturated Fat: .096 g. Cholesterol: 0 mg. Calcium: 21.6 mg. Iron: .956 mg. Potassium: 67.9 mg. Sodium: .958 mg. Vitamin K: 0 mcg. Folate: 40.7 mcg.

Nutrient Values per Bun Calories: 159.4 Protein: 5.11 g. Carbohydrate: 33.1 g. Dietary Fiber: 2.13 g. Total Sugars: 0 g. Total Fat: .509 g. Saturated Fat: .079 g. Monounsaturated Fat: .067 g. Polyunsaturated Fat: .191 g. Cholesterol: 0 mg. Calcium: 43.2 mg. Iron: 1.911 mg. Potassium: 135.8 mg. Sodium: 1.915 mg. Vitamin K: 0 mcg. Folate: 81.3 mcg.

❖ TRAIL MIX BREAD ❖

BREAD MACHINE KNEAD—HAND SHAPE—OVEN BAKE
NOT ADAPTABLE FOR DIABETICS

Nutty? You bet. But this bread also contains high fiber, a quick energy picker-upper, and a delightful flavor. I use either a cup of Don's Trail Mix or the ingredients listed below when adding them at the raisin buzzer.

MAKES 2 LOAVES (32 SLICES)

OR

MAKES 1 LOAF AND 6, 12, OR 18 MUFFINS
SODIUM PER RECIPE: 263.4 MG
SODIUM PER SLICE (32): 8.233 MG
SODIUM PER TEXAS-SIZE MUFFINS (12): 22 MG

1¾ cups nonfat milk (222.9 mg), at room temperature (70°F. to 80°F.)
 1 tablespoon honey (.84 mg)
 1 tablespoon apple cider vinegar (.15 mg)
 1 tablespoon natural maple syrup (1.8 mg)
 4 cups white best for bread flour (10 mg)
 1 cup whole wheat pastry flour (6 mg)
 1 level tablespoon vital wheat gluten (2.25 mg)
 2 tablespoons olive oil (trace)
 3 tablespoons white granulated sugar (.378 mg)
 1 teaspoon ground cinnamon (.606 mg)
 1 tablespoon Fleischmann's bread machine yeast (6 mg)
 ¼ cup unsalted Planter's dry-roasted peanuts (2.19 mg)
 ¼ cup seedless raisins or Sunmaid Baking Raisins (4.95 mg)
 ¼ cup flour-covered date bits* (1.56 mg)
 ¼ cup semisweet chocolate chips (4.758 mg)

*Dates, dusted in flour, can be purchased at Trader Joe's and other specialty stores. If you can't find them, replace with one of the following: Ocean Spray Craisins (dried cranberries), Zante currants, or golden seedless raisins.

Place all the dough ingredients (the first 11 ingredients) in your machine's bread pan in the order listed or in the order recommended by your machine's manufacturer and set on the Dough cycle. When the raisin buzzer sounds, add the peanuts, raisins, dates, and chocolate chips (or substitute 1 cup of Don's Trail Mix).

When the cycle is completed, transfer the dough to a lightly floured bread board and slice in half.

If making half the recipe into muffin-size rolls, break away or cut off 6 pieces for muffin dough. Place these in lightly greased and flour-dusted Texas-size muffin tins, filling them only halfway. Let rise in a warm place for 60 to 90 minutes, covered with wax paper.

Shape the other dough half into a loaf shape, and place in a lightly greased (olive oil) and flour-dusted bread pan, any size, and let rise, covered with wax paper, for 60 to 90 minutes.

Preheat the oven to 375°F. Bake the muffins at 375°F. for about 14 to 15 minutes. Test with a toothpick to make sure they have cooked through.

Lower the heat of the oven to 350°F. for the loaf and bake for about 22 to 23 minutes. Test for doneness with a toothpick or a clean sharp knife.

Nutrient Values per Slice Calories: 112.5 Protein: 3.304 g. Carbohydrate: 20.7 g. Dietary Fiber: 1.319 g. Total Sugars: 2.862 g. Total Fat: 2.059 g. Saturated Fat: .492 g. Monounsaturated Fat: 1.079 g. Polyunsaturated Fat: .361 g. Cholesterol: .268 mg. Calcium: 23.7 mg. Iron: 1.087 mg. Potassium: 93.7 mg. Sodium: 8.233 mg. Vitamin K: .416 mcg. Folate: 37.1 mcg.

Nutrient Values per Texas-size Muffin (12) Calories: 300.1 Protein: 8.809 g. Carbohydrate: 55.2 g. Dietary Fiber: 3.518 g. Total Sugars: 7.631 g. Total Fat: 5.598 g. Saturated Fat: 1.311 g. Monounsaturated Fat: 2.877 g. Polyunsaturated Fat: .962 g. Cholesterol: .715 mg. Calcium: 63.3 mg. Iron: 2.899 mg. Potassium: 249.8 mg. Sodium: 22 mg. Vitamin K: 1.11 mcg. Folate: 98.9 mcg.

❖ FLOUR TORTILLAS ❖

AS IS FOR DIABETICS

We grew up in Los Angeles, a city heavily influenced by citizens who emigrated from Mexico. With them came the tortillas, to be used in burritos, tostados, and other delicious recipes. This tortilla recipe was given to us by our good friend Dixie Guilan.

**MAKES 12 FLOUR TORTILLAS   SODIUM PER RECIPE: 16.9 MG
SODIUM PER TORTILLA: 1.408 MG**

4 cups unbleached bread flour (10 mg)
1 teaspoon Featherweight Baking Powder (4.5 mg)
½ cup extra virgin olive oil (trace)
1 teaspoon lime juice (.125 mg)
1½ cups unsweetened orange juice (3.731 mg), or water (0 mg) at
   room temperature (70°F. to 80°F.)

Combine the flour and baking powder in a medium-size mixing bowl. Mix in the olive oil and lime juice using a wooden spoon or fork. Add the orange juice or water slowly. Mix together while doing so, and when the dough cleans the side of the bowl stop adding the liquid. Too much water can make a tortilla tough.

Knead the dough about 5 turns only. Form a small ball and cover with plastic wrap or a light cloth. Let it sit in a warm place for about 30 minutes to 2 hours. You can also roll this ball into a log, if you like, and later cut the log into 12 pieces. After the dough has sat, cut the ball or log into 12 pieces, and roll each piece in your hands to form a ball. On a lightly floured or greased pan, set the balls apart from each other and cover. Let rest in a warm place for about ½ hour.

After resting, place the balls on a lightly floured breadboard. Press a ball of dough over your forefinger to create a hole. Set the ball on the breadboard, hole-side down, and roll out the dough with a pin. To make a circle, roll it once, then turn the dough 90 degrees, then roll again, and continue doing this until you've rolled it out thinly. Each ball of dough should make a 10- to-12-inch disk.

Heat an ungreased frypan on the stovetop to medium heat. When a splash of water hisses when it hits the pan, you are ready to cook the disks. You can roll one, cook, then roll while the first is cooking, or you can roll all disks and set them aside, one on top of the other with wax paper between layers. I prefer to cook while rolling. Cook the tortillas for about 20 to 30 seconds on each side. Turn when you see bubbles begin to pop up.

If holding for later, place on brown paper or a cloth towel or stack on a plate with brown or wax paper between them after they are cool. They can be rewarmed before serving. Serve hot. You can store these tortillas in zipper-type bags overnight, but no longer (because of the absence of salt). You may freeze these, however, and thaw them later either by setting them out or in the microwave.

Nutrient Values per Tortilla Calories: 246.5 Protein: 4.52 g. Carbohydrate: 35.5 g. Dietary Fiber: 1.191 g. Total Sugars: 3.112 g. Total Fat: 9.428 g. Saturated Fat: 1.282 g. Monounsaturated Fat: 6.672 g. Polyunsaturated Fat: .932 g. Cholesterol: 0 mg. Calcium: 44 mg. Potassium: 104.8 mg. Sodium: 1.408 mg. Vitamin K: 4.41 mcg. Folate: 77.9 mcg.

ADAPTABLE FOR DIABETICS

This new recipe (which includes topping for the benefit of pizza lovers) is easy to make and brings kudos from family and guests. Give it a try. You can add your own toppings, or make it just as is.* Bake it in a flat pizza pan or a deep dish.

MAKES 12 TO 18 SERVINGS
SODIUM PER RECIPE FOR PIZZA DOUGH: 157.9 MG
SODIUM PER COMPLETE PIZZA (INCLUDING CRUST)
RECIPE: 364.4 MG   SODIUM PER SERVING (12): 30.4 MG
SODIUM PER SERVING (18): 20.2 MG

You will make enough dough for 1 extra-large pizza or 2 medium-size ones.

THE DOUGH

  1 **cup reduced-fat, low-sodium buttermilk (see page 17)
     (130 mg)**
  2 **tablespoons light, reduced-fat, or regular sour cream (12.3 mg)**
  1 **tablespoon apple cider vinegar (.15 mg)**
  3 **cloves garlic (1.53 mg), minced**
  2 **tablespoons extra virgin olive oil (trace)**
  2 **teaspoons vital wheat gluten (1.5 mg)**
  3 **cups white best for bread machine flour (7.5 mg)**
  2 **teaspoons white granulated sugar (trace)**
2½ **teaspoons bread machine yeast (4.8 mg)**

To prepare the dough, warm the buttermilk to about 90°F. to 100°F. and place into the bread machine basket. Add the sour cream, vinegar, garlic, and olive oil, then the flours, sugar, and yeast. Set the machine on the Dough cycle.

THE TOPPINGS

  6 **to 10 cloves garlic (4.59 mg), minced**
  1 **large onion (4.5 mg), thinly sliced**
  2 **cups sliced mushrooms (5.8 mg)**
12 **ounces of Alpine Lace Low Swiss (191.9 mg), finely shredded**
  2 **tablespoons extra virgin olive oil, for spreading on dough
     (trace)**

*You can add no-salt-added (NSA) tomato sauce (see *The No-Salt, Lowest-Sodium Cookbook,* very low sodium pizza recipe), although this recipe was created without tomato sauce.

Prepare but do not mix the toppings above and set them aside. Prepare a shallow deep-dish or standard pizza pan by very lightly spritzing it with olive oil spray. (I use a pizza dish that has holes in the bottom, which helps the crust to bake more evenly.)

Preheat the oven to 425°F.

When the dough is ready, turn it out onto a lightly floured breadboard. If making two pizzas, slice dough in half. With a rolling pin, roll out the dough to the size and shape of your pizza pan. This dough is pliable. If you're a good "tosser," you may try your hand with it just like they do at Round Table Pizza.

When dough is in/on your pan, brush on the 2 tablespoons olive oil listed in the toppings ingredients. Evenly spread the minced garlic around the crust. Layer on the thinly sliced onions and the mushrooms. Sprinkle the grated cheese on top of this.

Bake for about 8 to 10 minutes, or until golden brown.

Nutrient Values per Serving (18 servings) Calories: 147.5 Protein: 6.012 g. Carbohydrate: 19.3 g. Dietary Fiber: .96 g. Total Sugars: .962 g. Total Fat: 5.597 g. Saturated Fat: 1.961 g. Monounsaturated Fat: 2.736 g. Polyunsaturated Fat: .453 g. Cholesterol: 8.106 mg. Calcium: 103.4 mg. Iron: 3.164 mg. Potassium: 104.6 mg. Sodium: 20.2 mg. Vitamin K: 1.638 mcg. Folate: 47.8 mcg.

❖ CALZONE Y EMPANADAS ❖

BREAD MACHINE KNEAD—OVEN BAKE
ADAPTABLE FOR DIABETICS

Calzones are great Italian turnovers or stuffed pies, while empanadas come from Spain and Mexico. The calzone usually is made with lots of ricotta or grated mozzarella cheese. Empanadas, on the other hand, can be made with various fillings, such as ground beef, turkey, chicken, or pork. The dough for each is slightly different.* As you can see, this is a flexible recipe offering you many choices for flavor, consistency and a terrific meal for the kids as well.

MAKES 6 TO 10 EMPANADAS
SODIUM PER RECIPE (BASED ON USING GROUND BEEF): 177.9 MG
SODIUM PER EMPANADA (6): 29.6 MG
SODIUM PER EMPANADA (10): 14.8 MG

*Sometimes I make a calzone dough (white flour, no sugar, some herbs), while other times the empanada dough, which is basically what we have here. You can make your own filling to your tastes for each one. To enhance this dough's flavor, you can add about ½ teaspoon fresh oregano or basil (trace amounts of sodium), and leave out the sugar to come closer to a calzone recipe. Calzones use just white flour instead of this whole wheat/white flour mix.

EMPANADA DOUGH

1 cup less 1 tablespoon unsweetened orange juice with calcium
   (2.323 mg), at room temperature (70°F. to 80°F.)
1 teaspoon apple cider vinegar (.05 mg)
1 cup whole wheat pastry flour (6 mg)
2 cups white unbleached flour (5 mg)
1 teaspoon vital wheat gluten (.7 mg)
1 tablespoon grated orange zest (trace)
2 tablespoons extra virgin olive oil (trace)
1 teaspoon white granulated sugar or Splenda Sugar Substitute
   (trace)
1 heaping teaspoon Ener-G Baking Soda (trace)
1½ teaspoons bread machine yeast (9 mg)

FILLING

8 ounces lean ground beef (149.7 mg)
   Or turkey (214.4 mg)
   chicken (214.4 mg)
   pork (126.6 mg)
1 tablespoon olive oil (trace)
¼ large red bell pepper (6.78 mg), chopped
2 level teaspoons ground coriander (1.271 mg)
1 teaspoon Don's Special Curry Mix (see next page) (trace)
1 chopped onion (4.5 mg), sautéed

Heat the orange juice to 115°F. to 125°F. and place it into bread machine first. Add the rest of the dough ingredients in the order listed. Make sure your yeast is at room temperature (about 70°F. to 75°F.). Set the machine on the Dough cycle.

While dough is nearing the end of its rising, assemble the filling in a nonstick pan. Using the olive oil, lightly brown the meat, add the pepper, spices, and onions, and sauté. Stir with meat, frequently. Set aside.

When the dough is ready, turn it onto a lightly floured board and break it into 6 or 10 (even up to 12) equal-size pieces. Roll each gently in your hands into a ball. Take each ball and press down on your lightly floured board and "roll" it out with a pin into a 6-to-12-inch disk (depending on the number you want to make). This dough is pliable and some of your disk may be stretched out more by tossing it like pizza dough or by stretching with a gentle pulling action. With a large spoon, spread the filling mix on half of each disk. Fold the other half over and pinch closed. Leave a ½-inch border around the edge.

Place these disks on a lightly greased baking dish or pizza pan and cover with a light cloth. Set in a warm place and let rise for 30 to 45 minutes.

Preheat your oven to 350°F. and bake disks for 20 to 22 minutes, or until golden brown.

DON'S SPECIAL CURRY MIX
  1 teaspoon dried thyme (.766 mg)
  1 teaspoon dried crushed marjoram (.462 mg)
  1 teaspoon ground cloves (5.099 mg)
  1 teaspoon ground coriander (1.266 mg)
  1 teaspoon curry powder (1.04 mg)

Grind the thyme and marjoram into a fine texture, then add the other spices and mix together in a small dish or bowl. Store in an empty spice jar or other small container.

Nutrient Values per Empanada (based on 10) Calories: 204 Protein: 7.945 g. Carbohydrate: 27.4 g. Dietary Fiber: 2.487 g. Total Sugars: .347 g. Total Fat: 7.144 g. Saturated Fat: 1.824 g. Monounsaturated Fat: 4.013 g. Polyunsaturated Fat: .597 g. Cholesterol: 13 mg. Calcium: 45.2 mg. Potassium: 207.1 mg. Sodium: 14.8 mg. Vitamin K: 1.904 mcg. Folate: 83.9 mcg.

Nutrient Values per Empanada (based on 6) Calories: 408 Protein: 15.9 g. Carbohydrate: 54.9 g. Dietary Fiber: 4.974 g. Total Sugars: .693 g. Total Fat: 14.3 g. Saturated Fat: 3.647 g. Monounsaturated Fat: 8.026 g. Polyunsaturated Fat: 1.194 g. Cholesterol: 26.1 mg. Calcium: 90.5 mg. Potassium: 414.2 mg. Sodium: 29.6 mg. Vitamin K: 3.808 mcg. Folate: 167.9 mcg.

Nutritional Information for Curry Mix Sodium per Batch: 8.003 mg Sodium per Teaspoon: 1.601 mg

Nutrient Values per Teaspoon Calories: 4.825 Protein: .161 g. Carbohydrate: .939 g. Dietary Fiber: .579 g. Total Sugars: 0 g. Total Fat: .233 g. Saturated Fat: .044 g. Monounsaturated Fat: .08 g. Polyunsaturated Fat: .055 g. Cholesterol: 0 mg. Calcium: 14.9 mg. Potassium: 19.5 mg. Sodium: 1.601 mg. Vitamin K: 0 mcg. Folate: 2.103 mcg.

❖ DON'S OWN BREAD DOUGH ENHANCER ❖

There are a few bread dough enhancers available on the market. See page 000 for a full detail of what bread dough enhancers are and where to obtain commercial brands. If you are unable to obtain bread dough enhancers, then make your own if you believe your recipe needs it. This enhancer will work with any and all of my yeast breads. In some cases, it may cause you to have to extend the baking time. You may want to lightly oil the lid of your bread machine if you're just making dough. Both baked breads and dough will generally push up against the lid if you use this enhancer.

MAKES 9 TEASPOONS   SODIUM PER RECIPE: 2.454 MG SODIUM PER TEASPOON: .273 MG

  1 tablespoon vital wheat gluten (2.25 mg)
  1 tablespoon grated orange or lemon zest (.36 mg), or 1 tablespoon lemon juice

2 teaspoons white granulated sugar or Splenda Sugar Substitute*
   (.126 mg)

Mix the ingredients together; add to yeast bread recipes.

Nutrient Values per Teaspoon Calories: 7.05 Protein: .642 g. Carbohydrate: 1.135 g. Dietary Fiber: .024 g. Total Sugars: .924 g. Total Fat: .015 g. Saturated Fat: 0 g. Monounsaturated Fat: 0 g. Polyunsaturated Fat: 0 g. Cholesterol: 0 mg. Calcium: .307 mg. Iron: .002 mg. Potassium: .374 mg. Sodium: .273 mg Vitamin K: 0 mcg. Folate: .029 mcg.

*If using Splenda, total sugars measure 0 g.

Muffins, Rolls, and Biscuits*

❖ ❖ ❖ ❖ ❖ ❖ ❖ ❖

❖ San Francisco Sandwich Buns ❖

BREAD MACHINE PREPARATION — OVEN BAKE
ADAPTABLE FOR DIABETICS

Sourdough is fun to work with. If you make a starter using yeast, or one of the commercial "starter" packages, which generally contain yeast, then set it on your kitchen sink near an open window. You want it bubble up, collapse, bubble up again. When it begins to smell sour, you've got it where you want it. Try it with these sandwich buns. Make the full recipe, shape into 18 buns, and freeze those you don't use the first day for future use. The vinegar is in the recipe to help keep them fresh a few days longer in zipper-type bags. This recipe can be made without sugar or with Splenda Sugar Substitute.

MAKES 18 LONG SANDWICH BUNS   SODIUM PER RECIPE: 30.5 MG
SODIUM PER BUN: 1.695 MG

1¼ cups unsweetened orange juice fortified with calcium
   (3.731 mg), at room temperature (70°F. to 80°F.)
5¼ cups best for bread white flour (13.1 mg)
 1 tablespoon extra virgin olive oil (trace)
 1 tablespoon apple cider vinegar (.05 mg)
 1 cup homemade Sourdough Starter (see page 57) (3.489 mg), at
   room temperature
 2 teaspoons vital wheat gluten (1.5 mg)
 1 tablespoon white granulated sugar† (.126 mg)
 1 tablespoon bread machine yeast (6 mg)
 ½ cup Albers, Quaker, or other cornmeal for dusting (2.064 mg)

---

*Many of the recipes in the Bread section can also be adapted for muffins or buns.
See the recipe descriptions for details.
†This recipe can be made without sugar. Simply add 1 additional teaspoon of dry
yeast to replace the sugar.

If you are storing your sourdough in the refrigerator, take it out the night before and set it on your countertop, covered with light cloth. Make sure it's not too watery. Drain any water on top and stir once before leaving it overnight.

Place the orange juice and 3 cups of the flour in your bread machine basket. Add the olive oil and vinegar. Next add the sourdough starter. Then add in the balance of flour and the gluten, and finally add the rest of the ingredients, except the cornmeal. Set the yeast on top in a dry area.

Set your machine on Dough cycle.

When done, turn dough out onto a lightly floured breadboard. Cut into three equal sections. Press each section out gently (never "punch" dough down). Cut each section into 6 lengthwise shapes for 6 sandwich buns. Place 9 buns on each of two lightly greased cooking sheets, using the cornmeal to generously dust the pans. The dough will sit on the cornmeal. Make a shallow lengthwise slice along the top of each. Cover with well-oiled paper or a light cloth, and let rise for up to 1 hour in a room temperature environment or in front of a closed window with the sun peeking through.

About 10 to 15 minutes before rising is completed, preheat oven to 350°F.

After rising, bake the buns on your center rack for 22 to 25 minutes, or until golden brown. Remove, cool on racks, and serve hot. You may cut them in half and store them in zipper-type bags for a few days, or you may freeze them. Thaw on the countertop. To reheat, place in the microwave and reheat for 20 seconds. Serve with plain pasta, lasagna, or any meat or chicken dish.

Nutrient Values per Bun Calories: 182.8 Protein: 4.959 g. Carbohydrate: 37.1 g. Dietary Fiber: 1.751 g. Total Sugars: .693 g. Total Fat: 1.382 g. Saturated Fat: .176 g. Monounsaturated Fat: .627 g. Polyunsaturated Fat: .257 g. Cholesterol: 0 mg. Calcium: 27.1 mg. Potassium: 94.8 mg. Sodium: 1.695 mg. Vitamin K: .368 mcg. Folate: 90.1 mcg.

❖ BUTTERMILK EGG BUNS ❖

BREAD MACHINE PREPARATION — OVEN BAKE
ADAPTABLE FOR DIABETICS
GREAT FOR HAMBURGERS, SANDWICHES, AND TOAST

When I worked in the film industry in southern California, I used to grab a "burger" for lunch. There was a place just down the road from the studio where I worked in the mid-seventies that served a giant burger on a giant "egg bun." It was called Don's Place. Of course I took a ribbing for that, but, wow, what a burger. Melted in my mouth. Fortunately, my work was the "physically intense" kind that automatically removed the calories.

These buns aren't high in fat, but the stuff you put between them might be. It is a great base for hamburgers, sandwiches, and toast. (For a good hamburger, use ¼ pound very lean ground round, thick slices of red onion, tomato, and fresh lettuce. Add a bit of no-salt-added ketchup, and you're in burger heaven.)

MAKES 12 BUNS   SODIUM PER RECIPE: 292.9 MG
SODIUM PER BUN: 16.9 MG

1 **cup reduced-fat, cultured, low-sodium buttermilk* (130 mg), at room temperature (70°F. to 80°F.)**
⅓ **cup orange juice with calcium (.821 mg), at room temperature (70°F. to 80°F.)**
1 **medium egg (55.4 mg)**
4 **cups white unbleached best for bread flour (10 mg)**
4 **tablespoons extra virgin olive oil (trace)**
4 **tablespoons white granulated sugar (.504 mg)**
1 **teaspoon vital wheat gluten (.72 mg)**
½ **cup quick oats (trace)**
1 **tablespoon bread machine yeast (6 mg)**

Warm the buttermilk in the microwave to about 100°F. Add all the ingredients to your bread machine in the order listed. Set on Dough cycle, and when the dough has risen, transfer it onto a lightly floured breadboard.

Press down hard with your palms until the dough is down to about ½ inch thick. With a large glass, cup, or shaped bun cutter, cut out 10 to 12 buns. To make the last few, you may have to roll up the dough and press down again.

Place these on lightly greased baking sheets (5 to 6 to a sheet) Cover with wax paper or a very light cloth and place in a warm spot for about 45 minutes (the oven would be good if heated to about 80°F. to 90°F.).

Preheat the oven to 425°F. while the buns are rising.

After rising, bake the buns at 450°F. on middle shelf for 6 to 8 minutes, or until golden brown.

Cool on rack. Serve warm or room temperature They will store in zipper-type bags for up to a week on your countertop or in your refrigerator and will freeze for up to a month.

Nutrient Values per Bun Calories: 235.6 Protein: 6.358 g. Carbohydrate: 40.3 g. Dietary Fiber: 1.682 g. Total Sugars: 4.991 g. Total Fat: 5.992 g. Saturated Fat: 1.084 g. Monounsaturated Fat: 3.602 g. Polyunsaturated Fat: .684 g. Cholesterol: 17.7 mg. Calcium: 41.1 mg. Potassium: 83.3 mg. Sodium: 16.9 mg. Vitamin K: 2.205 mcg. Folate: 92.3 mcg.

*Use Knudsen's if it is available in your area.

❖ ESKIMO BURGER BUNS ❖

(AN EGG BREAD)
WITH ONION FLAKES
BREAD MACHINE KNEAD—HAND SHAPE—OVEN BAKE
ADAPTABLE FOR DIABETICS

I love hamburgers. Some of my true-life tales were inspired by hamburgers. When healthy and working hard, I used to eat giant, humongous hamburgers. In Juneau, Alaska, during the sixties while working there for a month, I used to get a hamburger across the street from the Baronof Hotel called an "Eskimo Burger." It was as big and juicy and tasty as any you can imagine. The buns were huge, and they were just like these—only much larger. This recipe has honey, eggs, and oil in it. It can also be made using the sugar substitute Splenda in place of the honey.

MAKES 12 BUNS   SODIUM PER RECIPE: 212.7 MG
SODIUM PER BUN: 17.7 MG

THE DOUGH
  1 **cup orange juice fortified with calcium (2.488 mg), at room temperature (70°F. to 80°F.)**
  ¼ **cup honey (3.39 mg), at room temperature (70°F. to 80°F.)**
  1 **tablespoon apple cider vinegar (.15 mg)**
  2 **large eggs (126 mg)**
  5 **tablespoons extra virgin olive oil (trace)**
  4 **cups white unbleached bread machine flour (10 mg)**
  1 **teaspoon white granulated sugar (trace)**
1½ **teaspoons vital wheat gluten (1.1 mg)**
  1 **tablespoon bread machine yeast (6 mg)**

THE GLAZE
  1 **large egg, beaten with 1 teaspoon bottled water (63 mg)**
  1 **to 1½ tablespoons McCormick Minced Onion Flakes (1.575 mg)**

Place all the dough ingredients in your bread machine in the order listed.

Because this is an egg bread recipe, you'll want to let the first rise take about 2 to 2½ hours. After the dough has been kneaded in your bread machine, transfer it to a large warm mixing bowl, slightly greased, and cover with a light cloth. Set in a warm place (room temperature or slightly higher) for about 2 hours. It may double in size or get even larger. When it does, take it out of the bowl and place it on a flat warm cookie sheet and let it rise once again, covered with a light cloth, for about 1 hour to 1½ hours.

When the dough has risen a second time, gently press down on it, then cut it in half. Section off 6 pieces from each half and form into balls with your hands. Place on a lightly greased cooking sheet about 3 inches apart. Each sheet should hold 6 buns. (I've successfully made as many as 18 buns with this recipe.) Gently press down on the balls until they are about an inch or so thick, but don't let them get more than 3 inches in diameter. Cover lightly with a very light cloth.

Let the dough rise again for approximately 30 minutes. After 15 minutes, lightly press each one down just a bit. They will rise noticeably after that. These buns will increase in size in the oven while baking.

Preheat your oven to 350°F. about 10 minutes before the final third rise is complete.

Just before baking, brush on the glaze and sprinkle each bun with the McCormick Minced Onion Flakes.

Bake at 350°F. for about 15 to 20 minutes or a bit longer on the lower third shelf of your oven. They may not brown but may instead turn a cream color. If you prefer a darker bread, you may leave them longer until they brown.

Nutrient Values per Bun (12) Calories: 237.6 Protein: 6.466 g. Carbohydrate: 41.5 g Dietary Fiber: 1.448 g. Total Sugars: 5.997 g. Total Fat: 5.097 g. Saturated Fat: .915 g. Monounsaturated Fat: 3.028 g. Polyunsaturated Fat: .63 g. Cholesterol: 53.1 mg. Calcium: 40.2 mg. Potassium: 134.2 mg. Sodium: 17.7 mg. Vitamin K: 1.654 mcg. Folate: 1037 mcg.

❖ WHOLE WHEAT 'N WHITE BUNS ❖

BREAD MACHINE KNEAD — HAND SHAPE — OVEN BAKED
ESPECIALLY CREATED FOR DIABETICS

My father was a diabetic, long before much research had been done into the challenge of surviving it for a long life. He avoided sugar like it was a plague, but longed for sugar-laden items like chocolate, ice cream, and so on. A problem back then, and often today, is that bread is almost always made with some sugar. However, because of much research and new discoveries about sugar and diabetes, today's diabetics are better able to manage their daily intake, with some able to consume sugar and sugar products at small levels. This recipe (adaptable to real sugar), has no sugar or sugar ingredients (like raisins). It makes a great hamburger bun, dinner roll, or loaf of bread.

MAKES 12 HAMBURGER BUNS   MAKES 24 DINNER ROLLS
SODIUM PER RECIPE: 32.5 MG
SODIUM PER HAMBURGER BUN (12): 2.709 MG
SODIUM PER DINNER ROLL (24): 1.354 MG

THE DOUGH

1¾ cups less 1 tablespoon orange juice with calcium and pulp (4.353 mg), at room temperature (70°F. to 80°F.).
1 tablespoon apple cider vinegar (.15 mg)
2 cups pastry or Gold Medal Specialty whole wheat flour (12 mg)
3 cups best for bread white flour (7.5 mg)
1 level tablespoon vital wheat gluten (2.52 mg)
1 level tablespoon flaxseed meal (trace)
2 tablespoons olive oil (trace)
2 tablespoons Splenda Sugar Substitute* (trace)
1 tablespoon bread machine yeast (6 mg)

THE BUN GLAZE

1 large egg white (54.8 mg)
2 tablespoons sesame seeds or McCormick Minced Onion Flakes† (1.98 mg)

Heat the orange juice to 110°F. to 115°F. and place into your bread machine basket. Add the rest of ingredients in the order listed. Set the machine on Dough cycle.

When the dough is ready, turn it out onto a lightly floured breadboard. Cut in half. Press down the first half and cut out buns, or slice out dinner roll triangles (to roll up), or smaller bun sizes for dinner. Place on a lightly greased cookie sheet. (Do the same with the other half.)

To glaze, beat the egg white until it turns white. Brush some on top of each bun or roll. Sprinkle the sesame seeds or onion flakes on top.

Set the buns aside in a warm area, covered with lightly oil-spritzed wax paper, for about 45 minutes, or until they have at least doubled in size.

Preheat the oven to 425°F. Bake on the middle rack for 6 to 7 minutes. Don't overbake them. Cool on racks.

Serve them hot, or you can reheat them in the microwave. When reheating salt-free bread in the microwave, don't set for more than 10 seconds or the bread will become rock-hard.

Nutrient Values per Bun (12) Calories: 234 Protein: 7.202 g. Carbohydrate: 45.1 g. Dietary Fiber: 3.733 g. Total Sugars: 2.079 g. Total Fat: 3.196 g. Saturated Fat: .425 g. Monounsaturated Fat: 1.761 g. Polyunsaturated Fat: .478 g. Cholesterol: 0 mg. Calcium: 56.2 mg. Iron: 2.446 mg. Potassium: 204.6 mg. Sodium: 2.709 mg. Vitamin K: 1.103 mcg. Folate: 96.2 mcg.

Nutrient Values per Dinner Roll (24) Calories: 117 Protein: 3.601 g. Carbohydrate: 22.6 g. Dietary Fiber: 1.867 g. Total Sugars: 1.039 g. Total Fat: 1.598 g. Saturated Fat: .213 g. Monounsaturated Fat: .881 g. Polyunsaturated Fat: .239 g. Cholesterol: 0 mg. Calcium: 28.1 mg. Iron: 1.223 mg. Potassium: 102.3 mg. Sodium: 1.354 mg. Vitamin K: .551 mcg. Folate: 48.1 mcg.

*Replace with sugar.
†You may also try caraway seeds instead.

❖ OATMEAL RAISIN BUNS ❖

BREAD MACHINE PREPARATION — OVEN BAKE
ADAPTABLE FOR DIABETICS

A terrific sandwich bun for lunches or burgers.
MAKES 12 TO 18 BUNS   SODIUM PER RECIPE: 41.7 MG
SODIUM PER BUN (12 COUNT): 3.473 MG
SODIUM PER BUN (18 COUNT): 2.315

1¾ **cups orange juice fortified with calcium (4.353 mg)**
1 **cup quick oats (3.24 mg)**
4 **cups unbleached bread flour (10 mg)**
2 **tablespoons white granulated sugar (.672 mg)**
2 **teaspoons vital wheat gluten (1.5 mg)**
2 **tablespoons extra virgin olive oil (trace)**
1 **tablespoon bread machine yeast (6 mg)**

 At the sound of the buzzer add:
1 **cup unpacked raisins (17.4 mg), soaked**

Heat the orange juice to about 115°F. Place into your bread machine container first. Add the rest of the dough ingredients in the order listed, reserving the raisins. Set the machine on the Dough cycle.

Just before the dough is ready, preheat your oven to 80°F. to 100°F., then turn it off. Prepare two baking sheets by placing them in the warmed oven for 5 minutes. Then spray lightly with olive oil. (I use PAM olive oil spray).

Remove the dough from the bread machine and lay it gently on a floured breadboard. Cut in half and set one half aside. Press down gently on the first piece until the dough is about ½ inch thick for making 12 buns, ⅜ inch thick to make 18 buns. I use a large drinking glass with sharp edges to cut out the buns. Pick a size that will make the count you want. Cut either 6 or 9 from each half. Set buns on a warmed baking sheet about 2 inches apart. Repeat this with second dough half on another warmed baking sheet. Cover both with a light cloth and set into the warmed oven for about 45 minutes. If you have a single oven, remove the sheets gently and set them in warm place (a sunny window works well) while the oven heats up to 425°F.

Bake one tray at a time at 425°F. for 6 to 7 minutes.

Cool on rack. Serve warm or room temperature. They store in zipper-type bags for up to a week on your countertop or in your refrigerator and will freeze for up to a month.

Nutritional Values per Bun (12) Calories: 274.7 Protein: 6.403 g. Carbohydrate: 55.8 g. Dietary Fiber: 2.606 g. Total Sugars: 17.9 g. Total Fat: 3.207 g. Saturated Fat: .47 g. Monounsaturated Fat: 1.86 g. Polyunsaturated Fat: .537 g. Cholesterol: 0 mg. Calcium: 60.3 mg. Potassium: 248 mg. Sodium: 3.473 mg. Vitamin K: 1.103 mcg. Folate: 106 mcg.

Nutritional Values per Bun (18) Calories: 183.1 Protein: 4.269 g. Carbohydrate: 37.2 g. Dietary Fiber: 1.738 g. Total Sugars: 12 g. Total Fat: 2.138 g. Saturated Fat: .313 g. Monounsaturated Fat: 1.24 g. Polyunsaturated Fat: .358 g. Cholesterol: 0 mg. Calcium: 40.2 mg. Potassium: 165.3 mg. Sodium: 2.315 mg. Vitamin K: .735 mcg. Folate: 70.7 mcg.

❈ VANILLA RAISIN BUNS ❈

BREAD MACHINE PREPARATION — OVEN BAKE
ADAPTABLE FOR DIABETICS

Somewhat like our standard hamburger buns, but with a much different flavor, texture, and taste. These are great for sandwiches, dinner rolls, picnics, or toasting.

MAKES 14 BUNS   SODIUM PER RECIPE: 42.8 MG
SODIUM PER BUN: 3 MG

1¾ **cups less 2 tablespoons unsweetened orange juice fortified with calcium (4.104 mg), at room temperature (70°F. to 80°F.)**
1 **tablespoon apple cider vinegar (.15 mg)**
2 **tablespoons extra virgin olive oil (trace)**
5 **cups white best for bread flour (12.5 mg)**
1½ **teaspoons vital wheat gluten (1.12 mg)**
1 **tablespoon vanilla extract (1.17 mg)**
2 **teaspoons white granulated sugar (trace)**
1 **tablespoon yeast (6 mg)**

At the raisin buzzer add:
1 **cup black baking raisins (17.4 mg)**

Place all the dough ingredients into your bread machine in the order listed, or in the order your manufacturer suggests, reserving the raisins. Set the machine on the Dough cycle. When the raisin buzzer sounds, add the raisins.

When the dough is ready, transfer it to a lightly floured board and cut in half. Roll out one half at a time to about ½ inch to ¾ inch thick, and then cut out 6 to 9 buns from each half.

Place the buns on 2 lightly greased cooking sheets about 2 inches apart (half on each) and set them in a warm place, covered with a light cloth or lightly oil-spritzed wax paper. Let rise for about 45 minutes. (This dough will stick to wax paper if you don't lightly oil it.)

Preheat the oven to 425°F. about 10 to 15 minutes before dough is finished rising.

Bake the buns for 7 to 8 minutes, then set on racks to cool. Serve warm or room temperature. They will store in zipper-type bags for up to a week on your countertop or in your refrigerator and will freeze for up to a month. Thaw them on the countertop or put them in the microwave, cover with wax paper, and defrost for about 40 seconds.

Nutrient Values per Bun Calories: 236.9 Protein: 5.691 g Carbohydrate: 46.8 g Dietary Fiber: 1.862 g. Total Sugars: .594 g. Total Fat: 2.477 g. Saturated Fat: .352 g. Monounsaturated Fat: 1.487 g. Polyunsaturated Fat: .364 g. Cholesterol: 0 mg. Calcium: 50.2 mg. Iron: 2.475 mg. Potassium: 204.2 mg. Sodium: 3.056 mg. Vitamin K: .945 mcg. Folate: 102.7 mcg.

❈ APRICOT DINNER ROLLS ❈

BREAD MACHINE PREPARATION — OVEN BAKE

A special-flavor roll for special meals like Thanksgiving and other holidays. If you like apricots, you'll love this recipe.

MAKES 24 TO 36 DINNER ROLLS   SODIUM PER RECIPE: 43.4 MG
SODIUM PER ROLL (24): 1.807 MG
SODIUM PER ROLL (36): 1.205 MG

½ packed cup dried apricots* (6.5 mg), boiled, soaked, puréed
1 cup bottled water for soaking apricots (trace)
¾ cup orange juice fortified with calcium (1.866 mg), at room temperature (70°F. to 80°F.)
2 tablespoons nonfat milk (15.8 mg)
2 teaspoons apple cider vinegar (trace)
1 tablespoon extra virgin olive oil (trace)
4¾ cups white unbleached best for bread flour (11.9 mg)
1 tablespoon vital wheat gluten (2.25 mg)
1 level tablespoon grated lemon or orange zest (.36 mg)
2 teaspoons white granulated sugar (trace)
1 tablespoon bread machine yeast (6 mg)
½ cup unsalted walnut halves (5 mg), chopped in processor

In a medium-size saucepan, bring the apricots to a boil in the cup of water. Boil for 5 minutes, stirring. Turn the heat off, cover with a lid, and let the apricots sit for 1 hour in the water. After they have soaked, purée the apricots in the water, using your food processor (the Braun 550 Handheld Mixer is great for this).

Pour your puréed apricots into your bread machine pan along with the orange juice and the nonfat milk, all at room temperature (70°F. to 80°F.). Add in the vinegar and the olive oil.

Put all other ingredients into the pan in the order listed, reserving the

*Total sugars not listed by USDA. Carbohydrates for dried apricots = 40.1 grams.

walnuts. Set the machine for the Dough cycle, and when the raisin buzzer sounds add the walnuts.

When the dough is ready, turn it out onto a lightly floured breadboard. Cut in half. Spritz the dough with just a dab of olive oil spray. Fold over and roll out again, each time the dough gets thicker. Don't roll it flat like the first time. Now roll it out again. Fold again. You'll do this until your fold is about 1 inch wide but you've created a log about 12 to 18 inches long. You will have created "creases" in the dough that will split open when baking, giving the appearance of a Parker House roll.

Cut the log into 12 to 18 pieces, depending on how long your log is. Set these into lightly greased muffin tins or muffin cups in tins with the fold side down. Repeat with the second half of dough. Or, if you like, you can roll out the second half to about ⅛ inch thick, cut a bunch of triangles and roll up into crescent-shape rolls. These you will place on a lightly greased cooking sheet.

Cover each with lightly oil-spritzed wax paper and set in a warm spot. If your house isn't warm, then turn the oven on your "warmer" temperature for a minute or two, then turn it off and set the dough inside. The temperature in there shouldn't be more than 90°F. however. If for some reason your oven got too hot, open the door and let it cool down for a few minutes, then place the dough in the oven and close the door. Let it rise for about 45 minutes.

When the dough is ready, and if you used the oven, carefully take the sheets and tins out and set them on the stovetop or countertop.

Preheat oven to 425°F. When the oven is ready, bake each sheet or muffin tin by itself on the middle rack for about 6 to 7 minutes. To make sure they brown nicely, you can spritz them with a very light coating of olive oil before baking. Cool on rack. Serve warm or room temperature. They will store in zipper-type bags for up to a week on your countertop or in your refrigerator and will freeze for up to a month. Thaw them on the countertop or put them in the microwave, cover with wax paper, and defrost for about 40 seconds.

Nutrient Values per Roll (24) Calories: 123.2 Protein: 3.499 g. Carbohydrate: 22.4 g. Dietary Fiber: 1.172 g. Total Sugars: .401 g. Total Fat: 2.211 g. Saturated Fat: .248 g. Monounsaturated Fat: .642 g. Polyunsaturated Fat: 1.136 g. Cholesterol: .026 mg. Calcium: 18.3 mg. Iron: 1.432 mg. Potassium: 100.3 mg. Sodium: 1.9 mg. Vitamin K: .276 mcg. Folate: 55.6 mcg.

✦ ENGLISH MUFFINS ✦

BREAD MACHINE PREPARATION — OVEN BAKE
ADAPTABLE FOR DIABETICS

You can change this recipe to a crumpets recipe by adding more scalded milk. Open the English Muffins with a fork after they have cooled. When toasting, toast until just golden brown. The texture and flavor will remind you of a true old-fashioned English Muffin.

MAKES 8 TO 10 MUFFINS SODIUM PER RECIPE: 96.9 MG
SODIUM PER MUFFIN BASED ON 8 MUFFINS: 12.1 MG
SODIUM PER MUFFIN BASED ON 10 MUFFINS: 9.692 MG

1   teaspoon active dry yeast (3.5 mg)
2   tablespoons bottled water (trace), at room temperature (70°F. to 80°F.)
1   cup orange juice with calcium (2.488 mg), at room temperature (70°F. to 80°F.)
1   tablespoon apple cider vinegar (.15 mg)
½   cup scalded nonfat milk (63.1 mg)
2   teaspoons white granulated sugar (.084 mg)
1   tablespoon Featherweight Baking Powder (13.5 mg)
1½ tablespoons Ener-G Baking Soda (trace mg)
3   cups all-purpose flour (7.5 mg)
1   cup whole wheat pastry flour (6 mg)
⅓   cup Albers cornmeal (0 mg)

In a medium-size mixing bowl, dissolve the yeast in the water for about 5 minutes. Add the orange juice, vinegar, scalded milk, sugar, baking powder, and baking soda. Beat in slowly, with double beaters, ½ cup of the whole wheat and 1½ cups of the white flour. Cover the bowl with a cloth or plastic wrap and place in a warm location or in the oven with temperature about 85°F. to 90°F. for about 1½ hours.

After this rising period, scrape the dough from the bowl to a flour-dusted breadboard and knead in the balance of the flours. Knead by rolling—do not "punch" down. Knead until no folds show.

Lightly grease the inside of your muffin rings.* Place the rings on a cookie sheet that has been dusted generously with cornmeal (Albers is good for this), and fill each ring only halfway. Set in warm place, covered with a light cloth, for about 30 minutes.

Preheat your oven to 425°F.

Place the baking sheet with the muffin dough and rings into the oven

*You can buy muffin rings at most good kitchen ware stores or on-line at www.surlatable.com.

on the middle rack. Cook for 2 minutes. Open oven and turn each muffin over using a flat-blade pancake turner. Bake for 15 to 20 minutes, or until golden brown.

Place the sheet on a cooling rack. When cooled a few minutes, remove the rings.

Serve toasted. They will store in zipper-type bags for up to a week on your countertop or in your refrigerator and will freeze for up to a month. Thaw them on the countertop or put them in the microwave, cover with wax paper, and defrost for about 40 seconds.

To make crumpets, simply increase the scalded milk to 1⅔ cups.

Nutrient Values per Muffin (8) Calories: 260.8 Protein: 8.218 g. Carbohydrate: 55.7 g. Dietary Fiber: 3.633 g. Total Sugars: 1.039 g. Total Fat: .896 g. Saturated Fat: .148 g. Monounsaturated Fat: .108 g. Polyunsaturated Fat: .318 g. Cholesterol: .306 mg. Calcium: 205.5 mg. Iron: 3.605 mg. Potassium: 404.2 mg. Sodium: 12.1 mg. Vitamin K: .003 mcg. Folate: 113.6 mcg.

Nutrient Values per Muffin (10) Calories: 208.6 Protein: 6.574 g. Carbohydrate: 44.6 g. Dietary Fiber: 2.906 g. Total Sugars: .832 g. Total Fat: .717 g. Saturated Fat: .118 g. Monounsaturated Fat: .087 g. Polyunsaturated Fat: .254 g. Cholesterol: .245 mg. Calcium: 164.4 mg. Iron: 2.884 mg. Potassium: 323.3 mg. Sodium: 9.692 mg. Vitamin K: .002 mcg. Folate: 90.9 mcg.

❖ BASIC SCONES ❖

FROM SCRATCH—HANDMADE
ADAPTABLE FOR DIABETICS

You can use this recipe to experiment with. These are basic British-type scones—made with flour, water, baking soda, but without the salt. You won't be able to tell the difference. I suggest adding currants or a dried fruit of your choice. You can use raisins, chopped dates, chopped nuts, dried fruit pieces, or leave them out and have a hot, spreadable scone just as is. Basic often means little or no flavor other than flour, or, as with regular scones, salt. Try these with currants the first time, then add your own flavors next time. Remember: Don't overmix or overknead.

MAKES 8 LARGE SCONES   SODIUM PER RECIPE: 130.1 MG
SODIUM PER SCONE: 16.3 MG

2 **cups unbleached white flour (5 mg)**
1 **level tablespoon Featherweight Baking Powder (9 mg)**
1 **heaping tablespoon Ener-G Baking Soda (0 mg)**
1 **tablespoon white granulated sugar (.126 mg)**
2 **medium eggs (110.9 mg), beaten**
3 **tablespoons unsalted butter (4.686 mg), softened**
1 **tablespoon apple cider vinegar (.15 mg)**
½ **cup bottled water (trace), at room temperature (70°F. to 80°F.)**
   Optional: ½ cup currants (1.12 mg)

Preheat your oven to 425°F.

Combine and stir together with a wooden spoon the flour, baking powder, baking soda, and sugar. Lightly beat the eggs and butter together with the vinegar and water. Add the currants, if using. Stir. Combine the wet with the dry and stir with a wooden spoon just until the dough becomes crumbly. (We don't want to overmix).

With a soup spoon* drop 8 equal-size balls of dough onto a lightly greased baking sheet. These will take an irregular form, which is the sign of a good scone.

Bake at 425°F. for about 13 to 15 minutes, or until just turning golden brown. (Make sure to preheat the oven to prevent burning the bottom of the scone.) Serve hot out of the oven or store overnight in the refrigerator in zipper-type bag and reheat in the microwave. They also may be frozen for a few weeks for future use.

Nutrient Values per Scone Calories: 175.9 Protein: 4.649 g. Carbohydrate: 26.3 g. Dietary Fiber: .871 g. Total Sugars: 1.559 g. Total Fat: 5.733 g. Saturated Fat: 3.079 g. Monounsaturated Fat: 1.694 g. Polyunsaturated Fat: .441 g. Cholesterol: 58.4 mg. Calcium: 478.1 mg. Potassium: 176.3 mg. Sodium: 16.3 mg. Vitamin K: 0 mcg. Folate: 53.4 mcg.

❖ STREET VENDOR SCONES ❖

WITH ORANGE ZEST
FROM SCRATCH—HANDMADE
ADAPTABLE FOR DIABETICS

While filming in London once, I came across a street vendor who sold scones. I bought one. For the rest of that trip my search was one for the great English scone. Turned out that the best one I'd had was from that street vendor, who, of course, I could never find again. I think, finally, with the availability of Ener-G Baking Soda, we have recreated the great "Street Vendor Scone."

**MAKES 8 LARGE SCONES   SODIUM PER RECIPE: 145.5 MG
SODIUM PER SCONE: 18.2 MG**

2 **cups unbleached white flour (5 mg)**
1 **tablespoon Featherweight Baking Powder (9 mg)**
1 **heaping tablespoon Ener-G Baking Soda (0 mg)**
1 **tablespoon white granulated sugar (.126 mg)**
2 **egg yolks (for binding) (14.3 mg)**
1 **egg white (54.8 mg)**
3 **tablespoons unsalted butter (4.686 mg), softened**

*They are also nice shaped into triangles with fruit or nuts added in.

½ teaspoon of either vanilla extract or almond extract (trace)
1 tablespoon apple cider vinegar (.15 mg)
½ cup fresh orange juice from above orange or commercial unsweetened orange juice with calcium, or a mix of both (1.244 mg), at room temperature (70°F. to 80°F.)
1 heaping tablespoon grated zest of 1 medium or large orange (.18 mg)
½ cup currants (1.12 mg)

THE GLAZE PRIOR TO BAKING
1 egg white (54.8 mg)
1 tablespoon orange zest (.18 mg)

Preheat your oven to 425°F.

Combine and stir together with a wooden spoon the flour, baking powder, baking soda, and the sugar. Lightly beat the yolks, egg white, and butter together with the vanilla, vinegar, and orange juice. Add the currants and the orange zest. Stir. Combine the wet with the dry and stir with a wooden spoon just until the dough becomes crumbly. (We don't want to overmix.)

With a soup spoon, drop 8 equal-size balls of dough onto a lightly greased baking sheet. These will take an irregular form, which is the sign of a good scone.

To prepare the glaze, whisk together the egg white and orange zest. Brush the tops of the scones with the glaze mix. You can add 1 teaspoon sugar to the glaze mix if you like, but it's not necessary.

Bake in the preheated oven at 425°F for about 12 to 13 minutes. Serve the scones hot out of the oven or store them overnight in the refrigerator in a zipper-type bag and reheat in the microwave.

Nutrient Values Per Scone Calories: 268 Protein: 6.093 g. Carbohydrate: 49.2 g. Dietary Fiber: 2.546 g. Total Sugars: 23.3 g. Total Fat: 6.57 g. Saturated Fat: 3.501 g. Monounsaturated Fat: 1.772 g. Polyunsaturated Fat: .509 g. Cholesterol: 64.8 mg. Calcium: 544.6 mg. Potassium: 490.5 mg. Sodium: 21.6 mg. Vitamin K: .084 mcg. Folate: 63.4 mcg.

❖ WHOLE WHEAT SCONES ❖

FROM SCRATCH—HANDMADE
NOT ADAPTABLE FOR DIABETICS

Before CHF, I used to enjoy visiting a local boulangerie with my wife. We'd order a latte and I'd get a whole wheat scone with raisins. The local place is still there, expanded in fact, but I don't get in as much as before. It's tough to be a watching guest. So, here they are, as close as I've been able to figure them out. These seem just as tasty, although it's been a long time since tasting the real thing. (No kidding, the hypotenuse of the triangle is 3 inches.)

MAKES 12 LARGE 3-INCH TRIANGLE SCONES
SODIUM PER RECIPE: 264.8 MG   SODIUM PER SCONE: 22.1 MG

1½ cups unbleached white flour (3.75 mg)
1½ cups whole wheat bread flour (9 mg)
2 teaspoons vital wheat gluten (1.5 g)
1½ tablespoons Featherweight Baking Powder (20.2 mg)
2 heaping tablespoons Ener-G Baking Soda (trace)
1 tablespoon brown sugar (5.382 mg)
1 tablespoon white granulated sugar (.126 mg)
½ teaspoon ground cinnamon (.303 mg)
2 medium eggs (110.9 mg), beaten
1½ tablespoons apple cider vinegar (.15 mg)
6 tablespoons unsalted butter* (9.372 mg), softened
⅓ cup natural pure maple syrup (not the Log Cabin type) (41.6 mg), at room temperature (70°F. to 80°F.)
½ cup bottled water (trace), at room temperature (70°F to 80°F.)

Preheat your oven to 425°F.

With a wooden spoon, combine and stir together the flours, gluten, baking powder, baking soda, cinnamon, and brown and white sugars.

Beat the eggs lightly. Add the vinegar. With a wooden spoon stir in the butter, maple syrup, and water. Fold in the dry ingredients until the mixture becomes just crumbly.

Preheat your oven to 425°F.

Break the dough into 12 even pieces. Shape triangles about 1 inch thick and place onto a lightly greased cookie sheet.

Bake at 425°F. for about 13 to 15 minutes. Serve hot out of the oven, or store overnight in the refrigerator in zipper-type bags and reheat in the microwave. They also may be frozen for a few weeks for future use.

OPTIONAL GLAZE
1 teaspoon ground cinnamon (.303 mg)
1 teaspoon white granulated sugar (.126 mg)
1 egg white (54.8 mg), beaten

Stir together the sugar and cinnamon. Beat this into the beaten egg white until just mixed. Using a basting brush, baste each triangle just before baking.

Nutrient Values per Scone Using the Butter Calories: 194.6 Protein: 5.725 g. Carbohydrate: 27.6 g. Dietary Fiber: 2.345 g. Total Sugars: 3.194 g. Total Fat: 7.384 g. Saturated Fat: 4.027 g. Monounsaturated Fat: 2.157 g. Polyunsaturated Fat: .557 g. Cholesterol: 64.6

*You may substitute ⅔ cup flaxseed meal (trace) for the butter. This also cuts the fat content.

mg. Calcium: 106.6 mg. Iron: 1.697 mg. Potassium: 299.8 mg. Sodium: 22.1 mg. Vitamin K: .029 mcg. Folate: 36.8 mcg.

Nutrient Values Per Scone Using the Flaxseed Meal Calories: 168.7 Protein: 6.914 g. Carbohydrate: 29.3 g. Dietary Fiber: 4.012 g. Total Sugars: 3.194 g. Total Fat: 3.5 g. Saturated Fat: .442 g. Monounsaturated Fat: .494 g. Polyunsaturated Fat: .343 g. Cholesterol: 49 mg. Calcium: 104.9 mg. Iron: 1.685 mg. Potassium: 297.9 mg. Sodium: 21.3 mg. Vitamin K: .029 mcg. Folate: 36.6 mcg.

❖ DON'S BISCUITS ❖

HAND KNEAD—OVEN BAKE
ADAPTABLE FOR DIABETICS

Ever wonder what those sailors at sea used to munch on? Or the cowboys herding cattle between stops at the chuck wagon? Nope, no jerky. They had biscuits—tough, stale, highly salted (for preservation) biscuits. And all you military types, remember the C-rations of World War II, Korea, and the beginning of the Vietnam War? (MREs took over about then.) Those biscuits we used to call "John Wayne Biscuits" were about as tough as leather. But we ate them because they were biscuits and because you could load them up with that awful peanut butter that came in that awful tin. Well, no more C-rations. These are made without salt and preserve just fine, thank you— mostly because they get eaten up in a hurry. Make them 2 inches or 2½ inches and form by hand for that old-fashioned biscuit feel and look. You'll love 'em. I do freeze leftovers and they make great snacks at family picnics or during a long drive somewhere. Leave the butter at home; there's plenty in the biscuit.

MAKES 10 2½-INCH BISCUITS   SODIUM PER RECIPE: 170.1 MG
SODIUM PER BISCUIT: 17 MG

 1 **egg white (54.8 mg), beaten**
 6 **tablespoons unsalted butter (6.248 mg), softened**
 ¾ **cup reduced-fat, reduced-sodium cultured buttermilk
     (Knudsen's preferred) or ¾ cup nonfat milk* (94.6 mg)**
 2 **cups white best for bread flour or all-purpose flour
     (5 mg)**
 1 **tablespoon Ener-G Baking Soda (trace)**
1½ **teaspoons Featherweight Baking Powder (3 mg)**

*The buttermilk helps make these flakier. Nonfat milk tends to make them crispier, or a bit more like those John Wayne biscuits.

1 teaspoon sugar (.042 mg) or honey (.28 mg) or Splenda Sugar Substitute (0 mg)

Preheat your oven to 350°F.

Lightly beat the egg with the softened butter, then add the buttermilk and stir.

With a wooden spoon, stir together the flour, baking soda, and baking powder. Stir in the egg/buttermilk/butter mixture, adding the honey or sugar. Mix with a wooden spoon until slightly crumbly. Do not overmix. This is a quick stir until crumbly. Ener-G kicks in the batter and then in the oven; it can't be allowed to "sit."

With a large spoon, drop the dough onto a lightly greased baking sheet. Press down once slightly, pushing the ball down to about ¾ to 1 inch. If you want perfectly round biscuits, then roll the dough out once on a lightly floured board until about ¾ inch thick. Cut with a biscuit cutter and set the biscuits on the baking sheet.

Bake at 350°F. for about 20 minutes, or until golden brown. Serve hot out of the oven. Enjoy!

Nutrient Values per Biscuit Calories: 164.2 Protein: 3.633 g. Carbohydrate: 21 g. Dietary Fiber: .675 g. Total Sugars: .416 g. Total Fat: 7.189 g. Saturated Fat: 4.362 g. Monounsaturated Fat:2.027 g. Polyunsaturated Fat: .361 g. Cholesterol: 19 mg. Calcium: 358.6 mg. Potassium: 64.2 mg. Sodium: 17 mg. Vitamin K: .004 mcg. Folate: 39.8 mcg.

❄ SOFT BREADSTICKS ❄

WITH SESAME SEEDS
HAND KNEAD—OVEN BAKE
ADAPTABLE FOR DIABETICS

Who doesn't like breadsticks? These are great to take with you as snacks or to serve at the dinner table. I have a special fondness for them. Many years ago, after gaining too much weight traveling the country in airlines, staying in a different hotel or motel every night, wondering what town I woke in, I decided to go on a "crash" diet. I found breadsticks. Great. I could throw a pack in my briefcase, and when I felt the pangs of hunger, just nibble on one Of course, those had a ton of sodium in them, while these don't. If you prefer crunchy, hard breadsticks, leave out the yeast.

**MAKES 20 BREADSTICKS   SODIUM PER RECIPE: 78.5 MG
SODIUM PER BREADSTICK: 3.923 MG**

THE DOUGH

⅔ cup unsweetened orange juice fortified with calcium (1.657 mg), at room temperature (70°F. to 80°F.)

1½ teaspoons bread machine yeast (3 mg)
  ½ teaspoon white granulated sugar (.042 mg) (or Splenda)
  2 cups less 2 tablespoons white unbleached bread machine
      white flour (5 mg)
  2 level tablespoons cornstarch (1.44 mg)
  3 tablespoons extra virgin olive oil (trace)
  1 teaspoon apple cider vinegar (.15 mg), at room temperature
      (70°F. to 80°F.)

THE GLAZE
  1 egg white (54.8 mg), beaten
  ½ teaspoon white granulated sugar (.042 mg)
  6 to 8 tablespoons sesame seeds (12.5 mg)

This mix makes a pliable dough to work with after it rises. You'll need 2 baking sheets, lightly sprayed with olive oil. (If you don't use yeast, seeking a "crispier" breadstick, then of course the dough will not be "pliable.")

Float the yeast in the orange juice (you may substitute water or apple juice for the orange juice) along with the sugar for about 10 minutes, then stir the yeast in. When it doubles, it is ready.

In a medium-size mixing bowl, with a wooden spoon stir together the flour, and cornstarch. Stir in the olive oil, cider vinegar, and yeast and mix until well combined. Roll dough out onto a breadboard and hand knead for 5 to 8 minutes. When ready, press the dough down on the board with your hands to about 6 by 8 inches. Brush or lightly spritz with the olive oil and cover with a light cloth or wax paper. Set in a warm place for about 1 hour to rise.

To make the glaze, beat the egg white with the sugar until it nearly stiffens.* Pour it out onto a dinner plate or other surface where you can roll the sticks.

Spread the sesame seeds out on a dish or on a sheet of wax paper, so you can roll the sticks in them. Cut the dough in half (to about 3 inches by 4 inches), and then slice 8 to 10 three-inch-long pieces off each half. One by one, roll each piece in the palms of your hands until they stretch out to about 6 to 8 inches in length. You can try to stretch them up to 7 to 8 inches after you've "palmed" them to 6 inches.

Roll each first in the egg white glaze, then in the sesame seeds. Space each breadstick well apart (about 2 inches) from the next on your lightly greased (with olive oil spray) baking sheets. Cover with a light cloth or wax paper and let stand for about 20 minutes or so.

Preheat your oven to 400°F. Bake the breadsticks at 400°F. for 12 to 13

---

*You may leave the sugar out of this glaze—it's used as a sweetener only. You may substitute honey at room temperature (70°F. to 80°F.) for the sugar.

minutes. Roll them over on the opposite side at 6 minutes to prevent burning on one side. Place on, wire cooling racks when done. Enjoy!

Nutrient Values per Breadstick Calories: 75.8 Protein: 1.912 g. Carbohydrate 11.9 g. Dietary Fiber: .695 g. Total Sugars 1.037 g. Total Fat: 2.26 g. Saturated Fat: .312 g. Monounsaturated Fat: 1.305 g. Polyunsaturated Fat: .503 g. Cholesterol: 0 mg. Calcium: 14.3 mg. Potassium: 44.3 mg. Sodium: 3.923 mg. Vitamin K: .662 mcg. Folate: 31.5 mcg.

❈ SOFT CHEDDAR BREADSTICKS ❈

WITH GARLIC AND ONION
HAND KNEAD — OVEN BAKE
ADAPTABLE FOR DIABETICS

These are great to take with you as snacks or to serve at the dinner table. They can be made crispier by not using the yeast.

**MAKES 20 BREADSTICKS   SODIUM PER RECIPE. 81.1 MG
SODIUM PER BREADSTICK: 4.057 MG**

⅔ cup unsweetened orange juice fortified with calcium (1.657 mg), at room temperature (70°F. to 80°F.)
1½ teaspoons active dry yeast or bread machine yeast (3 mg)
1 teaspoon white granulated sugar (.042 mg)
2 cups minus 2 tablespoons best for bread flour (4.68 mg)
1 teaspoon Ener-G Baking Soda (trace)
2 tablespoons cornstarch (1.44 mg)
3 tablespoons extra virgin olive oil (trace)
2 cloves garlic (1.02 mg), minced
1 ounce grated Heluva Good low sodium Cheddar Cheese (10 mg)
1 egg white (54.8 mg), beaten
4 tablespoons McCormick Minced Onion Flakes (4.2 mg)

This mix makes a nice fluffy, soft dough to work with after it rises. You'll need 2 baking sheets lightly sprayed with olive oil. If you decide to make them without yeast, to obtain a crispier breadstick, then the dough will not be as pliable. (But first try them with yeast.)

Float the yeast in the warmed orange juice (about 80°F. not hot; hot liquid will "kill" the yeast) with the sugar for about 10 minutes, then stir the yeast in. When it doubles, it is ready.

In a medium-size mixing bowl with a wooden spoon stir together the flour, baking soda, and cornstarch. Stir in the olive oil, garlic, cheese, and yeast/juice and mix together with the spoon. When well combined, turn the dough out onto a breadboard and hand knead for 5 minutes. (At this stage the dough will be crumbly.) When ready, press the dough down on the board until it measures about 6 by 8 inches. Brush or lightly spray with olive oil (trace sodium) and cover with wax paper. Set in a warm place for about 1 hour to double in size.

Beat the egg white until foamy and then pour it onto a large dinner plate. Spread the onion flakes out on another dinner plate or a sheet of wax paper, so you can roll the sticks in them. (If you like caraway or sesame or other flavors, you can add a small portion of those to the onion flakes and mix them up.)

Cut the dough in half (to about 3 inches by 4 inches), and then slice 8 to 10 three-inch-long pieces off each half. One by one, roll each piece between your hands to lengthen them to about 6 inches. When done, stretch them just a bit to about 7 or 8 inches by pulling on each end. Be careful to not break them apart.

Roll each stick in beaten egg white first, then in the onion flakes. (If you go through the onion flakes quickly, just add more. The additional sodium is negligible.) Space each breadstick well apart from the next on your lightly greased (with olive oil spray) baking sheets. Cover with light cloth or wax paper and let stand in a warm place for about 10 minutes or so while they rise a bit more. (You may let them rise more or less—the longer they rise the softer; the less they rise the crispier.)

Preheat your oven to 350°F.

Bake the breadsticks at 350°F for 16 to 20 minutes. Roll them over halfway through the baking time to keep them from burning on the bottom side. Remove to wire cooling racks when done. Enjoy!

Nutrient values per Breadstick: Calories: 177.6 Protein: 2.099 g. Carbohydrate: 12.4 g. Dietary Fiber: .523 g. Total Sugars: .208 g. Total Fat: 13.4 g. Saturated Fat: 1.754 g. Monounsaturated Fat: 9.472 g. Polyunsaturated Fat: 1.133 g. Cholesterol: 1.25 mg. Calcium: 25.3 mg. Iron: .712 mg. Potassium: 55 mg. Sodium: 4.057 mg. Vitamin K: 6.284 mcg. Folate: 31.6 mcg.

❖ DON'S BEST SOFT PRETZELS ❖

HAND KNEAD—STOVETOP BOIL—OVEN BAKE
ADAPTABLE FOR DIABETICS

Remember the fairgrounds? Remember the hucksters who could hustle those little tools that could cut, peel, shape, dice, splice anything in your kitchen? Remember the Ferris wheels and other rides? Remember the sugar cones and the soft pretzels? Those pretzels were loaded with salt and were very, very high in sodium—yet they were yummy. They helped make the county fair a truly great experience. If you liked those, you'll love these. With this recipe, you'll think you taste salt, but there isn't any. The sodium count is so low you can eat more than one. They are best eaten right out of the oven or reheated within one day. You can also make some great breadsticks with this dough. This recipe takes a little planning and some work, but it's well worth it. We love them around here.

MAKES 12 PRETZELS   SODIUM PER RECIPE: 82 MG
SODIUM PER PRETZEL: 6.85 MG

THE YEAST SPONGE
- ¾ teaspoon active dry yeast (1.5 mg)
- 4 tablespoons bottled water (trace), at room temperature (70°F. to 80°F.)
- 1 tablespoon white flour (.156 mg)
- 1 teaspoon white granulated sugar (.042 mg) or Splenda Sugar Substitute

THE DOUGH MIX
- 1 teaspoon active dry yeast (1.98 mg)
- ⅔ cup bottled water (4.693 mg), at room temperature (70°F. to 80°F.)
- 3¼ cups flour (8.125 mg)
- 1½ teaspoons vital wheat gluten (1.5 mg)
- 1 tablespoon Featherweight Baking Powder (6 mg)
- 4 tablespoons unsweetened orange juice fortified with calcium (.622 mg), at room temperature (70°F. to 80°F.)
- 1 tablespoon lime juice (.38 mg), at room temperature (70°F. to 80°F.)
- 2 tablespoons extra virgin olive oil (trace)

THE GLAZE
- 1 egg white (54.8 mg), beaten
- 2 tablespoons McCormick Minced Onion Flakes (2.1 mg)

OPTIONAL TOPPINGS
- 2 level tablespoons caraway seeds (1.139 mg)
- 2 level tablespoons poppy seeds (3.696 mg)

Prepare the sponge in a small bowl by combining all the ingredients listed. Cover it tightly with plastic and let stand for 2 hours. This is somewhat the same recipe I use for making sourdough starter. We call this mixture a "sponge." After sitting for about 2 hours, the mix should be light and bubbly.

In a small bowl, mix the yeast with the water, making sure the water is at least lukewarm. In a large bowl, combine 3 cups of the flour with the gluten and the baking powder by stirring it with a wooden spoon or a fork. Add the yeast mixture (the sponge), the orange juice, lime juice, and olive oil, and mix all together. When it cleans the bowl, transfer the dough to a lightly floured breadboard and knead with your hands gently for a few turns. Place the dough into a lightly oiled bowl and cover tightly with plastic wrap and let it rise in a warm place. (I like to heat my oven slightly, turn off the heat, and let it rise in there. I never get it over 80°F., and it seems to work consistently.) Let it rise for about ½ hour or slightly more.

Transfer the risen dough to a lightly floured board and knead gently for just a few turns. Never punch it down. Place back into the bowl, tightly cover with plastic wrap, and let sit for another ½ hour.

Next roll the dough out onto your board and make a log about 12 inches long. Cut it into 12 different equal pieces. Now you are ready to make either pretzels or breadsticks. Roll each piece between your hands until you have about a 14-to-18-inch rope of dough.

Shape each rope into a pretzel, and set it on a lightly greased cookie sheet. You may get about 4 to 6 pretzels per sheet. Remember, when these boil later on, they will rise to much thicker shapes.

When you get all 12 done, place a light cloth or wax paper over them and let them rest for about 10 to 15 minutes at room temperature.

Bring a large pan of water to a boil, then turn heat to a low boil.

Preheat your oven to 375°F. (You may also like to bake these at 350°F. for a few minutes longer—the lower temperature results in a softer pretzel.)

When they have rested enough lower about 3 pretzels (I use a slotted pancake turner) into the water. Poach for about 3 or 4 minutes. Remove, using a spatula, a very large spoon, or a combination of 2 wooden spoons or large wooden forks to lift, letting the water drain off. When drained, place them on your lightly greased cooking sheet. Leave about 1 inch or more space between pretzels. I fit about 6 per sheet.

Brush the pretzels with the egg white glaze and then generously sprinkle minced onions, poppy seeds, sesame seeds, or caraway seeds on each of them.

Bake them for about 20 to 25 minutes at 375°F. until golden brown on top. Remove them from the oven when done and cool on racks. Serve the pretzels warm now or reheat within 24 hours. Store in zipper-type bags in the refrigerator for no more than a day.

Nutritional Values per Pretzel Calories: 159.4 Protein: 4.538 g. Carbohydrate: 29 g. Dietary Fiber: 1.326 g. Total Sugars: .347 g. Total Fat: 2.663 g. Saturated Fat: .367 g. Monounsaturated Fat: 1.724 g. Polyunsaturated Fat: .336 g. Cholesterol: 0 mg. Calcium: 291.6 mg. Potassium: 97.3 mg. Sodium: 6.849 mg. Vitamin K: 1.103 mcg. Folate: 195.3 mcg.

❖ POPPYSEED BAGELS ❖

WITH WHOLE WHEAT FLOUR
BREAD MACHINE KNEAD — STOVETOP BOIL — OVEN BAKE
ADAPTABLE FOR DIABETICS

This is an eggless, sugarless bagel but it does use 2 table-spoons honey. You can make these with water or orange or apple juice.

MAKES 8 BAGELS   SODIUM PER RECIPE: 32.2 MG
SODIUM PER BAGEL: 4.03 MG

1½ cups unsweetened orange juice fortified with calcium (8.731 mg), at room temperature (70°F. to 80°F.)
  2 tablespoons honey* (1.68 mg), at room temperature (70 F. to 80°F.)
  1 tablespoon apple cider vinegar (.15 mg)
2¼ cups whole wheat flour (13.5 mg)
  1 cup unbleached bread flour (2.5 mg)
  1 tablespoon vital wheat gluten (2.25 mg)
1½ tablespoons extra virgin olive oil (trace)
  2 teaspoons bread machine yeast (3.96 mg)

   At the raisin buzzer add:
2½ tablespoons poppy seeds (4.62 mg)

Place all the dough ingredients in your bread machine in the order listed, reserving the poppy seeds. Set the machine on the Dough cycle. When the raisin buzzer sounds, add the poppy seeds.

Five minutes before the dough is ready, bring a pan of water to boiling. You can add a bit of honey to the water if you like, but I've not found this necessary. (It's supposed to help the glazing.)

Preheat your oven to 350°F.

When dough is ready, transfer it to a lightly floured breadboard and break it into 8 pieces. Shape them into round balls, then press down gently. Now punch a center hole with your finger and thumb in one and drop it immediately into the boiling water. Repeat. Remove each in about a minute (they will have risen greatly) and set on a lightly greased cooking sheet. (You may also let it rise for 30 minutes before putting it into the water.)

When all 8 are ready, bake at 350°F. for about 20 minutes, or until golden (not dark) brown. Serve hot and fresh. These can be frozen. Thaw in the microwave.

*Diabetics may substitute 3 level tablespoons Splenda Sugar Substitute for the honey but must add ½ tablespoon cider vinegar when putting the ingredients into the bread machine.

Nutrient Values per Bagel Calories: 251.9 Protein: 8.165 g. Carbohydrate: 47 g. Dietary Fiber: 5.126 g. Total Sugars: 4.2 g. Total Fat: 4.634 g. Saturated Fat: .618 g. Monounsaturated Fat: 2.162 g. Polyunsaturated Fat: 1.393 g. Cholesterol: 0 mg. Calcium: 111.1 mg. Iron: 2.535 mg. Potassium: 283.8 mg. Sodium: 4.03 mg. Vitamin K: 1.24 mcg. Folate: 84.2 mcg.

❈ RAISIN CINNAMON ENGLISH MUFFINS ❈

WITH APPLE JUICE
BREAD MACHINE PREPARATION — OVEN BAKE
ADAPTABLE FOR DIABETICS*

Containing no salt, very little fat, these can also be made with no sugar. Toasted they are a great addition to your collection of no-salt bread recipes. Spread with a light jam or some honey.

MAKES 10 MUFFINS   SODIUM PER RECIPE: 54.1 MG
SODIUM PER SERVING: 5.409 MG

THE DOUGH
1¼ cups unsweetened apple juice (1.162 mg), at room
        temperature (70°F. to 80°F.)
  1 tablespoon apple cider vinegar (.15 mg)
3½ cups white best for bread flour (8.75 mg)
1½ teaspoons Featherweight Baking Powder (9 mg)
  1 teaspoon vital wheat gluten (.72 mg)
  1 teaspoon ground cinnamon (.606 mg)
  1 teaspoon extra virgin olive oil (trace)
2¼ teaspoons (1 package) bread machine yeast (3.5 mg)

   At the raisin buzzer add:
  ¾ cup (not packed) seedless black raisins (13 mg)

   Dust the baking pan with:
  1 teaspoon cornmeal (trace)

Place all the dough ingredients in your bread machine in the order listed. Set on the Dough cycle. When the raisin buzzer sounds, add the raisins. When the dough is ready, transfer it to a lightly floured breadboard and roll it over once, pressing down gently. Knead once or twice, then flatten. Roll the dough out with a pin until about ½ inch thick. Using a 2½-inch cutter, cut and place the English muffins on a slightly warmed cooking

*Diabetics may substitute bottled water if apple juice is too high in sugar for their diet.

sheet dusted with the cornmeal. Lay a light cloth over the sheet and put it in a warm place to rise (the oven heated to about 90°F. works well with this recipe).

After 45 minutes, bake at 425°F. for about 7 minutes. Turn each English muffin over and bake for another 7 or 8 minutes. Serve halved, toasted or warmed with honey or jam.

Nutritional Values per Muffin Calories: 214.5 Protein: 5.213 g. Carbohydrate: 46.6 g. Dietary Fiber: 1.956 g. Total Sugars: 7.884 g. Total Fat: 1.001 g. Saturated Fat: .156 g. Monounsaturated Fat: .389 g. Polyunsaturated Fat: .246 g. Cholesterol: 0 mg. Calcium. 379.6 mg. Potassium: 259 mg. Sodium: 5.409 mg. Vitamin K: .218 mcg. Folate: 84.4 mcg.

❖ RAISIN APPLE JUICE BUNS ❖

BREAD MACHINE KNEAD—HAND SHAPE—OVEN BAKE

You can play with this one and change the flavors, too. Add cinnamon if you like, or vanilla extract or almond or maple extract (about 2 teaspoons).

**MAKES 12 TO 18 BUNS   SODIUM PER RECIPE (12): 51.3 MG
SODIUM PER SERVING (12): 4.275 MG**

THE DOUGH
- 1 **cup orange juice (2.488 mg), at room temperature (70°F. to 80°F.)**
- ¾ **cup plus 1 tablespoon unsweetened apple juice with vitamin C (5.58 mg), at room temperature (70°F. to 80°F.)**
- 1 **tablespoon apple cider vinegar (.15 mg)**
- 4 **cups unbleached best for bread machine flour (10 mg)**
- 1 **cup best for bread whole wheat flour (6 mg)**
- 3 **tablespoons white granulated sugar (.378 mg)**
- 1 **level tablespoon vital wheat gluten (2.25 mg)**
- 1½ **tablespoons extra virgin olive oil (trace)**
- **Zest of 1 orange (.54 mg)**
- 1 **tablespoon bread machine yeast (6 mg)**

   At the raisin buzzer add:
- 1 **cup (not packed) raisins (17.4 mg)**

   Dust the baking pan with:
- 2 **tablespoons cornmeal (.516 mg)**

Place all the dough ingredients in your warmed bread machine pan. Set for the Dough cycle. Add the raisins at the sound of the raisin buzzer.

When the dough is ready, transfer it to a breadboard and flatten it with your hands until it's rectangular and about ½-inch thick (or slightly more).

Form buns with large drinking glass or cup by pushing down the open end and pulling away the dough shaped as a bun. Place the buns on a warmed baking sheet which you have dusted with cornmeal. Use large cookie sheets and place 6 to 9 buns per sheet. Lay a light cloth over the sheet and let buns rise for about 45 minutes to 1 hour in a warm (about 75°F. to 90°F.), draft-free area (the oven heated to about 90°F. with the door closed works well).

When ready, bake at 425°F. for 5 to 6 minutes. Cool on rack. Serve toasted or as a lunchtime sandwich with unsalted peanut butter and jam, or spread with strawberry jam in the morning when toasted. Makes a good dinner roll, also. Store in zipper-type bags on the countertop for up to 3 days and in the freezer for up to 1 month. Thaw them on the countertop or cover them with wax paper and defrost for up to 2 minutes in the microwave.

Nutrient Values per Bun (12) Calories: 277.9 Protein: 7.22 g. Carbohydrate: 57.9 g. Dietary Fiber: 3.36 g. Total Sugars: 3.118 g. Total Fat: 2.451 g. Saturated Fat: .357 g. Monounsaturated Fat: 1.34 g. Polyunsaturated Fat: .427 g. Cholesterol: 0 mg. Calcium: 45 mg. Iron: 2.86 mg. Potassium: 260.5 mg. Sodium: 4.275 mg. Vitamin K: .827 mcg. Folate: 102.5 mcg.

❖ SOPAIPILLAS ❖

HANDMADE
ADAPTABLE FOR DIABETICS

Sometimes hand kneading is enjoyable, especially when it doesn't take much effort. While traveling many years ago, ferrying aircraft from Wichita, Kansas, to other states, I stopped in El Paso, Texas, for an overnight during one of the flights. At the motel I was told to eat at a place down the street that served great sopaipillas. I could barely remember the word but headed to the restaurant. Wow! What a great bread. I poured endless amounts of honey on each one I ate and returned to the motel wanting more. Unfortunately, the real thing is a fried bread with way too much fat—and need I add?— too much sodium. I think you'll like these, however. It's a modified version using my basic yeast "pastry" dough with an egg added in. Note, too, that I use olive oil instead of the standard butter that real sopaipillas use— this adds a touch of flavor and cuts the saturated fat way down. Enjoy!

MAKES 20 SOPAIPILLAS   SODIUM PER RECIPE: 174.9 MG
SODIUM PER SOPAIPILLA: 8.774 MG

THE YEAST
¼ cup bottled water (trace), at room temperature (about 80°F.)
1 tablespoon bread machine or other active dry yeast (5 mg)
1 level teaspoon white granulated sugar (.042 mg)

THE DOUGH
2¾ cups white unbleached bread flour (6.875 mg)
2 tablespoons white granulated sugar (.252 mg)
1 teaspoon vital wheat gluten (.72 mg)
1 large egg (63 mg)
¾ cup low-sodium reduced-fat buttermilk* (97.5 mg), at room
    temperature (70°F. to 80°F.)
1 tablespoon grated orange or lemon zest (.36 mg)
1 tablespoon apple cider vinegar (.15 mg)
1 tablespoon vanilla extract (1.17 mg)
2 tablespoons extra virgin olive oil (trace)

FOR THE BREADBOARD
¼ cup white bread flour (.625 mg)

Spoon the yeast into a small bowl with the warm bottled water. Add the sugar, stir, and let stand for 10 minutes. It will bubble and rise, forming a "foamy" mass. If it doesn't, your yeast is dead and you should replace it. (**Note**: Do not use tap water if you have chlorine in your system.)

Combine the flour, sugar, and gluten, stirring once with a wooden spoon or sifting them into a larger bowl. Stir in the egg, zest, buttermilk, vinegar, vanilla, olive oil, and yeast mixture (when ready).

Mix all together with a wooden spoon, but don't over mix. Roll the dough out onto a lightly floured breadboard and knead in the ¼ cup of remaining flour. Do this 1 tablespoon at a time. If the dough won't take it all in 10 kneads, that's okay; you can use the rest when you roll out the dough after it's risen. Place this ball into a large deep bowl, lightly spritz with olive oil spray, roll it over and do it again. Cover the bowl tightly with plastic wrap, and let it stand for 60 minutes at room temperature. It can stand a bit longer if you need the time for other things.

About 40 minutes into the rising, preheat your oven to 500°F. The cooking rack should be set in the center of the oven.

When the dough has risen, place it on the breadboard (lightly floured) and divide it into two pieces. Using your rolling pin, roll each piece one at a time, gently until it's about an ⅛ inch thin. Then lightly spritz the dough with olive oil spray, fold it over, and roll it again. Lightly spritz the dough

*You may substitute orange juice (1,866 mg) fortified with calcium for the buttermilk.

again with the olive oil, fold it over, and roll it out again. Do this for a total of four times. Set it aside to rest while you do the other half. Then with a sharp knife or pizza cutting wheel, cut each section into squares or triangles (about 10 per section). Work with the dough quickly. You don't have to be perfect with the cuts—various shapes make them more interesting. (You can store them in the refrigerator for up to one day at this point.)

Place the dough pieces at least 1 inch or more apart on 2 separate insulated greased cooking sheets, or if you don't have the insulated type, use 2 cookies sheets tacked one upon the other. Let them stand, covered with wax paper, for about 10 minutes. Prepare the second batch while the first stands. When done, put the first sheet into the oven while the second stands with the wax paper over it.

After taking the first sheet out of oven, let the oven reheat for a minute before putting the second sheet in. Bake for 6 to 8 minutes, or until lightly golden brown. Serve hot, warm, or microwave reheated (about 20 seconds under a paper towel), with honey or jam.

Nutritional Values per Sopaipilla using Buttermilk: Calories: 89.6 Protein: 2.706 g. Carbohydrate: 15.4 g. Dietary Fiber: .597 g. Total Sugars: 1.793 g. Total Fat: 2 g. Saturated Fat: .402 g. Monounsaturated Fat: 1.118 g. Polyunsaturated Fat: .219 g. Cholesterol: 11.6 mg. Calcium: 15.4 mg. Potassium: 33.2 mg. Sodium: 8.744 mg. Vitamin K: .662 mcg. Folate: 38.9 mcg.

Nutritional Values per Sopaipilla using Orange Juice: Calories: 97.3 Protein: 2.501 g. Carbohydrate: 17.2 g. Dietary Fiber: .658 g. Total Sugars: 1.455 g. Total Fat: 1.813 g. Saturated Fat: .293 g. Monounsaturated Fat: 1.12 g. Polyunsaturated Fat: .226 g. Cholesterol: 10.6 mg. Calcium: 16.2 mg. Iron: 1.009 mg. Potassium: 52.6 mg. Sodium: 3.957 mg. Vitamin K: .662 mcg. Folate: 45.4 mcg.

❖ POLENTA MUFFINS ❖

WITH ZANTE CURRANTS
HANDMADE—OVEN BAKE
ADPATABLE FOR DIABETICS

Serve these as a snack or with dinner
**MAKES 6 TEXAS-SIZE MUFFINS   SODIUM PER RECIPE: 234.4 MG
SODIUM PER SERVING: 39.1 MG**

1 **cup white unbleached bread flour (2.5 mg)**
1 **cup Golden Pheasant polenta* (4.14 mg)**
2 **tablespoons Featherweight Baking Powder (27 mg)**
¼ **cup white granulated sugar (.5 mg)**
1 **teaspoon vital wheat gluten (.8 mg)**
1 **teaspoon lemon or orange zest (.12 mg)**
1 **medium egg (55.4 mg), beaten**

*This recipe was developed using Golden Pheasant Polenta. Albers and Quaker cornmeal also work. Corn grits don't do well here.

1 cup reduced-fat, low sodium buttermilk (130 mg)
¼ cup extra virgin olive oil (trace)
¼ cup Zante currants (2.88 mg)

Preheat your oven to 425°F.

Into a large mixing bowl, sift together the flour, polenta, baking powder, sugar, gluten, and zest, sifting three times at least. Set this aside.

Beat the egg and stir it into the dry ingredients, along with the buttermilk and olive oil. Mix with a beater at medium speed just until ingredients are smooth. Fold in the currants. Spoon the batter into 6 medium to large lightly oiled and flour-dusted muffin cups.

Place muffin tin on a larger cookie sheet and bake on the middle rack at 425°F for 20 minutes.

Nutrient Values per Muffin Calories: 312.6 Protein: 9.715 g. Carbohydrate: 47 g. Dietary Fiber: 2.375 g. Total Sugars: 9.75 g. Total Fat: 11.9 g. Saturated Fat: 2.061 g. Monounsaturated Fat: 7.064 g. Polyunsaturated Fat: 1.125 g. Cholesterol: 39.6 mg. Calcium: 273.1 mg. Potassium: 574.8 mg. Sodium: 39.1 mg. Vitamin K: 4.41 mcg Folate: 79 mcg.

❖ HIGH-FIBER LOW-FAT POLENTA MUFFINS ❖

HANDMADE—OVEN BAKE
ADAPTABLE FOR DIABETICS

Serve as a snack or with dinner.
**MAKES 6 OR 12 MUFFINS   SODIUM PER RECIPE: 197.1 MG
SODIUM PER SERVING (6 MUFFINS): 33.4 MG
SODIUM PER SERVING (12 MUFFINS): 16.9 MG**

1 large egg white (54.8 mg), beaten
1 cup white unbleached bread flour (2.5 mg)
2 teaspoons vital wheat gluten (1.5 mg)
½ cup polenta* (2.07 mg)
½ cup crude wheat bran or 10-grain, unsalted cereal (1.15 mg)
1 tablespoon Featherweight Baking Powder (9 mg)
¼ cup white granulated sugar (.5 mg)
1 tablespoon apple cider vinegar (.15 mg)
1 cup reduced-fat, low-sodium buttermilk (130 mg)
½ cup Zante currants (5.76 mg)
½ cup diced fresh apple (trace)

*I use Golden Pheasant polenta. It's best to not use corn grits (also called polenta at times). You may use Albers or Quaker cornmeal, but you won't quite get the same polenta flavor.

Beat the egg white until almost stiff. Set it aside.

Preheat your oven to 425°F.

Combine the flour, gluten, polenta, wheat bran, baking powder, and sugar, mixing them together with a wooden spoon. Stir in the buttermilk and vinegar, then the beaten egg white and diced apples. Mix with a wooden spoon until the batter is smooth. Fold in the currants. Spoon the batter into 6 or 12 medium to large oiled and flour-dusted muffin cups.

Bake at 425°F. for 18 to 20 minutes. Use a toothpick to test for doneness. Cool on rack. Serve hot or warm. Serve with chicken or beef entrée. Serve alone with strawberry jam or fresh honey. Don't freeze. Store in zipper-type bags for up to 2 days.

Nutrient Values per Muffin (12) Calories: 103.4 Protein: 3.227 g. Carbohydrate: 23.5 g. Dietary Fiber: 2.149 g. Total Sugars: 4.875 g. Total Fat: .733 g. Saturated Fat: .296 g. Monounsaturated Fat: .051 g. Polyunsaturated Fat: .148 g. Cholesterol: 2.083 mg. Calcium: 33 mg. Potassium: 107.1 mg. Sodium: 16.4 mg. Vitamin K: 0 mcg. Folate: 29.4 mcg.

❖ OAT MUFFINS ❖

WITH FLAXSEED
HANDMADE — OVEN BAKE
ADAPTABLE FOR DIABETICS

I remember while doing some childhood growing up on a farm in the Southern California desert that we had acres upon acres of flax. I always thought the crop was just for linseed oil and paper. Now, I know differently. Ground flaxseed meal is good enough to use in all baked goods as a replacement for cooking oil. Try these. I think you'll enjoy their nutty flavor and their low fat content. (You may halve this recipe to make just 12 muffins.)

**MAKES 24 2½-INCH MUFFINS   SODIUM PER RECIPE: 356.1 MG
SODIUM PER MUFFIN:* 14.8 MG**

1½ **cups unbleached white flour (3.75 mg)**
¾ **cup flaxseed meal (trace)**
¾ **cup Quaker 1-Minute Oats† (trace)**
¼ **cup white granulated sugar (1.5 mg), or brown sugar
(unpacked) (42.5 mg), or Splenda Sugar Substitute (0 mg)**

*The total figures are based on using highest-sodium ingredients instead of the lower-sodium alternatives.

†If you have raw or Quaker regular oats, then put enough into your Braun handheld processor or favorite processor with a metal blade and cut the oats into a small or almost oat bran size. (You can do this with any raw oats or Quaker oats to obtain oat bran.)

½ cup lightly packed brown sugar (Splenda may be substituted
    for this) (42.9 mg)
1 tablespoon plus 1 teaspoon Ener-G Baking Soda (.384 mg)
2 teaspoons Featherweight Baking Powder (27 mg)
1 tablespoon ground cinnamon (1.791 mg)
¼ teaspoon ground cloves (1.275 mg)
8-ounce can Dole crushed pineapple in its own juice (20 mg)
1 medium apple (trace), shredded or finely diced, skin on
1 cup SunMaid Baker's black seedless raisins (9.9 mg), or
    currants
½ cup chopped unsalted walnuts (1.2 mg)
1 cup shredded carrots (38.5 mg)
2 medium eggs (110.9 mg), beaten
¾ cup low-sodium buttermilk (97.5 mg), or if allergic to dairy
    products, use ¾ cup unsweetened apple juice (3.72 mg)
1½ teaspoons vanilla extract (.567 mg)

Preheat your oven to 350°F.

Prepare the muffin cups. Since this recipe has no oil, lightly spritz the cups with Pam olive oil spray (trace sodium).

Mix together the flour, flaxseed meal, oats, sugar, baking soda, baking powder, cinnamon, and cloves.

In another bowl, mix together the pineapple, apple, raisins, walnuts (optional), and carrots, and set aside.

In a small bowl, beat the eggs for about ½ minute or so with an electric beater. Add the buttermilk and vanilla and stir.

Mix the fruit with the flour mix, then add the liquid ingredients. Don't overstir.

Spoon the batter into muffin cups to about ¾ full. They will rise to the top of the cup, sometimes just over the cup.

Bake at 350° F for 20 to 25 minutes. Test with a toothpick or fork. Set on a cooling rack when done. Bake the second batch right away.

Serve hot or with a light frosting (the kids love it that way).

Nutrient Values per Muffin Calories: 140.6 Protein: 2.251 g. Carbohydrate: 21.1 g. Dietary Fiber: 1.253 g. Total Sugars: 6.88 g. Total Fat: 6.023 g. Saturated Fat: .744 g. Monounsaturated Fat: 1.133 g. Polyunsaturated Fat: 3.709 g. Cholesterol: 16.4 mg. Calcium: 263.5 mg. Potassium: 229.8 mg. Sodium: 14.8 mg. Vitamin K: .229 mcg. Folate: 176 mcg.

❦ LONG-LASTING BRAN MUFFINS ❦

HEARTY, FILLING
HANDMADE — OVEN BAKE
NOT ADAPTABLE FOR DIABETICS

I call this long-lasting because eating just one will carry you for hours, even on a long walk. The oat bran and wheat bran make this a fairly heavy muffin.

MAKES 24 REGULAR MUFFINS OR 12 JUMBO MUFFINS
SODIUM PER RECIPE: 604 MG
SODIUM PER SERVING (24 REGULAR MUFFINS): 25.2 MG
SODIUM PER SERVING (12 JUMBO MUFFINS): 50.4 MG

1 **cup black seedless raisins (not packed) (17.4 mg), plumped in hot water for about 5 minutes, then drained**
½ **cup dates or date bits (2.67 mg), coarsely chopped**
2½ **cups unbleached white flour (6.25 mg)**
5 **level teaspoons Ener-G Baking Soda (trace)**
1 **level tablespoon Featherweight Baking Powder (13.5 mg)**
2 **teaspoons ground cinnamon (1.211 mg)**
3 **large eggs (189 mg), lightly beaten**
¾ **cup extra virgin light olive oil (trace)**
2 **tablespoons honey (.84 mg)**
1¼ **cups light brown sugar, packed firm (about 7 to 8 oz.) (107.2 mg)**
1½ **teaspoons pure vanilla extract (.567 mg)**
¾ **teaspoon pure maple extract or flavoring (283 mg)**
2 **cups reduced-fat, lowered-sodium buttermilk (130 mg)**
1 **cup Bob's Red Mill or other oat bran* (3.76 mg)**
.1 **cup Bob's Red Mill or other whole wheat (natural) bran (1.16 mg)**

Prepare raisins (plump in very hot water for about 5 minutes, then drain well; or use SunMaid Baking Raisins). Chop the dates. Set both aside.

In a medium bowl, combine the flour, baking soda, baking powder, and cinnamon. Set aside.

In a larger bowl, thoroughly whisk the eggs. Blend in the oil, brown sugar, honey, and vanilla and maple extracts until well combined. Too much beating will hurt this recipe. Stir in the buttermilk, then fold in the two brans. Allow to rest for 10 to 15 minutes.

---

*If you don't have oat bran in stock, then using your food processor (I use the Braun 550 Handheld Mixer with its processor unit) grind 1 cup Quaker Quick Oats into a flour or bran grade. It works wonderfully. If you want a nuttier flavor, substitute flaxseed meal (trace) for the oat bran.

Add the dry ingredients from the medium bowl to the oil and sugar mixture, and partially blend with wooden spoon. Add the dates and raisins, mixing them well into the batter.

Cover the batter bowl tightly with plastic wrap. Let the batter rest for at least 1 hour in your refrigerator. (The batter may also be held in the refrigerator overnight.)

To bake, preheat your oven to 400°F.

Very lightly spritz the sides of two nonstick 12-cup muffin pans (or two 6-cup Texas-size muffin pans). You may use muffin cups if you like. Lightly dust the pans if you aren't going to use cups. Shake the muffin pans until all sides are lightly lined with the flour. (I use whole wheat flour to do this one, since white might discolor the sides of the muffins.) Spoon the muffin batter evenly into the prepared muffin pans. Fill them only halfway.

Place the muffins on the uppermost rack and bake for 20 minutes, then reduce the heat to 375°F. and bake until done, about another 10 to 12 minutes. Cool on rack. Serve hot or warm. Serve with jam or honey. Use as a snack during the day or with any meat or fish entrée. Store in zipper-type bags for up to 3 days in the refrigerator or on the countertop. These don't freeze well.

Baker's Tip: When measuring honey with a tablespoon, first dip the spoon into the recipe's oil. Then pour the honey onto the spoon. It will slip right off into the mixture.

Nutrient Values per Muffin (24): Calories: 211.3 Protein: 4.208 g. Carbohydrate: 34.9 g. Dietary Fiber: 2.628 g. Total Sugars: 16.9 g. Total Fat: 8.352 g. Saturated Fat: 1.46 g. Monounsaturated Fat: 5.34 g. Polyunsaturated Fat: .879 g. Cholesterol: 28.6 mg. Calcium: 305.6 mg. Potassium: 246.5 mg. Sodium: 25.2 mg. Vitamin K: 3.307 mcg. Folate: 27.8 mcg.

❖ HEARTY, HIGH-FIBER BRAN MUFFINS ❖

HANDMADE — OVEN BAKE
ADAPTABLE FOR DIABETICS

Most high-fiber muffins are without flavor and sometimes taste a bit like wood. Not these. I use Bob's Red Mill wheat bran, a popular bran from Oregon. Fortunately, the sodium count is also very low.

MAKES 12 MUFFINS   SODIUM PER RECIPE: 48.9 MG
SODIUM PER MUFFIN: 4.079 MG

3 **cups unprocessed (or raw crude) wheat bran (1.74 mg)**
1 **cup best for bread whole wheat flour (6 mg)**
1 **teaspoon ground cinnamon (.606 mg)**
1½ **tablespoons Featherweight Baking Powder (20.2 mg)**
2 **teaspoons vital wheat gluten (1.5 mg)**

¼ cup (unpacked) brown sugar* (28.3 mg)
2 teaspoons apple cider vinegar (trace)
    8-ounce can (1 cup) crushed pineapple in its own juice or
        water (2.49 mg)
¾ cup Homemade Applesauce† (see page 206) (.284 mg)
¼ cup bottled water (trace)
1 cup unsweetened frozen blueberries (1.55 mg)

Preheat your oven to 400°F.

Combine the wheat bran, flour, cinnamon, baking powder, gluten, sugar, and vinegar in a medium-sized bowl. Fold in the pineapple, applesauce, and water and mix until completely "wet." Fold in the still-frozen blueberries—do not thaw them.

Spoon the batter into lightly oil-spritzed and flour-dusted muffin cups. The oil and flour dusting will add no appreciable sodium.

Bake at 400°F. for about 20 to 25 minutes. Serve hot or cooled. Serve with low-sugar jam, if you like.

Nutrient Values with Sugar and Pineapple: Calories: 109.9 Protein: 3.805 g. Carbohydrate: 28.6 g. Dietary Fiber: 8.486 g. Total Sugars: 3.814 g. Total Fat: .967 g. Saturated Fat: .143 g. Monounsaturated Fat: .133 g. Polyunsaturated Fat: .459 g. Cholesterol: 0 mg. Calcium: 105.7 mg. Potassium: 462.7 mg. Sodium: 4.079 mg. Vitamin K: 0 mcg. Folate: 18.2 mcg.

Nutrient Values with Splenda Sugar Substitute and Sugarless Applesauce Calories: 93.8 Protein: 3.8 g. Carbohydrate: 24.4 g. Dietary Fiber: 8.432 g. Total Sugars: 0 g. Total Fat: .961 g. Saturated Fat: .141 g. Monounsaturated Fat: .132 g. Polyunsaturated Fat: .457 g. Cholesterol: 0 mg. Calcium: 100.6 mg. Potassium: 387.7 mg. Sodium: 2.32 mg. Vitamin K: 0 mcg. Folate: 18.1 mcg.

PINEAPPLE PRUNE BRAN MUFFIN

HANDMADE—OVEN BAKE
NOT ADAPTABLE FOR DIABETICS
MAKES 12 MUFFINS   SODIUM PER RECIPE: 133.3 MG
SODIUM PER MUFFIN: 11.1 MG

1 cup wheat bran (1.16 mg)
½ cup oats (1.88 mg)
1 cup whole wheat flour (6 mg)
1 tablespoon vital wheat gluten (2.25 mg)
½ cup seedless raisins (9.9 mg)

*Or use an equal amount of Splenda Sugar Substitute.
†Use the Homemade Applesauce recipe on page 206. Diabetics, you can make the applesauce using Splenda or leave the sugar out altogether. Or you may substitute flaxseed meal.

½ cup dried, pitted prunes (3.4 mg), chopped
½ cup canned crushed pineapple in its own unsweetened juice
  (1.25 mg)
 2 teaspoons Featherweight Baking Powder (9 mg)
½ cup (packed) brown sugar (42.9 mg)
¼ cup chopped unsalted dry-roasted pecans (.142 mg)
 1 egg (55.4 mg), beaten
 1 teaspoon vanilla extract (.378 mg)
¾ cup prune juice (7.624 mg)
½ cup Homemade Applesauce* (see page 206) (.189 mg)

Stir the dry ingredients together in a medium bowl. In another medium or a larger bowl, beat the egg. Add liquid ingredients, vanilla, prune juice, and applesauce, and beat slightly. Pour wet into dry and mix with a wooden spoon.

Lightly grease a muffin pan. Spoon the batter into 12 standard muffin cups and set the cups into the pan.

Bake at 400°F. for 15 minutes. Cool on rack. Serve hot or warm. These don't freeze well. You can store them for up to 2 days in zipper-type bags in your refrigerator.

Nutrient Values per Muffin Calories: 168 Protein: 3.925 g. Carbohydrate: 38.8 g. Dietary Fiber: 5.227 g. Total Sugars: 16.9 g. Total Fat: 2.028 g. Saturated Fat: .322 g. Monounsaturated Fat: .836 g. Polyunsaturated Fat: .617 g. Cholesterol: 15.6 mg. Calcium: 31.4 mg. Potassium: 334.5 mg. Sodium: 11.1 mg. Vitamin K: .073 mcg. Folate: 15.5 mcg.

❧ OAT BRAN AND DATE MUFFINS ❧

FROM SCRATCH—OVEN BAKE
NOT ADAPTABLE FOR DIABETICS

What a neat way to sneak a date into our diets. Just follow the recipe and then enjoy.

MAKES 12 MUFFINS   SODIUM PER RECIPE: 232.7 MG
SODIUM PER MUFFIN: 19.4 MG

2¼ cups oat bran (8.46 mg)
¼ cup (packed) brown sugar (21.5 mg)
 1 tablespoon Featherweight Baking Powder (13.5 mg)
 2 teaspoons vital wheat gluten (1.5 mg)
 1 teaspoon granulated white sugar (trace)
 2 teaspoons ground cinnamon (1 mg)
 1 tablespoon apple cider vinegar (.15 mg)

*You may substitute 1 cup flaxseed meal and ¼ cup water for the applesauce.

2 tablespoons extra virgin olive oil* (trace)
2 large egg whites (109.6 mg)
½ cup nonfat milk (63.7 mg)
¾ cup frozen unsweetened apple juice concentrate fortified with added Vitamin C (12.5 mg)
12 Majoul dates (2.88 mg)

Preheat your oven to 425°F.

Mix together the bran, sugar, baking powder, gluten, sugar, and cinnamon, then stir in the vinegar, oil, egg whites, milk, and apple juice concentrate until smooth.

Spoon only half the batter into lightly greased muffin cups. Place a date on top of the batter in each cup, then top them off with the other half of the batter.

Bake for 15 to 16 minutes at 425°F. Allow the muffins to cool in the pan for about 10 minutes. Remove to a wire rack and cool. These muffins can be refrigerated or frozen.

Nutrient Values per Muffin Calories: 119.4 Protein: 4.178 g. Carbohydrate: 25.5 g. Dietary Fiber: 3.645 g. Total Sugars: 4.792 g. Total Fat: 3.576 g. Saturated Fat: .571 g. Monounsaturated Fat: 2.098 g. Polyunsaturated Fat: .685 g. Cholesterol: .184 mg. Calcium: 89.4 mg. Potassium: 339.6 mg. Sodium: 19.4 mg. Vitamin K: 1.105 mcg. Folate: 11.1 mcg.

❖ BLUEBERRY BRAN MUFFINS ❖

FROM SCRATCH—OVEN BAKE
NOT ADAPTABLE FOR DIABETICS

Most high-fiber muffins are without flavor and sometimes taste a bit like wood. Not these. I use Bob's Red Mill wheat bran, a popular bran from Oregon, as well's as Bob's whole wheat pastry flour, available from www.bobsredmill.com. Fortunately, the sodium count is also very low.

MAKES 12 MUFFINS   SODIUM PER RECIPE: 33 MG
SODIUM PER MUFFIN: 2.746 MG

2 cups raw crude wheat bran (2.32 mg)
1⅓ cups whole wheat pastry flour (7.98 mg)
1 teaspoon ground cinnamon (.606 mg)
1 tablespoon Featherweight Baking Powder (13.5 mg)
¼ cup (unpacked) brown sugar (14.1 mg)
   8-ounce can crushed pineapple in its own juice (2.49 mg)

*You may substitute homemade applesauce for the oil, but the muffins won't be as soft nor rise as high.

1 tablespoon apple cider vinegar (.15 mg)
¾ cup Homemade Applesauce (see page 206) (.284 mg)
1 cup unsweetened frozen blueberries (1.55 mg)

Preheat your oven to 400°F.

Combine the bran, flour, cinnamon, baking powder, and sugar in a medium-sized bowl. Fold in the pineapple, vinegar, and applesauce, and mix until completely "wet."

Beat egg whites in a smaller bowl until just stiff. Fold in still frozen blueberries.

Spoon the batter into 12 lightly greased and flour-dusted muffin cups.

Bake at 400°F. for about 20 to 25 minutes. Serve hot or cooled. Serve with low-sugar jam, if you like.

Nutrient Values per Muffin Calories: 97.1 Protein: 3.451 g. Carbohydrate: 23.7 g. Dietary Fiber: 6.571 g. Total Sugars: 3.52 g. Total Fat: .906 g. Saturated Fat: .133 g. Monounsaturated Fat: .191 g. Polyunsaturated Fat: .378 g. Cholesterol: 0 mg. Calcium: 313.2 mg. Potassium: 253.9 mg. Sodium: 2.746 mg. Vitamin K: .055 mcg. Folate: 15.2 mcg.

❈ BLUEBERRY MUFFINS ❈

NOT ADAPTABLE FOR DIABETICS

You can substitute olive oil for the flaxseed meal if you want a really moist muffin.

MAKES 12 MUFFINS   SODIUM PER RECIPE: 101.3 MG
SODIUM PER MUFFIN: 8.444 MG

1½ cups white unbleached bread flour (3.75 mg)
½ cup best for bread whole wheat pastry flour (3 mg)
¼ cup flaxseed meal (trace)
2 level teaspoons vital wheat gluten (1.5 mg)
2 teaspoons ground cinnamon (1.196 mg)
¼ teaspoon ground cloves (1.3 mg)
1 tablespoon Featherweight Baking Powder (13.5 mg)
½ cup white granulated sugar or Splenda Sugar Substitute (1 mg)
1 large egg white (54.8 mg)
1 cup bottled water (trace)*
1 tablespoon apple cider vinegar (.15 mg)
1 16.5-ounce can Oregon canned blueberries (7.58 mg), syrup drained, set aside

Preheat your oven to 400°F.

Open can of blueberries.

*Start with ½ cup. If the batter is smooth and creamy, don't use the balance. If crumbly, slowly add the rest of the water until creamy.

In a medium-size mixing bowl, stir together the flour, flaxseed meal, gluten, cinnamon, cloves, baking powder, and sugar, then set aside.

In a smaller bowl, beat the egg white until nearly stiff. Mix together the egg white and flour mixture, blending with a wooden spoon. Add the blueberries at the end.

Lightly grease and flour-dust a 12-cup muffin pan and its cups. Bake at 400°F. for 20 minutes. The muffins will darken a bit.

You may serve these directly out of the oven, or refrigerate or freeze them and reheat later.

Nutrient Values per Muffin Calories: 141.6 Protein: 3.57 g. Carbohydrate: 30.9 g. Dietary Fiber: 2.297 g. Total Sugars: 8.25 g. Total Fat: 1.105 g. Saturated Fat: .053 g. Monounsaturated Fat: .038 g. Polyunsaturated Fat: .142 g. Cholesterol: 0 mg. Calcium: 118.7 mg. Iron: 1.357 mg. Potassium: 305.8 mg. Sodium: 8.444 mg. Vitamin K: 1.28 mcg. Folate: 26.9 mcg.

BECKY'S BRAN MUFFINS
❖ WITH BLUEBERRIES ❖

FROM SCRATCH—OVEN BAKE
ESPECIALLY FOR DIABETICS

This fruity muffin comes from my younger sister. Her recipes are envied by us all. I first understood her devotion to the kitchen when I was a sophomore in college and she was about three. Mother asked me to fix the drain at the kitchen sink, so I dutifully knelt down to work on the pipes under the sink. Next thing I knew I was flat on my front side, a bit unconscious, and in a lot of pain. My three-year-old-sister Becky had whacked me on the back side of my head with a 12-inch iron skillet. Kind of like, "Get out of my kitchen." (Smile.) Here's her version of a high-fiber, very-low-fat muffin with only 46 calories. Diabetics can use olive oil or flaxseed meal (1 cup flaxseed is the substitute) instead of the applesauce, or make the applesauce with Splenda Sugar Substitute. These have good flavor, but a bit on the rough side.

MAKES 6 JUMBO TEXAS-SIZE MUFFINS OR 12 REGULAR MUFFINS
SODIUM PER RECIPE: 35.2 MG
SODIUM PER MUFFIN (12): 2.98 MG

1½ **cups crude wheat bran (1.74 mg)**
 ⅓ **cup whole wheat pastry flour (1.98 mg)**
 2 **teaspoons vital wheat gluten (1.5 mg)**
 1 **tablespoon Featherweight Baking Powder (13.5 mg)**

½ cup flaxseed meal (trace)
¼ cup Splenda Sugar Substitute* (trace)
   8-ounce can unsweetened crushed pineapple in its own juice†
   (1.245 mg)
 1 tablespoon apple cider vinegar (.15 mg)
 1 cup frozen, unsalted, unsweetened blueberries‡ (1.55 mg)
   Olive oil spray for muffin tins (trace)

Preheat your oven to 400°F.

Mix all the ingredients together in a medium-size bowl, stirring with a wooden spoon. Pour the batter into the muffin tins, which you have spritzed with olive oil spray.

Bake at 400°F. for 22 to 30 minutes, or until golden brown. Test for doneness with a toothpick. This recipe makes 6 jumbo muffins or 12 regular ones.

Tip from Chef Don: Don't thaw the blueberries. Mix them into the batter last—right out of the freezer. This way they will remain whole and not burst into juice.

Nutrient Values per Muffin (12) Calories: 53.9 Protein: 2.499 g. Carbohydrate 12.3 g. Dietary Fiber: 4.659 g. Total Sugars: 0 g. Total Fat: 1.228 g. Saturated Fat: .066 g. Monoun-saturated Fat: .067 g. Polyunsaturated Fat: .228 g. Cholesterol: 0 mg. Calcium: 117.3 mg. Iron: 1.158 mg. Potassium: 372.4 mg. Sodium: 2.93 mg. Vitamin K: 0 mcg. Folate: 8.602 mcg.

For each muffin in a batch of 6 jumbo muffins, double the numbers.

❖ CHOCOLATE CHIP BRAN MUFFINS ❖

HANDMADE—OVEN BAKE
NOT ADAPTABLE FOR DIABETICS
MAKES 12 MUFFINS   SODIUM PER RECIPE: 256.4 MG
SODIUM PER MUFFIN: 21.4 MG

1¼ cups raw Bob's Red Mill (or other) oat bran (4.7 mg)
 1 cup Bob's Red Mill (or other) whole wheat pastry
   flour (6 mg)
 1 level tablespoon vital wheat gluten (2.25 mg)
¼ cup (packed) brown sugar (21.5 mg)
 2 tablespoons flaxseed meal (trace)
 1 tablespoon Featherweight Baking Powder (13.5 mg)

*You may substitute granulated sugar (trace) with Splenda.
†You may substitute fresh grated carrots for the pineapple.
‡1 cup unsweetened blueberries has 18.9 g carbohydrates. The USDA has not yet listed the sugar count.

1 teaspoon granulated white sugar (trace)
2 teaspoons ground cinnamon (1.211 mg)
½ cup nonfat milk (63.1 mg)
2 medium egg whites (109.6 mg)
1 tablespoon apple cider vinegar (.15 mg)
¾ cup plus 1 tablespoon apple juice concentrate (17.6 mg) or
    orange juice concentrate (1.866 mg)
2 tablespoons grated orange zest (.36 mg)
½ cup Nestle semisweet chocolate chips (16 mg)

Preheat your oven to 425°F.

Mix together the bran, flour, gluten, sugars, flaxseed meal, baking powder, and cinnamon, then stir in the milk, egg whites, vinegar, juice concentrate, zest, and chocolate chips.

Fill lightly greased (olive oil spray) and flour-dusted bake cups inserted into a muffin pan. Bake at 425°F for 15 to 16 minutes.

Allow the muffins to cool in the pan for about 10 minutes, then remove and cool on a rack. Any muffins not eaten immediately can be refrigerated or frozen.

Nutrient Values per Muffin (Figured Using Apple Juice): Calories: 154.8 Protein: 5.125 g. Carbohydrate: 29.6 g. Dietary Fiber: 3.824 g. Total Sugars: 9.886 g. Total Fat: 3.961 g. Saturated Fat: 1.85 g. Monounsaturated Fat: .997 g. Polyunsaturated Fat: .596 g. Cholesterol: .204 mg. Calcium: 91.2 mg. Iron: 1.68 mg. Potassium: 329.1 mg. Sodium: 21.4 mg. Vitamin K: .003 mcg. Folate: 11.9 mcg.

❖ CARROT MUFFINS ❖

HANDMADE — OVEN BAKE
NOT ADAPTABLE FOR DIABETICS

This recipe uses a special whole wheat pastry flour. Many local mills will manufacture a lighter whole wheat flour for use in pastries. In the West, a mill in Milwaukee, Oregon, known as Bob's Red Mill makes a terrific whole wheat pastry and white flour that I use often (www.bobs redmill.com). I've not tried this recipe with the coarser and standard whole wheat, but if you can find only that, it should work, although it may come out of the oven a bit "heavier."

MAKES 12 TO 16 REGULAR MUFFINS OR 8 TEXAS-SIZE MUFFINS
SODIUM PER RECIPE: 234.2 MG
SODIUM PER MUFFIN (12): 19.5 MG

1 cup grated carrots (about 2 medium) (38.5 mg)
¼ cup walnuts (3 mg), chopped or ground in the processor

½ cup white granulated sugar (or Splenda Sugar Substitute)
(2 mg)

½ cup brown sugar (or Sugar Twin substitute, or Splenda Sugar
Substitute) (42.9 mg)*

½ cup extra virgin olive oil (trace)

1 tablespoon apple cider vinegar (.15 mg)

2 medium egg whites (109.6 mg)

1 medium egg yolk (7.138 mg)

1½ teaspoons ground cinnamon (.908 mg)

1 cup whole wheat pastry flour (6 mg)

2 teaspoons vital wheat gluten (1.5 mg)

1½ tablespoons Featherweight Baking Powder (13.5 mg)

2 teaspoons Ener-G Baking Soda (trace)
8-ounce can crushed pineapple (we recommend Dole in own
juice (1.245 mg)

½ cup golden seedless raisins (8.7 mg)

2 teaspoons vanilla extract or flavoring (.756 mg)

Preheat your oven to 350°F.

Shred the carrots, set aside. Chop the walnuts, set aside.

Using a wooden spoon, combine the sugars, oil, vinegar and egg whites and yolk, mixing well. Add in the remaining ingredients one at a time, mixing as you go.

When ready, spoon or ladle the batter into muffin cups, filling them about ¾ of the way up. Set the muffin pan (12 regular cups or 6 jumbo) on a cookie sheet and bake in the 350°F oven on the middle or lower middle rack for 30 minutes for the smaller muffins, for about 32 minutes for the larger muffins. Test with a toothpick or sharp knife for doneness.

Cool on rack. Store them in zipper-type bags for up to 4 days. Reheat when serving. Serve with jam or plain. Great for snacks.

Nutrient Values per Muffin (16) Calories: 250.8 Protein: 5.339 g. Carbohydrate: 59.3 g. Dietary Fiber: 2.431 g. Total Sugars: 21.1 g. Total Fat: 5.406 g. Saturated Fat: .346 g. Monounsaturated Fat: .894 g. Polyunsaturated Fat: 2.593 g. Cholesterol: 20.3 mg. Calcium: 122.9 mg. Iron: 5.344 mg. Potassium: 404.9 mg. Sodium: 27.5 mg. Vitamin K: 0 mcg. Folate: 48.3 mcg.

*You may substitute the brown sugar for white sugar or the brown sugar for Splenda Sugar Substitute. Diabetics may choose to leave the raisins out. If substituting, your sodium levels can be counted as "0 mg."

❧ APPLE STREUSEL MUFFINS ❧

MUFFIN IS OKAY FOR DIABETICS
(STREUSEL TOPPING: SUBSTITUTE SPLENDA FOR THE SUGAR)

This muffin is low in fat and sodium. You can modify this recipe for more fiber by substituting ½ cup wheat bran or 7-grain cereal for the ½ cup flour. This muffin is a bit spongier than muffins cooked with oil. Serve hot at breakfast with a glass of orange juice. The Texas-size muffin makes a complete meal. Add ½ cup shredded carrots (reduce the raisin total by ½ cup) and get some beta carotene.

MAKES 12 REGULAR-SIZE MUFFINS OR 6 TEXAS-SIZE MUFFINS
SODIUM PER RECIPE: 330.3 MG
SODIUM PER MUFFIN (12): 27.5 MG
SODIUM PER MUFFIN (6): 53.5 MG

THE BATTER

    1   medium egg (55.4 mg)
    2   tablespoons finely grated orange zest (.36 mg)
 1⅓   cups (not packed) light brown sugar (75.2 mg)
    2   teaspoons vanilla extract (.756 mg)
  ⅔   cup Homemade Applesauce (see page 206) (.25 mg)
    1   cup 1%-fat, low-sodium Knudsen or other suitable buttermilk
         (130 mg)
 2½   cups all-purpose or best for bread unbleached flour (6.25 mg)
    1   tablespoon Featherweight Baking Powder (13.5 mg)
    1   level teaspoon ground cinnamon (.606 mg)
 1½   cups seedless golden raisins (26.1 mg)

THE TOPPING
(You can use your own version of streusel topping, if you like, but without salt added; here's mine)
    1   tablespoon unsalted butter (1.562 mg)
  ⅓   cup (not packed) brown sugar (18.7 mg)
  ¾   teaspoon ground cinnamon (.454 mg)
  ½   cup finely chopped unsalted walnuts (6 mg)

Prepare the topping first. Soften the butter and mix all the ingredients together with a fork. When it comes mostly together, use your fingers to complete the process. Set aside.

Preheat your oven to 400°F.

To prepare the batter, in a medium to large bowl with a wooden spoon combine the egg, orange zest, sugar, vanilla, and applesauce. Stir in the buttermilk.

In a separate bowl, sift together the flour, baking powder, and cinnamon, then stir into the batter until smooth. Fold in the raisins, stirring again with the wooden spoon.

Spoon the batter into muffin tins or a muffin pan. If you use paper cups, make sure to spritz them lightly with olive oil spray and dust each with flour.

Crumble the streusel mix over each muffin. If you're short of streusel mix, make more. You can make this mix and store it in the refrigerator in an airtight container for up to a week and use it on other baked goods from waffles and pancakes to cakes and pies.

Place the muffin tins on a large baking sheet. Bake for 15 minutes at 400°F. Reduce the temperature to 350°F. and bake for another 12 minutes if making 12 regular muffins; if making Texas-size muffins, bake for another 15 to 18 minutes. Test for doneness with a knife or toothpick at the above times. Bake longer if necessary.

Nutrient Values per Muffin (12) Calories: 290.9 Protein: 5.338 g. Carbohydrate: 59 g. Dietary Fiber: 2.403 g. Total Sugars: 34.3 g. Total Fat: 5.401 g. Saturated Fat: 1.345 g. Monounsaturated Fat: .894 g. Polyunsaturated Fat: 2.592 g. Cholesterol: 29.3 mg. Calcium: 344 mg. Potassium: 278.6 mg. Sodium: 25.8 mg. Vitamin K: 0 mcg. Folate: 48.3 mcg.

❈ HOLIDAY CRANBERRY STREUSEL ❈

HANDMADE—OVEN BAKE
NOT ADAPTABLE FOR DIABETICS

This one will get you going again with muffins. With a glass of orange juice, it's a complete noontime meal or breakfast during the holidays. I have provided two versions here for you. One is with olive oil, the other without oil but with applesauce as the substitute for the oil. The fat is lowered greatly in the applesauce version. If serving to healthy friends, the olive oil's unsaturated fats won't harm them and indeed some olive oil is good for us all. If you want to enjoy the full robust flavor of this muffin, then eat only half or make and eat one when the balance of your day hasn't tipped the 30 percent total fats level.

MAKES 12 REGULAR MUFFINS OR 6 TEXAS-SIZE MUFFINS
SODIUM PER RECIPE: 332.1 MG
SODIUM PER MUFFIN (12): 27.7 MG
SODIUM PER MUFFIN (6): 55 MG

THE BATTER
 1 **medium egg (55.4 mg)**
 ⅔ **cup extra virgin light olive oil* (trace)**

*You may substitute ⅔ cup flaxseed meal and ¼ cup of bottled water (trace) for half the oil. This will cut fat and calories down.

2 tablespoons finely grated orange zest (.36 mg)
1⅓ cups light brown sugar (114.1 mg), packed firm
   2 teaspoons vanilla extract (.756 mg)
   1 cup reduced-fat, cultured, low-sodium buttermilk (Knudsen or other) (130 mg)
   1 tablespoon apple cider vinegar (.15 mg)
2½ cups all-purpose flour (6.25 mg)
2½ teaspoons vital wheat gluten (1.87 mg)
   1 tablespoon Featherweight Baking Powder (13.5 mg)
   1 level teaspoon ground cinnamon (.606 mg)
   1 cup Ocean Spray Craisins (cranberry raisins) (9 mg)

OPTIONAL TOPPING
(You can use your own version of streusel topping, but without salt added, of course.)
   1 tablespoon unsalted butter (1.562 mg)
   ⅓ cup brown sugar (28.3 mg)
   ¾ teaspoon ground cinnamon (.454 mg)
   ½ cup finely chopped unsalted walnuts (6 mg)

Preheat your oven to 400°F.

To prepare the batter, spritz nonstick muffin pans (the regular or Texas-size pan) with olive oil spray, then dust with flour.

Prepare the topping. Soften the butter and mix together the ingredients with a fork. When mostly together, use your fingers to bring them completely together. Set aside.

In a medium to large bowl, whisk or gently beat together with your handheld beater the egg, orange zest, sugar, and vanilla. Do not overbeat. When together in somewhat a paste form, add the buttermilk and the vinegar, stirring with a wooden spoon.

In a separate bowl, sift together the flour, gluten, baking powder, and cinnamon. Stir the flour mixture into batter. If it doesn't fold in well, lightly use the handheld blender for no more than 1 minute. Fold in the Craisins with a wooden spoon.

Spoon the batter into the muffin tins or muffin pan. If you use paper cups, make sure to use the nonstick type, or spritz lightly with olive oil spray and dust with flour.

Crumble the streusel mix over each muffin. If you're short of streusel mix, make more. You can make this mix and store it in the refrigerator in an airtight container for up to 1 week, and use it on other baked goods from waffles and pancakes to cakes and pies.

Bake the muffins for 15 minutes at 400°F. Reduce the heat to 350°F. and bake for another 10 to 12 minutes if making regular-size muffins; if making Texas-size muffins, bake at 350°F. for another 15 to 18 minutes.

The muffins should spring back when pressed lightly. Let them sit in the pan 5 minutes before removing. Cool on rack. Store them in zipper-type bags for up to 4 days. Reheat when serving. Serve warm, with jam or plain.

Nutrient Values per Muffin with Olive Oil (12) Calories: 340.3 Protein: 4.344 g. Carbohydrate: 54 g. Dietary Fiber: 1.441 g. Total Sugars: 32.2 g. Total Fat: 12.9 g. Saturated Fat: 2.01 g. Monounsaturated Fat: 8.919 g. Polyunsaturated Fat: 1.158 g. Cholesterol: 17.7 mg. Calcium: 108.7 mg. Iron: 4.821 mg. Potassium: 248.3 mg. Sodium: 27.7 mg. Vitamin K: 5.821 mcg. Folate: 42.4 mcg.

Nutrient Values per Muffin with Flaxseed Meal Instead of Olive Oil (12) Calories: 287.8 Protein: 4.344 g. Carbohydrate: 54 g. Dietary Fiber: 1.441 g. Total Sugars: 32.2 g. Total Fat: 7.002 g. Saturated Fat: 1.263 g. Monounsaturated Fat: 4.542 g. Polyunsaturated Fat: .659 g. Cholesterol: 17.7 mg. Calcium: 108.7 mg. Iron: 4.798 mg. Potassium: 243.3 mg. Sodium: 27.7 mg. Vitamin K: 2.911 mcg. Folate: 42.4 mcg.

❖ CRANBERRY RAISIN MUFFINS ❖

HANDMADE — OVEN BAKE
NOT ADAPTABLE FOR DIABETICS

I have always enjoyed cranberries—not just during the holidays, but during the rest of the year also. I will buy the frozen bags during the Thanksgiving season and freeze many of them for the rest of year, since they are seasonal. When the dried cranberry "raisin" began to appear in stores in abundance, I began to use them for breakfast cereal, salads, and now this muffin. The fresh cranberry sauce in the recipe is made from some of those frozen cranberries. This makes a terrific holiday muffin to serve guests as well.

**MAKES 12 REGULAR MUFFINS   SODIUM PER RECIPE: 321.8 MG
SODIUM PER MUFFIN: 26.8 MG**

2 **medium egg whites, beaten (109.6 mg)**
1 **teaspoon apple cider vinegar (trace)**
1 **teaspoon vanilla extract (.378 mg)**
¾ **cup (unpacked) brown sugar (42.4 mg)**
½ **cup fresh cranberry sauce (1.077 mg)**
1 **cup nonfat milk (126.2 mg)**
   Zest of 1 medium orange (.18 mg), grated
2 **cups whole wheat pastry flour (12 mg)**
2 **teaspoons vital wheat gluten (1.5 mg)**
1 **tablespoon Featherweight Baking Powder (13.5 mg)**
4½ **teaspoons Ener-G Baking Soda (trace)**
1½ **cups Ocean Spray Craisins or other dried cranberries (13.5 mg)**
½ **cup chopped pecans (.54 mg)**

Whisk together the eggs, vinegar, vanilla, sugar, cranberry sauce, and milk.

In a separate bowl with a wooden spoon, stir together the remaining ingredients.

Blend the two mixes together until the batter is smooth. Spoon it into lightly greased and flour-dusted muffin cups until the batter reaches the top.

Bake at 400°F. for 20 minutes. Cool on rack. Store them in zipper-type bags for up to 4 days. Reheat when serving. Serve warm, with jam or plain.

Nutrient Values per Muffin Calories: 221.1 Protein: 4.464 g. Carbohydrate: 45.2 g. Dietary Fiber: 4.091 g. Total Sugars: 26.8 g. Total Fat: 3.666 g. Saturated Fat: .368 g. Monounsaturated Fat: 1.892 g. Polyunsaturated Fat: 1.135 g. Cholesterol: .367 mg. Calcium: 511 mg. Potassium: 303.7 mg. Sodium: 26.8 mg. Vitamin K: .005 mcg. Folate: 11.3 mcg.

❖ DATE MUFFINS WITH PINEAPPLE ❖

HANDMADE—OVEN BAKE
NOT ADAPTABLE FOR DIABETICS

Dates are very low in sodium and fat and have no cholesterol. These muffins are high in fiber, flavor and low in fat and sodium.

MAKES 12 REGULAR MUFFINS   SODIUM PER RECIPE: 137.5 MG
SODIUM PER MUFFIN: 11.5 MG

- 1 **cup wheat bran (1.16 mg)**
- ½ **cup oat bran (.118 mg)**
- 1 **cup Bob's Red Mill or other whole wheat pastry flour (6 mg)**
- 1 **tablespoon Featherweight Baking Powder (13.5 mg)**
- 1 **level tablespoon vital wheat gluten (2.25 mg)**
- ½ **cup (packed) brown sugar (42.9 mg)**
- 1 **medium to large egg, beaten (55.4 mg)**
- ½ **cup crushed canned pineapple in its own unsweetened juice (1.25 mg)**
- 1 **teaspoon vanilla flavoring or extract (.378 mg)**
- ½ **cup Homemade Applesauce (.189 mg)**
- ¾ **cup unsweetened prune juice (7.624 mg)**
- 1 **tablespoon apple cider vinegar (.15 mg)**
- 1 **cup chopped pitted dates (6.24 mg)**
- ¼ **cup chopped unsalted, dry-roasted pecans (.275 mg)**

In a medium-small bowl, mix the wheat and oat brans, flour, baking powder, gluten, and sugar, then set aside. In a large bowl, beat the egg, add the pineapple, applesauce, vanilla, prune juice, and vinegar into the egg and beat. Next spoon the flour mixture into wet mixture, stirring with wooden spoon as you do. Stir in the dates and pecans.

Pour the batter into 12 standard muffin cups and bake at 400°F on the middle or lower middle rack for 15 to 17 minutes. Cool on a rack. Serve warm or hot or reheated.

Nutrient Values per Muffin Calories: 176.3 Protein: 3.816 g. Carbohydrate: 32.1 g. Dietary Fiber: 5.554 g. Total Sugars: 9.572 g. Total Fat: 2.643 g. Saturated Fat: .386 g. Monounsaturated Fat: 1.175 g. Polyunsaturated Fat: .798 g. Cholesterol: 15.6 mg. Calcium: 82.5 mg. Iron: 1.836 mg. Potassium: 453.4 mg. Sodium: 11.5 mg. Vitamin K: 0 mcg. Folate: 13.6 mcg.

❖ Don's Pumpkin Muffin ❖

Adaptable for Diabetics

One of our young granddaughters asked after eating her first Don's Pumpkin Muffin, "Who's Don?" So much to learn. I had a half a can of Libby's pumpkin left over after making only one pumpkin pie, and a bit of Bob's Red Mill Whole Wheat Pastry Flour, so, on a whim, I decided to create a new pumpkin muffin. It took a few more tries than that first "whim," however, since I felt more spices were needed and a bit more pumpkin. If you think I've added too many spices, then, please, cut them back to fit your tastes. But it's a good recipe as it stands now and I think you'll enjoy it.

Makes 12 regular muffins or 6 Texas-size muffins
Sodium per Recipe: 258.7 mg
Sodium per Muffin (12): 21.6 mg*

 2 **cups white unbleached bread flour (5 mg)**
 ¾ **cup whole wheat pastry flour (4.5 mg)**
 1½ **tablespoons Featherweight Baking Powder† (20.2 mg)**
 1 **teaspoon vital wheat gluten (.8 mg)**
 ½ **teaspoon grated nutmeg (.178 mg)**
 1 **teaspoon ground cinnamon (.303 mg)**
 1 **teaspoon ground ginger (.584 mg)**
 ½ **teaspoon cloves (2.55 mg)**
 ½ **cup white granulated sugar (1 mg)**
 2 **medium or large egg whites (109.6 mg)**
 1 **egg yolk (7.138 mg)**

*Double all nutrient values for each Texas-size muffin.
†You may add ¼ teaspoon double-acting baking powder for extra kick. Add 121 mg sodium to recipe total.

¼ cup extra virgin olive oil (trace)
⅔ cup reduced-fat, low-sodium buttermilk (Knudsen's or other) (85.8 mg)
1½ teaspoons vanilla extract (.567 mg)
1 teaspoon apple cider vinegar (.05)
½ cup (packed) golden seedless raisins (9.9 mg), or use Zante currants
1 cup Libby's or other canned no-salt-added or unsalted pumpkin (12.2 mg)

Prepare a 12-muffin tin or a Texas-size 6-muffin tin by oiling the cups with olive oil or a bit of melted unsalted butter; these oils will add a trace of fat— no sodium. Dust these cups with whole wheat pastry flour after oiling them.

Preheat your oven to 425°F.

Sift together the flours, baking powder, gluten, nutmeg, cinnamon, ginger, cloves, and sugar in a small or slightly large bowl. Stir together using a wooden spoon.

Beat the egg whites to peaks in a medium mixing bowl. Add the olive oil, yolk, buttermilk, vanilla, vinegar, and raisins or currants and stir gently. Stir in the pumpkin.

With a wooden spoon, beat in the dry ingredient mix a bit at a time until the batter is well mixed and smooth. Do not use a mixer, only a wooden spoon.

Spoon the batter into muffin cups, filling them about ¾ of the way up.

Bake on the middle or lower middle rack at 425°F for 18 to 22 minutes. (The smaller muffins might bake in 18 to 20 minutes, while the larger ones might take 20 to 22 minutes.) Use a dry toothpick to test for doneness.

Remove the muffins from the tins, cool on a rack, then serve warm, reheated, or at room temperature. You may store these in the freezer. Do not bake them in foil cups, as the bottoms will burn.

Nutrient Values per Muffin Calories: 213.9 Protein: 4.955 g. Carbohydrate: 38.1 g. Dietary Fiber: 2.524 g. Total Sugars: 13.1 g. Total Fat: 5.705 g. Saturated Fat: 1.034 g. Monounsaturated Fat: 3.53 g. Polyunsaturated Fat: .604 g. Cholesterol: 19.1 mg. Calcium: 116.9 mg. Potassium: 344 mg. Sodium: 21.6 mg. Vitamin K: 5.5 mcg. Folate: 40.5 mcg.

❈ PINEAPPLE MUFFIN TOPS ❈

HANDMADE—OVEN BAKE

This muffin is very low in fat. You can modify this recipe to add more fiber by substituting ½ cup wheat bran or 7-grain cereal for ½ cup of the flour. This muffin is a bit spongier than muffins cooked with oil. Serve them hot at breakfast with a glass of orange juice. Muffin Tops are baked in a special muffin top pan. I found mine at Sur La

Table, in Oakland, California. You can find one at www. surlatable.com or at your local kitchenware store. It's made by Farberware.

MAKES 8 TO 10 MUFFIN TOPS   SODIUM PER RECIPE: 332.2 MG
SODIUM PER MUFFIN TOP (10): 33.2 MG
SODIUM PER MUFFIN TOP (8): 41.5 MG

THE BATTER

1 large egg white (54.3 mg)
1 tablespoon oil (trace)
½ cup unsweetened orange juice with calcium (1.244 mg)
1⅓ cups light brown sugar, not packed (75.2 mg)
2 teaspoons vanilla extract (.756 mg)
½ cup cultured, reduced-fat, lowered-sodium buttermilk
   (65 mg)
8-ounce can Dole crushed pineapple in its own juice (2.49 mg)
2½ cups best for bread unbleached flour (6.25 mg)
1 tablespoon Featherweight Baking Powder (13.5 mg)
1 level teaspoon ground cinnamon (.606 mg)
1½ cups (not packed) seedless golden raisins (26.1 mg)

TOPPING

(You can use your own version of streusel topping, if you like, but without salt added)

1 tablespoon unsalted butter (1.562 mg)
⅓ cup (not packed) brown sugar (18.7 mg)
¾ teaspoon ground cinnamon (.454 mg)
½ cup finely chopped unsalted pecans (.567 mg)

Prepare the topping first. Soften the butter, mix all the ingredients together with a fork. When it comes together, use your fingers to complete the process. Set aside.

Preheat your oven to 400°F.

To prepare the batter, in a medium to large bowl with a wooden spoon, combine the egg, oil, orange juice, sugar, and vanilla. Stir in the buttermilk and pineapple.

In a separate bowl, sift together the flour, baking powder, and cinnamon, then stir into the batter until smooth. Fold in the raisins, stirring again with the wooden spoon.

Spoon batter into a muffin-top tin or muffin pan. If you use paper cups, make sure to spritz them lightly with olive oil spray and dust with flour.

Crumble the streusel mix over each muffin. If you're short of streusel mix, make more. You can make this mix and store it in the refrigerator in an airtight container for up to 1 week, and use it or other baked goods from waffles and pancakes to cakes and pies.

Place the muffin-top tin on a large baking sheet.

Bake for 15 minutes at 400°F. Reduce the oven to 350°F. and bake for another 12 minutes, if you are making regular muffin tops. If you are making Texas size muffins instead of muffin tops, bake at 350°F. for another 15 to 18 minutes. Test for doneness with a knife or toothpick at the above times. Bake longer if necessary.

Nutrient Values per Muffin Top (10) Calories: 352 Protein: 5.974 g Carbohydrate: 72.7 g Dietary Fiber: 2.728 g Total Sugars: 24.5 g Total Fat: 6.316 g Saturated Fat: 1.46 g Monounsaturated Fat: 2.86 g Polyunsaturated Fat: 1.379 g Cholesterol: 5.608 mg Calcium: 158.7 mg Potassium: 516.9 mg Sodium: 33.2 mg Vitamin K: 0 mcg. Folate: 56.9 mcg.

❖ POPPY SEED PUFF-UPS ❖

BREAD MACHINE KNEAD—OVEN BAKE
ADAPTABLE FOR DIABETICS

During the 1940s and 1950s, a truck from a well-known bakery came by our house once a week. This was the way bread was delivered to nearly everyone in our area. The driver would open up the back door of that van-type truck, and the aromas would make you lick your lips and roll your eyes. Everything from cream puffs to cookies, cakes and pies rode around in that truck. I had some favorites, too, like everyone else. Poppy seed buns were one of my favorites. This recipe attempts to duplicate that old Helms Bakery recipe, but of course we can't quite get the "salt" flavor; so I've replaced that flavor by using orange zest, almond extract, and low-sodium baking powder and baking soda. Bingo! These are great. You can make these "puff-ups," or turn them into dinner rolls or even sandwich buns.

Your children will love these, too! A dash of their favorite jam and these hit the spot. (Warm before serving, or serve hot out of the oven.) You can make this recipe into puff-ups in a muffin tin, in foil-lined muffin cups, sitting on a cookie sheet, or you can make pull-a-parts or bread for slicing in a loaf pan. These rise high during the second rising. Dough for pull-a-parts in a loaf pan should sit only at the bottom third.

MAKES 24 PUFF-UPS*   SODIUM PER RECIPE: *300.8 MG* SODIUM PER PUFF-UP (24): *12.5 MG*

*You can also make 2 loaves of bread (9.6 mg per slice).

THE DOUGH

¾ **cup lowered-sodium buttermilk (see page 17) (130 mg) at room temperature (80°F.)**

¼ **cup plus 3 tablespoons orange juice (1 mg), at room temperature (70°F. to 80°F.)**

2 **tablespoons extra virgin olive oil (trace)**

1 **tablespoon apple cider vinegar (trace)**

2 **teaspoons vanilla extract (.756 mg)**

½ **teaspoon almond extract (trace)**

1 **large egg (63 mg)**

The zest of 1 medium to large orange (.18 mg), grated

3 **cups white unbleached bread flour (7.5 mg)**

1 **cup whole wheat bread flour (6 mg)**

1 **tablespoon poppy seeds (1.848 mg)**

1 **tablespoon vital wheat gluten (2.25 mg)**

¼ **cup (packed) brown sugar (21.5 mg)**

2 **tablespoons white granulated sugar* (.252 mg)**

1 **tablespoon bread machine yeast (6 mg), at room temperature (70°F.)**

THE TOPPING

1 **large egg white (54.8 mg), beaten**

2 **tablespoons poppy seeds (3.696 mg)**

(If you get overgenerous using this egg mix, then double it next time.)

Place all the dough ingredients in your bread machine in the order listed. Make sure you first warm the buttermilk to between 90°F. and 100°F., and that the yeast is at least at 70°F. (room temperature). Set the machine on the Dough cycle (approximately 1½ hours).

While dough is working, prepare one or two muffin tins with muffin cups. (Or "foil" muffin cups on a cookie sheet.) Lightly spray the tins and paper cups with olive oil spray—you'll only add a trace of sodium and and negligible fats.

If using Texas-size muffin cups, do the same thing. Make the dough balls twice as large. If making a loaf for pull-a-parts, lightly spray a loaf pan. I like to make 12 small muffins or 6 Texas-size and 1 loaf from the same batch.

When the dough is ready, preheat your oven to about 100°F. and turn it off.

Just before the dough is ready, beat the egg white until nearly stiff. Add in the poppy seeds and stir.

---

*Optional, used only to make the puff-ups sweeter.

To make 24 puff-ups: Using your hands, gently press down on the dough. Pull 24 equal-size pieces off the large dough ball and roll them in your hands to form evenly shaped balls. Roll each ball in the beaten egg/poppy seed mix. Set each ball into a separate cup lightly spritzed with olive oil spray.

To make 12 standard or 6 Texas-size muffins and a loaf: Cut the dough in half, pull the needed number of balls off one half and roll them in your hands to form evenly shaped balls. Roll each ball in the beaten egg/poppy seed mix. Set each ball into a separate cup lightly spritzed with oil from a spray can. Form the second half of the dough into a loaf shape and roll it into a lightly oil-spritzed loaf pan.

To make a pull-apart loaf: Pull 12 balls from half of the dough, set the balls on the bottom of 7- or 9-inch loaf pan, barely touching each other, and then stack.

For any of the above: Let the dough rise in the warmed oven for about 45 minutes, lightly covered with a cloth or wax paper. Remove gently from the oven if you have only one oven, and set oven to 350°F.

When baking muffins: Bake them on a large cookie or baking sheet, on the middle rack at 350°F. for about 8 to 10 minutes, or until they begin to turn golden.

When baking loaves: If you're making a loaf or pull-aparts, bake it in a loaf pan for about 14 to 18 minutes, or until golden brown. Cool on rack. Store them in zipper-type bags for up to 4 days. Reheat when serving. Serve warm, with jam or plain.

Nutrient Values per Muffin (24) (Double for Texas-Size Muffins) Calories: 111.2 Protein: 3.985 g. Carbohydrate: 19.4 g. Dietary Fiber: 1.282 g. Total Sugars: 3.051 g. Total Fat: 2.411 g. Saturated Fat: .439 g. Monounsaturated Fat: 1.017 g. Polyunsaturated Fat: .566 g. Cholesterol: 9.896 mg. Calcium: 41.3 mg. Potassium: 76.8 mg. Sodium: 12.5 mg. Vitamin K: .551 mcg. Folate: 41.7 mcg.

❖ JAM SURPRISE WHEAT MUFFINS ❖

HANDMADE — OVEN BAKE
ADAPTABLE FOR DIABETICS WITH LOW-SUGAR OR SUGARLESS JAM

High in fiber, low in fat and sodium, these are great for breakfast or as a midday snack.

MAKES 12 MUFFINS   SODIUM PER RECIPE: 144.2 MG
SODIUM PER MUFFIN: 12 MG

  2 **cups unprocessed wheat (crude) bran (2.32 mg)**
⅓ **cup best for bread whole wheat flour (1.98 mg)**
¼ **cup (packed) brown sugar (21.5 mg)**
  1 **teaspoon vital wheat gluten (.72 mg)**
  1 **tablespoon Featherweight Baking Powder (6 mg)**

1 teaspoon granulated white sugar (trace)
2 level teaspoons ground cinnamon (1.211 mg)
2 medium egg whites (109.6 mg)
½ cup Homemade Applesauce* (see page 206) (.189 mg)
¾ cup water (0 mg)
12 heaping teaspoons low-sugar jam or jelly of your choice†
(1.44 mg)

Preheat your oven to 425°F.

Mix together the bran, flour, sugar, gluten, baking powder, sugar, and cinnamon. Add the eggs, applesauce, and water, and stir with a wooden spoon.

Fill bake cups inserted into a muffin pan half full with batter. Spoon in 1 heaping teaspoon jam per muffin, then cover that with more dough until topped and three-quarters full in baking cup.

Bake for 15 to 16 minutes at 425°F. Allow to cool in tin for about 10 minutes, then remove and cool on a rack. These can be refrigerated or frozen.

Nutrient Values per Muffin Calories: 81. 2 Protein: 2.626 g. Carbohydrate: 20.4 g. Dietary Fiber: 5.23 g. Total Sugars: 5.382 g. Total Fat: .55 g. Saturated Fat: .081 g. Monounsaturated Fat: .077 g. Polyunsaturated Fat: .267 g. Cholesterol: 0 mg. Calcium: 19.3 mg. Potassium: 176.8 mg. Sodium: 12 mg. Vitamin K: .001 mg. Folate: 10.4 mcg.

❖ YAM MUFFINS ❖

HANDMADE—OVEN BAKE
ADAPTABLE FOR DIABETICS

No sugar, no cholesterol, low in fat, these muffins are loaded with nutrients because of the yams used. Yams, like yellow squash, can be used in pies, soups, breads, and muffins. If you want to lower the fat in this recipe, then use ½ the olive oil and substitute 2 tablespoons unsweetened applesauce or cranberry sauce or 6 tablespoons flaxseed meal for the missing oil.

MAKES 12 MUFFINS   SODIUM PER RECIPE: 173 MG
SODIUM PER MUFFIN: 14.4 MG

½ cup unsweetened apple juice (8.365 mg)
1 cup (not packed) raisins (17.4 mg)

*You may replace this with either unsalted butter or flaxseed meal, if desired.
†Blueberry or strawberry jam make the best muffins, but use your favorite jam or jelly. Many jams have fewer mg of sodium. A good low-sugar jam will also work as well. Serve hot or cooled.

2 eggs, whites only (109.6 mg)
1 cup yam (18.9 mg) baked until soft (about 2 medium yams or 1 large)
1 tablespoon apple cider vinegar (.15 mg)
4 tablespoons olive oil* (trace)
¾ teaspoon ground cloves (3.825 mg)
¾ teaspoon ground cinnamon (.454 mg)
1½ teaspoons Featherweight Baking Powder (3 mg)
1 cup best for bread whole wheat pastry flour (6 mg)
2 cups best for bread white flour (5 mg)
1 teaspoon vital wheat gluten (.72 mg)

Preheat your oven to 400°F. or preheat your convection oven to 375°F.

Warm the apple juice (I use Hanson's Unsweetened Apple Juice) and soak the raisins in the juice until you are ready to use them.

Beat the egg whites until stiff. With a wooden spoon, mix in the softened yam, vinegar, oil, ground cloves and cinnamon, and the baking powder. When well mixed, stir in the flour and gluten and the raisins with the juice.

Using nonstick muffin cups in a metal muffin pan, fill each with batter using a spoon. The muffins will rise from ½ to a full inch above the lip.

Bake at 400°F. in a standard oven for about 25 minutes, or until the tops spring back or a toothpick test proves them done. In a convection oven, bake on the middle rack at 375°F. for about 25 minutes.

To make these sweeter, add ½ cup white granulated sugar (1 mg), or ½ cup Splenda Sugar Substitute (trace) when mixing dry ingredients. If you add the sugar, the calorie count will jump up by 40 per muffin.

Nutrient Values per Muffin with 4 Tablespoons Olive Oil Calories: 215 Protein: 4.792 g. Carbohydrate: 39.1 g. Dietary Fiber: 3.123 g. Total Sugars: 0 g. Total Fat: 5.019 g. Saturated Fat: .707 g. Monounsaturated Fat: 3.364 g. Polyunsaturated Fat: .585 g. Cholesterol: 0 mg. Calcium: 32.5 mg. Potassium: 350.6 mg. Sodium: 14.4 mg. Vitamin K: 2.206 mcg. Folate: 41.3 mcg.

Nutrient Values per Muffin with 2 Tablespoons Olive Oil and 2 More Tablespoons Unsweetened Apple Juice Calories: 195.3 Protein: 4.792 g. Carbohydrate: 39.2 g. Dietary Fiber: 3.123 g. Total Sugars: 0.g Total Fat: 2.769 g. Saturated Fat: .403 g. Monounsaturated Fat: 1.706 g. Polyunsaturated Fat: .396 g. Cholesterol: 0 mg. Calcium: 32.6 mg. Iron: 1.836 mg. Potassium: 351.8 mg. Sodium: 14.4 mg. Vitamin K: 1.103 mcg. Folate: 41.2 mcg.

*You can use just 2 tablespoons of oil and 4 tablespoons of flaxseed meal instead.

WAFFLES

✦ BASIC BELGIAN AND STANDARD WAFFLES ✦

HAND PREPARE—WAFFLE IRON COOK
ADAPTABLE FOR DIABETICS

This is a delicious Belgian waffle, and it's made without salt or real baking soda. Serve it with hot homemade applesauce (made with either real sugar or Splenda), low-sodium syrup, or jam.

MAKES 4 STANDARD 7-INCH WAFFLES
SODIUM PER RECIPE: 189.8 MG   SODIUM PER WAFFLE: 46.3 MG

1 cup white unbleached best for bread flour or all-purpose flour (2.5 mg)
¾ cup reduced-fat, reduced-sodium, cultured buttermilk (130 mg per cup or less) (130 mg)
¼ cup orange juice* (.622 mg)
2 tablespoons extra virgin olive oil (trace)
1 teaspoon Ener-G Baking Soda (trace)
1 teaspoon natural vanilla extract (.378 mg)
1 large egg, separated (63 mg)
1 tablespoon white granulated sugar (.126 mg) or Splenda Sugar Substitute

Stir the flour, buttermilk, orange juice, oil, baking soda, and vanilla together with a wooden spoon until smooth. Beat the egg whites to a stiff peak, adding the sugar (or Splenda) in as you do so. Fold the beaten egg whites and the yolk into batter gently with a wooden spoon until the batter is light and smooth. Ladle ½ cup batter onto your hot nonstick waffle iron. (If it's not a nonstick, then use a spritz of olive oil spray to make sure the waffle doesn't stick.) The batter will be "thin" but will bake nicely into a thick golden waffle. (**Note:** Some nonstick waffle makers may need a spritz of oil also.)

Bake on hot cycle until done. Serve hot. If you want to make many waffles for a group, preheat your oven to 150°F. to 200°F. and set the cooked waffles on a lightly greased cookie sheet. Do not stack them on

*Or use nonfat milk (31.5 mg) or apple juice with vitamin C and calcium added (4.334 mg) instead.

top of each other or they will turn soggy. If you want really crisp waffles, substitute 2 tablespoons cornstarch for 2 tablespoons of the flour. You can also freeze these waffles and heat them in the toaster later.

Nutrient Values per Waffle Calories: 233.4 Protein: 6.797 g. Carbohydrate: 31.9 g. Dietary Fiber: .875 g. Total Sugars: 3.118 g. Total Fat: 8.279 g. Saturated Fat: 1.374 g. Monounsaturated Fat: 5.451 g. Polyunsaturated Fat: .852 g. Cholesterol: 47.9 mg. Calcium: 379.6 mg. Potassium: 179.3 mg. Sodium: 46.3 mg. Vitamin K: 3.32 mcg. Folate: 63.3 mcg.

❧ OLD-FASHIONED BUTTERMILK WAFFLES ❧

DIABETIC READY
HANDMADE—WAFFLE IRON BAKE

This recipe is right out of my mother's original, hand-written cookbook. We've cut the sodium way down by using Ener-G Baking Soda, which is obtainable at www.healthyheartmarket.com. We've cut the buttermilk in half and mixed it with orange juice. This produces a flavored waffle. You may use all buttermilk in place of the orange juice, but if you do, add 65 mg sodium to the total recipe (if using bottled buttermilk) but only 42.5 mg sodium with Bob's Red Mill Buttermilk Powder. Of course you can cut your sodium down even more by eating only half a waffle. ☺

MAKES 2 LARGE WAFFLES   SODIUM PER RECIPE: 124.4 MG
SODIUM PER WAFFLE: 62.2 MG

1   cup white best for bread flour (2.5 mg)
½   cup low-fat, cultured low-sodium buttermilk* (see page 17) (65 mg)
½   cup unsweetened orange juice fortified with calcium (1.244 mg)
1   medium egg (55.4 mg)
2   teaspoons Ener-G Baking Soda (.192 mg)

Preheat your waffle iron at a high setting.

Combine all the ingredients in a medium-size bowl and stir vigorously with a wooden spoon. When well mixed, use a measuring cup (½ cup if your waffle iron is small) to pour half the batter on the iron for the first waffle, then make the second. Serve hot with natural maple syrup or your favorite jam.

*You may use Knudsen's, Crowley, Darigold, Finast, Friendship unsalted, A&P, Borden, and any other 1% lowered-sodium buttermilk. Bob's Red Mill Buttermilk Powder also works great with this recipe.

Nutrient Values per Waffle Calories: 299.5 Protein: 11.9 g. Carbohydrate: 57.2 g. Dietary Fiber: 1.812 g. Total Sugars: 8.475 g. Total Fat: 4.104 g. Saturated Fat: 1.533 g. Monounsaturated Fat: .899 g. Polyunsaturated Fat: .566 g. Cholesterol: 99.8 mg. Calcium: 1267 mg. Potassium: 211.6 mg. Sodium: 62.2 mg. Vitamin K: 0 mcg. Folate: 133.8 mg.

❈ HEAVENLY SOURDOUGH WAFFLES ❈

FOR BELGIAN AND STANDARD WAFFLE MAKERS
ADAPTABLE FOR DIABETICS

These treats are low-fat, low-sodium, and you can also make them without the sugar.

MAKES 5 ROUND WAFFLES   SODIUM PER RECIPE: 121.2 MG
SODIUM PER WAFFLE: 24.2 MG

1½ **cups orange juice fortified with calcium (3.731 mg)**
 ½ **cup whole wheat pastry or whole wheat specialty flour (3 mg)**
1½ **cups white unbleached bread flour (3.75 mg)**
 1 **teaspoon vanilla extract or flavoring (.378 mg)**
 ½ **teaspoon white granulated sugar (.021 mg)**
 ½ **cup Sourdough Starter (see page 57) (.057 mg)**
 1 **tablespoon grated orange zest (.18 mg)**
 2 **egg whites (109.6 mg), beaten stiff**
  Spritz of olive oil (trace)

Preheat your waffle iron.

Heat the orange juice to about 90°F. to 100°F. and pour it into a large mixing bowl. Add both flours, vanilla, sugar, and mix with a single or double beater. Fold in the sourdough. Stir in the zest. If you have the time, set it aside, covered with plastic wrap, for about 45 minutes.

Beat the egg whites until stiff; fold them into mixture. Place about ½ cup batter onto the lightly greased waffle iron (spritzed with olive oil) and bake at medium-high setting.

Serve hot with hot natural maple syrup and sliced bananas or strawberries.

Nutrient Value per Waffle Calories: 229 Protein: 7.551 g. Carbohydrate: 47.6 g. Dietary Fiber: 3.148 g. Total Sugars: .416 g. Total Fat: .786 g. Saturated Fat: .122 g. Monounsaturated Fat: .17 g. Polyunsaturated Fat: .272 g. Cholesterol: 0 mg. Calcium: 108.8 mg. Potassium: 261.6 mg. Sodium: 24.2 mg. Vitamin K: .067 mcg. Folate: 98.4 mcg.

❈ BELGIAN WAFFLES SUPREME ❈

HANDMADE—WAFFLE IRON COOK
DIABETIC APPROVED

Serve these with natural maple syrup, fresh fruit, or a dollop of sour cream. Yum.

MAKES 4 BELGIAN WAFFLES   MAKES 4 ROUND WAFFLES
SODIUM PER RECIPE: 252.3 MG
SODIUM PER WAFFLE (4 SERVINGS): 63.1 MG
SODIUM PER ½ WAFFLE (8 SERVINGS): 31.5 MG

2   **medium to large egg whites (109.6 mg), beaten until nearly stiff**
1   **cup white unbleached flour (2.5 mg)**
1   **teaspoon Featherweight Baking Powder (4.5 mg)**
2   **teaspoons Ener-G Baking Soda (trace)**
1   **teaspoon cornstarch (.238 mg)**
1   **cup nonfat milk (126.2 mg)**
1   **teaspoon apple cider vinegar (.05 mg)**
1   **egg yolk (7.138 mg)**
1   **teaspoon vanilla extract (.378 mg)**
½   **teaspoon almond extract (.189 mg)**
1   **tablespoon unsalted butter (1.562 mg), melted**
½   **teaspoon extra virgin olive oil (trace)**

Preheat your waffle iron. You may use either your Belgian (recommended) or your standard waffle maker.

Beat the egg whites until nearly stiff. Set aside.

With a wooden spoon, stir the flour, baking powder, baking soda, and cornstarch together. Add the rest of the ingredients, stirring as you do. When ready, stir in the beaten egg whites.

Pour ½ cup of the batter onto your nonstick (slightly greased with olive oil) waffle iron. If you are making many waffles, keep the cooked ones on a flat baking sheet, unstacked, in your oven at about 100°F. to 150°F. They will remain warm and crisp.

Nutrient Values per Waffle (4 Servings) Calories: 197.2 Protein: 7.803 g. Carbohydrate: 28.5 g. Dietary Fiber: .877 g. Total Sugars: 0 g. Total Fat: 5.14 g. Saturated Fat: 2.385 g. Monounsaturated Fat: 1.786 g. Polyunsaturated Fat: .463 g. Cholesterol: 62 mg. Calcium: 192.2 mg. Potassium: 293.4 mg. Sodium: 63.1 mg. Vitamin K: .37 mcg. Folate: 58 mcg.

COOKIES

❖ ❖ ❖ ❖ ❖ ❖ ❖ ❖

❖ ALMOND POPPYSEED BISCOTTI ❖

ADAPTABLE FOR DIABETICS

Here is a low-sodium treat for after dinner or as a snack at midday.

MAKES 25 COOKIES   SODIUM PER RECIPE: 337.7 MG
SODIUM PER COOKIE: 13.5 MG

3 cups white unbleached bread flour (7.5 mg)
1 tablespoon Featherweight Baking Powder (13.5 mg)
1 teaspoon cornstarch (.238 mg)
5 egg whites (273.9 mg)
1 cup sugar or Splenda Sugar Substitute (2 mg)
1½ tablespoons almond extract (1.701 mg)
1 tablespoon poppy seeds (1.848 mg)
5 egg yolks (35.7 mg)
1 cup roasted unsalted whole almonds (15.2 mg)

Preheat your oven to 375°F. Lightly spray oil on two large baking sheets. Set one aside. You'll do your initial baking with just one sheet.

Sift the flour with the baking powder and cornstarch and set it aside.

In a larger bowl, beat the egg whites until peaks just form. Sprinkle in sugar (or Splenda), almond extract, and poppy seeds over the whites and continue to blend with beaters until stiffer but not hard. Fold in the yolks.

Using a wooden spoon, stir in the flour mixture and almonds until the mixture becomes a batter. When the dough becomes too thick, knead it with your hands.

Move the batter to a baking sheet and form it into a 3 × 14-inch shape, about ½ inch thick, or one 6 × 10 inches (you will slice down the middle after the first baking).

Bake at 375°F for about 25 to 30 minutes. Test with toothpick or knife to make sure it's baked through. Remove the 'cake" from the oven. If you've made a shorter "cake," then slice in half and then slice it into ½- to ¾-inch pieces at a radical diagonal. You're trying to get 25 to 30 cookies out of this. Lay these cookie slices on their sides on 2 separate baking sheets. Return them to the oven and bake for 10 minutes at 375°F then turn them over to other cut side and bake another 8 to 10 minutes. Be careful that they don't burn.

Cool on racks. Serve cold, hot, or warm. Serve with tea, coffee, or as a side to a salad. These can also be frozen for future use.

Nutrient Values per Cookie Calories: 138.1 Protein: 4.093 g. Carbohydrate: 21.2 g. Dietary Fiber: 1.106 g. Total Sugars: 8.19 g. Total Fat: 4.248 g. Saturated Fat: .581 g. Monounsaturated Fat: 2.283 g. Polyunsaturated Fat: 1.009 g. Cholesterol: 42.5 mg. Calcium: 53.1 mg. Potassium: 138.8 mg. Sodium: 13.5 mg. Vitamin K: .067 mcg. Folate: 30.2 mcg.

❧ ANISE BISCOTTI ❧

"ANISE TOAST"
ADAPTABLE FOR DIABETICS

This version of biscotti was served at our house for many years. It has been modified to bring the sodium down to a very low level. Notice the absence of butter in this version. Easy to prepare and cook.

MAKES 30 COOKIES   SODIUM PER RECIPE: 335.1 MG
SODIUM PER COOKIE: 11.2 MG

3 cups best for bread flour (7.5 mg)
1 tablespoon Featherweight Baking Powder (13.5 mg)
5 egg whites (273.9 mg)
1 cup white granulated sugar (2 mg)
5 egg yolks (35.7 mg)
1 tablespoon anise extract (1.17 mg)
1 cup toasted unsalted almonds (1.38 mg), sliced

Preheat your oven to 375°F. Grease 2 baking sheets.

Sift the flour with the baking powder and set aside.

In a large bowl, beat the egg whites until soft peaks form. Sprinkle the sugar over whites; continue beating until mixture is stiff.

With wooden spoon, fold in the egg yolk, anise extract, and almonds, blending well.

Sprinkle the flour mixture gradually over the egg mixture, folding it in well after each addition. When the dough becomes too heavy to work with a spoon, use your hands in a kneading action.

Roll the dough onto a lightly greased cookie sheet, forming a 3×12×1-inch rectangle. Bake at 375°F. until a cake tester inserted in the center comes out clean—about 30 minutes.

Remove from the oven and cool for 5 minutes or so. Cut slices at a diagonal across rectangle anywhere from ½-inch thick to 1 inch thick. Place the slices on their sides on an ungreased baking sheet and toast at 375°F. until lightly browned on the first side—4 to 10 minutes, then turn over and bake for another 8 to 10 minutes. These can be frozen for future use.

Cool on racks. Serve cold, hot, or warm.

❄ GINGER BISCOTTI ❄

WITH ALMONDS AND CRYSTALLIZED GINGER

I love gingersnaps. I guess I really enjoy ginger. Not too long ago I was in a produce market in one of America's smallest villages, and hanging on a hook was a bag of crystallized ginger bits. "Drop into your tea," the package said. I smiled, picked up the package, all the while knowing I had another use for them. Hope you like these biscotti.

MAKES 40 COOKIES   SODIUM PER RECIPE: 314.6 MG
SODIUM PER COOKIE: 7.865 MG

1 **cup white granulated sugar (2 mg)—Splenda works well, too**
½ **teaspoon ground ginger (.584 mg)**
1 **tablespoon Featherweight Baking Powder (13.5 mg)**
3 **cups all-purpose or bread flour (7.5 mg)**
5 **large egg whites (273.9 mg), beaten to peaks**
1 **tablespoon almond extract (1.17 mg)**
1 **egg yolk (7.138 mg)**
⅓ **cup crystallized or dry ginger chunks (10.4 mg), diced**
1 **cup unsalted sliced almonds (1.08 mg)**

Preheat your oven to 375°F. Lightly grease 1 baking sheet.

Stir together the sugar and ground ginger, then set aside.

Stir together the flour and baking powder, then set aside.

In a large bowl, beat the egg whites until soft peaks form. Sprinkle the sugar-ground ginger mixture and the almond extract over the whites while beating until the mixture is stiff.

With a wooden spoon, fold in the egg yolk, diced ginger, and almonds, blending well.

Sprinkle the flour mixture gradually over the batter, folding in well with a wooden spoon after each addition. When dough becomes too heavy to work with the spoon, use your hands in a kneading action and knead lightly.

*For diabetics: Splenda Sugar Substitute works well with this recipe. Replace the crystallized ginger with Zante currants or your own favorite sugarless fruit treat, diced, or try raw gingerroot, finely diced or minced.

Transfer the dough to a lightly greased cookie sheet, forming a 3×12×¾-inch rectangle. Shape with your hands. Quickly put in the preheated oven. Bake on the middle rack at 375°F. until a cake tester inserted in center comes out dry—about 25 to 30 minutes.

Remove from the oven and cool for 5 minutes or so on the baking sheet. Using a very good serrated knife, cut slices straight across very thinly (about ¼ to ⅜ inch). Place the slices on their sides on an ungreased baking sheet and toast on "bake" temperature of 375°F. until lightly golden brown—10 minutes on one side, then flip over and bake for 8 to 10 minutes on other side.

Cool on a rack. Break or cut each piece in half before serving, to make 40 cookies. These can be frozen for future use.

Nutrient Values per Cookie Calories: 78.4 Protein: 2.274 g. Carbohydrate: 14.1 g. Dietary Fiber: .586 g. Total Sugars: 6.13 g. Total Fat: 1.526 g. Saturated Fat: .12 g. Monounsaturated Fat: .877 g. Polyunsaturated Fat: .37 g. Cholesterol: 0 mg. Calcium: 24.7 mg. Potassium: 74.7 mg. Sodium: 7.865 mg. Vitamin K: 0 mcg. Folate: 15.4 mcg.

❖ CHOCOLATE DIPPED ALMOND BISCOTTI ❖

Just because we're on a no-salt or low-salt lifestyle plan, doesn't mean we can't enjoy the finer things in life. This treat is perfect for after dinner or while entertaining friends. Delicious cookies you'll make over and over.

MAKES 40 COOKIES   SODIUM PER RECIPE: 384.8 MG
SODIUM PER COOKIE (40): 9.62 MG

3 **cups white unbleached bread flour (7.5 mg)**
1 **tablespoon Featherweight Baking Powder (13.3 mg)**
5 **egg whites (273.9 mg)**
1 **cup sugar (2 mg)**
5 **egg yolks (35.7 mg)**
1 **tablespoon cider vinegar (.15 mg)**
2 **tablespoons almond extract (2.34 mg)**
1 **cup roasted unsalted whole almonds (18.7 mg)**
1 **tablespoon poppy seeds (1.848 mg)**

AFTER BAKING
1 **package Nestle's semi-sweet chocolate chips, melted in double boiler (48 mg)**

Preheat oven to 375°F. Lightly spray oil on two large baking sheets. Set one aside. You'll do your initial baking with just one sheet. Sift flour with the baking powder and set aside.

In a large bowl, beat the egg whites until soft peaks form. Sprinkle sugar over the whites while continuing to blend together.

When the egg whites slightly thicken, use a wood spoon and stir in the rest of the ingredients until the mixture becomes a batter.

Move the batter to a baking sheet and form into a 3×14-inch rectangle. Bake at 375°F. for about 25 minutes. Test with a toothpick or a knife to make sure it's cooked. Slice ½- to ¾-inch pieces at a radical diagonal. You're trying to get 25 to 40 cookies out of this. You can make 20 long cookies and cut them in half after baking.

Lay these on their sides on two separate baking sheets. Return to the oven and bake on each side for 12 minutes each, at 375°F. Cool on racks.

While cookies are baking on their sides, melt a package of semi-sweet chocolate chips in a double boiler pan. Spread on a dinner plate or in a 9-inch pie shell (for flatness). Keep this dish or the pan over the double-boiler hot water to keep the chocolate from setting too quickly. Dip the finished cookie bottoms into the chocolate and let them cool upside down on the rack. They will take up to 2 hours to harden.

Serve cold, hot, or warm. Serve with tea, coffee, or as a side to a salad. Can be frozen for future use.

Nutrient Values per Cookie Calories: 120.1 Protein: 3.096 g. Carbohydrate: 13.7 g. Dietary Fiber: 1.078 g. Total Sugars: 4.666 g. Total Fat: 5.891 g. Saturated Fat: 1.522 g. Monounsaturated Fat: 2.565 g. Polyunsaturated Fat: 1.047 g. Cholesterol: 26.6 mg. Calcium: 40.7 mg. Iron: 1.037 mg Potassium: 121.3 mg. Sodium: 9.62 mg. Vitamin K: 042 mcg. Folate: 20.1 mcg.

❧ CHOCOLATE CHIP BISCOTTI ❧

ADAPTABLE FOR DIABETICS

Here is a low-sodium and low-fat treat for you and your children.

MAKES 20 TO 30-PLUS COOKIES   SODIUM PER RECIPE: 373.9 MG
SODIUM PER COOKIE (20): 18.7 MG
SODIUM PER COOKIE (30): 12.5 MG

1 **orange (1.4 mg), puréed**
   Zest of 1 orange (.72 mg)
3 **cups white unbleached bread flour (7.5 mg)**
1 **tablespoon Featherweight Baking Powder (13.3 mg)**
1 **teaspoon cornstarch (.238 mg)**
5 **egg whites (273.9 mg)**
1 **cup white granulated sugar (2 mg)**
1 **teaspoon almond extract (.378 mg)**
1 **tablespoon vanilla extract (.378 mg)**

1 **tablespoon olive oil (trace)**
1 **cup semisweet chocolate chips (32 mg)**
  Olive oil spray (trace)

Preheat your oven to 375°F. Lightly spritz 2 large baking sheets with olive oil spray. Set one aside. You'll do your initial baking with just 1 sheet.

Zest your orange and set the zest aside. Purée the balance of the orange in your processor.

Sift the flour with the baking powder and cornstarch into a medium-size bowl, and set aside.

In a larger bowl, beat the egg whites until they form peaks. Sprinkle the sugar over whites while continuing to beat (after they peak). Add the almond and vanilla extracts when done and stir.

Use a wooden spoon and stir in the olive oil, the dry ingredient mix, pureed orange, chocolate chips, and orange zest, until the mixture becomes a thick batter. (The egg whites will loosen during this.)

Transfer the batter to a lightly greased baking sheet and form into a 3×14-inch rectangle. Push down on it with the palms of your hands (or lightly use a rolling pin), so that it's no more than ⅜ inch thick. It will rise in the oven. Bake at 375°F. for about 25 to 30 minutes. Test with toothpick or knife to make sure it's done. Remove the "cake" from the oven, slice ½-to-¾-inch pieces (widthwise of the cake) at a radical diagonal. (I like to use a very sharp serrated knife for this, since the "cake" will be hot.) You're trying to get 20 to 30 cookies out of this. Lay these slices on their sides, using 2 separate lightly greased baking sheets (spritz olive oil spray on the sheets first) to accommodate them. Return cookies to the oven and bake for 10 minutes on one side and about 8 minutes on the other at 375°F.

Cool on racks. Serve either cold, hot, or warm. Serve with tea, coffee, or as a side to a salad.

These can be frozen for future use.

Nutrient Values per Cookie (20) Calories: 242.9 Protein: 5.62 g. Carbohydrate: 34.9 g. Dietary Fiber: 2.14 g. Total Sugars: 16.6 g. Total Fat: 9.169 g. Saturated Fat: 2.821 g. Monounsaturated Fat: 4.236 g. Polyunsaturated Fat: 1.603 g. Cholesterol: 53.2 mg. Calcium: 76 mg. Potassium: 229.6 mg. Sodium: 18.7 mg. Vitamin K: .415 mcg. Folate: 41.5 mcg.

Nutrient Values per Cookie (30) Calories: 161.9 Protein: 3.746 g. Carbohydrate: 23.3 g. Dietary Fiber: 1.427 g. Total Sugars: 11 g. Total Fat: 6.113 g. Saturated Fat: 1.88 g. Monounsaturated Fat: 2.824 g. Polyunsaturated Fat: 1.069 g. Cholesterol: 35.4 mg. Calcium: 50.7 mg. Potassium: 153.1 mg. Sodium: 12.5 mg. Vitamin K: .276 mcg. Folate: 27.7 mcg.

Handmade—Oven Bake

Make these only if you have enough people to consume them right away. The danger with this cookie is that you may want to do that job alone—and, well, they do have calories. You may cut calories by leaving out nuts, almond paste, and white sugar, replacing sugar with Splenda.

MAKES 16 COOKIES   SODIUM PER RECIPE: 171.1 MG
SODIUM PER COOKIE: 10.7 MG

¾ cup white granulated sugar (1.5 mg)
6 tablespoons unsalted butter (9.372 mg)
1½ teaspoons almond extract (.567 mg)
2 tablespoons almond filling or paste (marzipan) (2.552 mg)
3 tablespoons orange juice with calcium (.1465 mg)
1½ cups best for bread white flour (3.75 mg)
2 large egg whites (109.6 mg), well beaten in cream of tartar until stiff
1 teaspoon cream of tartar (1.56 mg)
¾ cup (unpacked) brown sugar (42.4 mg)
almonds

Preheat your oven to 350°F.

Cream the white sugar, butter, almond extract, almond filling, and orange juice until smooth. Mix in the flour with the creamed mixture. Press this mix into an 8×8-inch lightly greased glass baking dish.

Beat eggs with cream of tartar until stiff.

Fold the brown sugar and almond paste into the egg whites gradually.

Spread this over the mixture in the baking pan. Bake at 375°F. for 25 to 30 minutes. Cool on rack for 15 minutes before cutting into 16 squares. Serve fresh. They will store for a day on a loosely covered dish or in a zipper-type bag overnight.

Nutrient Values Using Nuts and Almond Paste Calories: 167.1 Protein: 2.352 g. Carbohydrate: 26.6 g. Dietary Fiber: .662 g. Total Sugars: 16 g. Total Fat: 6.066 g. Saturated Fat: 2.841 g. Monounsaturated Fat: 2.303 g. Polyunsaturated Fat: .585 g. Cholesterol: 11.7 mg. Calcium: 21.7 mg. Potassium: 71.2 mg. Sodium: 19.6 mg. Vitamin K: 0 mcg. Folate: 21.8 mcg.

Nutrient Values Without Using Sugar, Nuts, and Almond Paste Calories: 146.3 Protein: 1.716 g. Carbohydrate: 25.3 g. Dietary Fiber: .323 g. Total Sugars: 15.9 g. Total Fat: 4.436 g. Saturated Fat: 2.707 g. Monounsaturated Fat: 1.258 g. Polyunsaturated Fat: .200 g. Cholesterol: 11.7 mg. Calcium: 12.9 mg. Potassium: 57.2 mg. Sodium: 10.5 mg. Vitamin K: 0 mcg. Folate: 19.8 mcg.

❧ ALMOND MERINGUE COOKIES ❧

ADAPTABLE FOR DIABETICS*

You can make these flat or twirl them up into peaks that resemble giant Hershey Kisses. Whichever way you do it, these are a real treat for no-salt diets. These cookies have zero cholesterol and high flavor.

MAKES 25 TO 50 COOKIES   SODIUM PER RECIPE: 167.8 MG
SODIUM PER COOKIE (25): 6.71 MG

¾ **cup unsalted whole almonds (11.4 mg)**
3 **egg whites (164.3 mg) well beaten**
¼ **teaspoon cream of tartar (.39 mg)**
1 **cup white granulated sugar (2 mg)**
1 **teaspoon almond extract (trace)**

Preheat your oven to 300°F.

Chop the almonds by hand with a chopping blade or Cuisinart or with the Braun MultiQuick Handheld Mixer (280-watt version) until chunky. Set aside.

Beat the egg whites at high speed with double beaters, adding the cream of tartar as you do. When they begin to stiffen, add in the sugar (or Splenda) slowly. Fold in the almond extract and chopped almonds.

Drop the batter by spoonfuls onto lightly greased large cookie sheet(s). If making 25 (2-inch) drops, use 1 sheet. If making 40 to 50 (1-inch) drops, use 2 cookie sheets. You can make flat cookies by folding in the extract and nuts vigorously, or coned cookies by gently folding in the extract and nuts. The baking time is the same for both.

Bake at 300°F for 20 minutes. The cookies will turn a light golden brown. Cool on rack. Serve fresh. Store loosely in a plastic container, covered, for up to 3 days.

Nutrient Values for per Cookie (25) Calories: 57.8 Protein: 1.336 g. Carbohydrate: 8.85 g. Dietary Fiber: .489 g. Total Sugars: 8.123 g. Total Fat: 2.187 g. Saturated Fat: .168 g. Monounsaturated Fat: 1.393 g. Polyunsaturated Fat: .524 g. Cholesterol: 0 mg. Calcium: 11.3 mg. Potassium: 41.7 mg. Sodium: 6.71 mg. Vitamin K: 0 mcg. Folate: 1.486 mcg.

*Substitute Splenda Sugar Substitute for the sugar in the recipe.

❂ CHOCOLATE MERINGUE KISSES ❂

ADAPTABLE FOR DIABETICS

These cookies have zero cholesterol and high flavor. Diabetics can substitute sugarless solid chocolates available in most supermarkets for the Hershey Kisses; they can also substitute Splenda for the sugar.

MAKE 30 MERINGUE KISSES   SODIUM PER RECIPE: 299.7 MG
SODIUM PER COOKIE: 9.99 MG

   3 **egg whites (164.3 mg), well beaten**
  ¼ **teaspoon cream of tartar (.39 mg)**
  ½ **cup white granulated sugar (1 mg), or Splenda Sugar Substitute (0 mg)**
   1 **teaspoon almond extract (trace)**
  ¾ **cup unsalted whole almonds (11.4 mg)**
  30 **Hershey Kisses (123 mg), or sugarless chocolate drops**

Preheat your oven to 300°F.

Beat the egg whites at high speed with a double beater, adding the cream of tartar at the beginning. When they begin to stiffen, add the sugar (or Splenda Substitute) very slowly, then the almond extract. When they have reached the peak stage, you're ready.

If you don't have an insulated pan, then double up your baking sheets. We don't want the bottoms of these kisses to burn. Spritz your baking pan very lightly with oil, wiping it with a towel to make sure the oil is thin and evenly spread.

Spoon a little egg white mixture in 15 to 16 locations on the baking sheet. Set a Hershey Kiss onto each one. Next, spoon over each Hershey Kiss (or use a decorator's squeeze) enough of the beaten egg white to form a cone. You should be able to get 15 per large cookie sheet.

Bake at 300°F for 20 minutes. The cookies will turn a light golden brown.

Nutrient Values Per Cookie, When Made with Hershey Kisses Calories: 60.9 Protein: 1.458 g. Carbohydrate: 7.01 g. Dietary Fiber: .547 g. Total Sugars: 5.969 g. Total Fat 3.353 g. Saturated Fat: 1.059 g. Monounsaturated Fat: 1.66 g. Polyunsaturated Fat: .482 g. Cholesterol: 1.1 mg. Calcium: 19 mg Potassium: 54 mg. Sodium: 9.658 mg. Vitamin K: 0 mcg. Folate: 1.589 mcg.

Nutrient Values Per Cookie, When Made with Sugarless Chocolate Drops and Splenda Calories: 22.3 Protein: 1.113 g. Carbohydrate: .715 g. Dietary Fiber: .407 g. Total Sugars: .169 g. Total Fat: 1.823 g. Saturated Fat: .14 g. Monounsaturated Fat: 1.161 g. Polyunsaturated Fat: .436 g. Cholesterol: 0 mg. Calcium: 9.379 mg. Potassium: 34.6 mg. Sodium: 5.525 mg. Vitamin K: 0 mcg. Folate: 1.239 mcg.

A dessert treat, I was served this at a relative's home. When I visit, they are kind enough to make a special meal just for me. Their daughter Rebecca, "Becca"—who was visiting from her job as a journalist in Moscow—whipped up this apple crisp. Her sister, upon learning of this, informed me that her own recipe was different. She added grated lemon zest to the apples as well as the juice from a lemon squeezed over them. You can add the lemon, too, if you like lemon flavor. I like it both ways, so I now make it half with lemon, half without.

MAKES 8 SERVINGS   SODIUM PER RECIPE: 68.9 MG
SODIUM PER SERVING: 8.613 MG

4   cups (about 6) sliced, cored apples (trace)
⅔   cup (packed) brown sugar (57.1 mg)
½   cup flour (1.25 mg)
½   cup rolled oats (1.56 mg)
1   teaspoon ground cinnamon (.606 mg)
⅓   cup unsalted butter (8.24 mg), softened
⅛   teaspoon unsalted butter for greasing pan (.109 mg)

OPTIONAL
    The grated peel of 1 lemon (trace)
    The juice of the above lemon (.47 mg)
    (Add in sodium amount to individual servings when using; also adds .4 g calcium.)

Preheat your oven to 350°F.

Slice the apples, then spread and layer in the bottom of an 8×8-inch lightly greased pan. (If using the optional lemon zest and juice, mix them with the apples.) In a medium-size bowl, mix together the rest of the ingredients with a wooden spoon. Spread this mixture over the apples. Bake for 25 minutes at 350°F. Cool in a pan on the rack. Cut into bar cookies, after cooling for 15 minutes. Serve fresh. Store, covered, in the refrigerator. Reheat or bring to room temperature. Makes a dish serving or a handheld cookie dessert treat.

Nutrient Values per Serving Calories: 235.4 Protein: 2.628 g. Carbohydrate: 38.6 g. Dietary Fiber: 2.446 g. Total Sugars: 17.8 g. Total Fat: 8.625 g. Saturated Fat: 4.951 g. Monounsaturated Fat: 2.451 g. Polyunsaturated Fat: .617 g. Cholesterol: 20.8 mg. Calcium: 30 mg. Potassium: 179.6 mg. Sodium: 8.613 mg. Vitamin K: .22 mcg. Folate: 18.2 mcg.

❖ CHOCOLATE OAT AND HONEY COOKIES ❖

NOT ADAPTABLE FOR DIABETICS

We are fortunate enough to have fresh honey from my sister's beehives. But any good clover honey will work with this recipe.

MAKES 12 COOKIES   SODIUM PER RECIPE: 127.5 MG
SODIUM PER COOKIE: 10.6 MG

- 5 **tablespoons unsalted butter (7.81 mg)**
- ⅓ **cup honey (4.62 mg)**
- 2 **cups Quaker instant oats (6.48 mg)**
- ⅓ **cup brown sugar (28.3 mg)**
- ¼ **cup unbleached best for bread flour (.625 mg)**
- ½ **tablespoon extra virgin olive oil (trace)**
- 6 **Baker's Semi Sweet Chocolate Squares (5.999 mg)**
- ¼ **cup nonfat evaporated milk (73.6 mg)**

Preheat your oven to 350°F.

Melt the butter and honey over low heat in a medium-size saucepan. Remove the pan from the stove and stir in the oats, brown sugar, and flour. Lightly grease a large cookie sheet with the olive oil, and spoon the mixture onto the cookie sheet in 24 evenly sized balls. Gently press down with your spoon or thumb to slightly flatten them. Make sure they are 1 inch or more apart. Bake for about 12 minutes at 350°F., or until brown.

In a double boiler, melt the chocolate with the evaporated milk. Stir while it melts over the near boiling water until smooth. Refrigerate this mixture for about ½ hour or more, or until it is easy to spread on half of the baked cookie bottoms. Marry 2 cookies together to make a chocolate sandwich. Cool in a pan on the rack. Serve fresh. May freeze in zipper-type bags for up to a month. Bring to room temperature for thawing.

Nutrient Values per Cookie Calories: 232.4 Protein: 3.911 g. Carbohydrate: 33.6 g Dietary Fiber: 1.771 g. Total Sugars: 20.3 g. Total Fat: 10.7 g. Saturated Fat: 5.924 g. Monounsaturated Fat: 3.674 g. Polyunsaturated Fat: .747 g. Cholesterol: 13.1 mg. Calcium: 35.5 mg. Potassium: 153.2 mg. Sodium: 10.6 mg. Vitamin K: .276 mcg. Folate: 9.708 mcg.

SUGARLESS STRAWBERRY
❋ OATMEAL COOKIES ❋

LOW SODIUM, LOW FAT, SUGARLESS
SUITABLE FOR DIABETICS

You already know how hard it is to make a sweet-tasting, healthy, and enjoyable cookie without sugar, sodium, or fat. After all, the three main flavors of a delicious cookie are sodium, fat, and sugar. If you are diabetic and must have low-sodium as well as low-sugar foods, here's your chance to bake a basketful of cookie snacks. Add or subtract fruity flavors, or bake them just the way given here.

MAKES 24 (4-INCH) COOKIES   MAKES 32 (3-INCH) COOKIES
SODIUM PER RECIPE: 200.1 MG
SODIUM PER COOKIE (24): 8.336 MG
SODIUM PER COOKIE (32): 6.252 MG

2   **egg whites (109.6 mg), beaten until nearly stiff**
1   **cup fresh sliced strawberries (1.66 mg), puréed**
1   **cup unsweetened Homemade Applesauce (see page 206) (4.88 mg)**
¾   **cup Splenda Sugar Substitute (trace)**
1   **teaspoon natural (nonalcoholic) vanilla extract (.378 mg)**
1   **cup white unbleached flour (2.5 mg)**
½   **cup whole wheat flour (3 mg)**
2   **teaspoons Featherweight Baking Powder (9 mg)**
½   **teaspoon cornstarch (.072 mg)**
2   **teaspoons ground cinnamon (1.211 mg)**
3   **cups quick or raw oats (9.72 mg)**
1   **cup pitted prunes (6.8 mg), diced**
½   **cup finely chopped walnuts (.625 mg)**
½   **cup chopped dates (2.67 mg)**

Preheat your oven to 350°F.

Beat the egg whites until nearly stiff and set aside. Using your Braun purée attachment or another puréeing device, purée the strawberries. Using your Braun single-beater mixer or other double-beater with one blade attached, beat together the applesauce, strawberries, Splenda, and vanilla.

Add the flours, baking powder, cornstarch, and cinnamon and combine using a wooden spoon. With the wooden spoon next stir in the oats, prunes, walnuts, and dates. Spoon in and stir the egg whites until just mixed. Drop by spoonfuls onto a lightly greased cookie sheet and bake for about 12 to 15 minutes at 350°F., or until they turn light brown. Cool on a rack.

Nutrient Values per Cookie (24) Calories: 119.8 Protein: 3.753 g. Carbohydrate: 22.4 g. Dietary Fiber: 2.825 g. Total Sugars: 0 g. Total Fat: 2.301 g. Saturated Fat: .237 g. Monounsaturated Fat: .577 g. Polyunsaturated Fat: 1.275 g. Cholesterol: 0 mg. Calcium: 38.4 mg. Potassium: 208.5 mg. Sodium: 8.336 mg. Vitamin K: .051 mcg. Folate: 16.2 mcg.

Nutrient Values per Cookie (32) Calories: 89.9 Protein: 2.815 g. Carbohydrate: 16.8 g. Dietary Fiber: 2.119 g. Total Sugars: 0 g. Total Fat: 1.726 g. Saturated Fat: .178 g. Monounsaturated Fat: .432 g. Polyunsaturated Fat: .956 g. Cholesterol: 0 mg. Calcium: 28.8 mg. Potassium: 156.3 mg. Sodium: 6.252 mg. Vitamin K: .038 mcg. Folate: 12.2 mcg.

❖ COWBOY COOKIES ❖

LOW SODIUM, LOWERED FAT
ADAPTABLE FOR DIABETICS

You can serve these to your guests and they'll never know they are made without salt or baking soda, but they will guess you're a great cookie maker. Diabetics may use Splenda to replace the regular sugar.

MAKES 24 (4-INCH) COOKIES   MAKES 40 (2-INCH) COOKIES
SODIUM PER RECIPE: 262.3 MG
SODIUM PER COOKIE (24): 11 MG
SODIUM PER COOKIE (40): 6.575 MG

½ cup (1 stick) unsalted butter (12.5 mg)*
½ cup white granulated sugar (1 mg)
 1 cup (packed) brown sugar (85.8 mg)
 2 egg whites (109.6 mg)
 1 teaspoon natural (nonalcoholic) vanilla extract (.378 mg)
½ cup Homemade Applesauce (see page 206) (trace)
 1 cup white unbleached flour (2.5 mg)
½ cup whole wheat flour (3 mg)
¼ teaspoon cornstarch (072 mg)
 2 teaspoons ground cinnamon (1.211 mg)
 3 cups quick or raw oats (9.72 mg)
 1 cup chocolate chips (13.5 mg)
½ cup finely chopped walnuts (.625 mg)
 1 cup (not packed) black seedless raisins (17.4 mg)

Preheat your oven to 350°F.

Using your Braun or other single-beater mixer, beat together the butter, sugars, egg whites, vanilla (or applesauce if you are substituting it for the butter). Mix in the flours, cornstarch, cinnamon (and flaxseed meal if substituting this for the butter) using the Braun single-beater.

*You can use 1 cup flaxseed meal (52.7 mg) as an optional substitute for the butter.

With a wooden spoon, stir in the oats, chocolate chips, walnuts, and raisins.

Drop by the spoonful onto a lightly greased cookie sheet and bake for about 12 to 13 minutes at 350°F., or until they turn light brown. Cool on a rack.

Nutrient Value per Cookie (24) Calories: 220.9 Protein: 3.964 g. Carbohydrate: 35.4 g. Dietary Fiber: 2.408 g. Total Sugars: 17 g. Total Fat: 8.176 g. Saturated Fat: 3.861 g. Monounsaturated Fat: 2.349 g. Polyunsaturated Fat: 1.47 g. Cholesterol: 10.3 mg. Calcium: 25.1 mg. Potassium: 184.2 mg. Sodium: 11 mg. Vitamin K: 0 mcg. Folate: 14.8 mcg.

Nutrient Values per Cookie (40) Calories: 132.6 Protein: 2.378 g. Carbohydrate: 21.3 g. Dietary Fiber: 1.445 g. Total Sugars: 10.2 g. Total Fat: 4.905 g. Saturated Fat: 2.317 g. Monounsaturated Fat: 1.41 g. Polyunsaturated Fat: .882 g. Cholesterol: 6.206 mg. Calcium: 15.1 mg. Potassium: 110.5 mg. Sodium: 6.575 mg. Vitamin K: 0 mcg. Folate: 8.903 mcg.

❖ HOLIDAY CRANBERRY COOKIES ❖

NOT ADAPTABLE FOR DIABETICS
MAKES 24 (4-INCH) COOKIES   MAKES 36 (3-INCH) COOKIES
SODIUM PER RECIPE: 298.3 MG
SODIUM PER COOKIE (24): 12.4 MG
SODIUM PER COOKIE (36): 8.30 MG

1½ **cups (packed) brown sugar (128.7 mg)**
 1 **tablespoon white granulated sugar (.126 mg)**
 2 **egg whites (109.6 mg)**
 ½ **cup unsalted butter (12.5 mg)—optional***
 1 **cup Ocean Spray or freshly made cranberry sauce† (.378 mg)**
 1 **teaspoon vanilla extract (.378 mg)**
1½ **cups unbleached white flour (3.75 mg)**
 1 **tablespoon Featherweight Baking Powder (13.5 mg)**
 2 **teaspoons ground cinnamon (1.211 mg)**
 1 **cup (loosely packed) shredded coconut flakes, packaged or**
   canned without salt (15.4 mg)—optional
 ½ **cup finely chopped walnuts (12 mg)**
 ½ **cup golden raisins packed or Ocean Spray Craisin raisins, or**
   dried cranberry raisins‡ (9.9 mg)

*If you leave out the butter, you can reduce the total fat by 3.83 g per cookie (92 g total for the recipe). You can also reduce the caloric intake by 33.879 per cookie, making the total per cookie 138.21 calories. However, if making these cookies for guests, they taste best with the butter.
†You may use canned whole berry sauce, but the sodium count is much higher at 80.3 mg to 140 mg per cup depending upon the brand used.
‡Prepare the cranberries according to recipe on the Ocean Spray package.

Preheat your oven to 350°F.

Combine and beat together the sugars, egg whites, butter if you use it, cranberry sauce, vanilla. Add the flour, baking powder, cinnamon, walnuts, coconut flakes, and raisins and mix together with wooden spoon.

Very lightly spritz the cookie sheet with olive oil spray. Make sure it's a very light coating. For large cookies, use your ice cream scoop to make each cookie. For smaller cookies, use a tablespoon to drop the batter for each cookie. The cookies will flatten out.

Bake at 350°F. for about 10 to 13 minutes. If top of the cookie is not sticky, then it is done. Don't overbake them. Cool cookies on a rack. They will seem limp or soft at first, but will harden as they cool down.

Nutrient Values Per Cookie (24): Calories: 176.9 Protein: 1.774 g. Carbohydrate: 29.1 g. Dietary Fiber: 1 g. Total Sugars: 17.6 g. Total Fat: 6.594 g. Saturated Fat: 3.462 g. Monounsaturated Fat: 1.385 g. Polyunsaturated Fat: 1.376 g. Cholesterol: 10.4 mg. Calcium: 48.7 mg. Iron: 1.112 mg. Potassium: 176.4 mg. Sodium: 12.4 mg. Vitamin K: 0 mcg. Folate: 15.3 mcg.

Nutrient Values Per Cookie (36) Calories: 118 Protein: 1.182 g. Carbohydrate: 19.4 g. Dietary Fiber: .667 g. Total Sugars: 11.7 g. Total Fat: 4.396 g. Saturated Fat: 2.308 g. Monounsaturated Fat: .923 g. Polyunsaturated Fat: .917 g. Cholesterol: 6.905 mg. Calcium: 32.5 mg. Iron: .742 mg. Potassium: 117.6 mg. Sodium: 8.287 mg. Vitamin K: 0 mcg. Folate: 10.2 mcg.

✺ DON'S ENERGY BARS ✺

BREAD MACHINE PREPARATION — OVEN BAKE
ADAPTABLE FOR DIABETICS

I designed these to munch on while rowing long before I began my no-salt lifestyle. They're great for flavor and quick energy without consuming a lot of sugar. They'll remind you of some of the commercial "energy bars," but without the high sodium—these are not sweet or "crunchy" hard. They have consistency of a dense bread almost like a bagel.

MAKES 20 BARS   SODIUM PER RECIPE: 80.5 MG
SODIUM PER BAR: 4.026 MG

THE DOUGH

1¼ cups plus 1 tablespoon orange juice fortified with calcium (3.607 mg), at room temperature [70°F. to 80°F.)

1 tablespoon apple cider vinegar (.15 mg)

1 cup 10-grain cereal (20 mg)

1 cup best for bread whole wheat flour (6 mg)

1 teaspoon vital wheat gluten (.72 mg)

1 cup best for bread white flour (2.5 mg)

1 tablespoon Ener-G Baking Soda (trace)

2 tablespoons (unpacked) brown sugar (7.02 mg) sugar substitutes work as well

¼ teaspoon ground cinnamon (.151 mg)
2½ teaspoons bread machine yeast (4.8 mg)

At the raisin buzzer, add
½ cup chopped unsalted walnut halves (6 mg)
1 cup (unpacked) golden seedless raisins (17.4 mg)
1 cup cranberry raisins (or Ocean Spray Craisins) (9 mg)
½ cup (unpacked) black seedless raisins (8.3 mg)

Heat the orange juice to about 115°F. Add the dough ingredients to your bread machine basket. Set the machine on the Dough cycle. When the raisin buzzer sounds, add the nuts and raisins.

When the dough is ready, transfer it to a lightly floured board and cut or break it into 20 pieces. Shape these into squares or rectangular roll shapes (whichever you prefer). Set on baking sheet lightly spritzed with olive oil spray (trace sodium). You can place these within ½ inch of each other. They won't rise too much.

Cover with lightly spritzed wax paper or with a light cloth, set in a warm place, and let rise for about 45 minutes.

Preheat your oven to 425°F.

Bake for about 10 to 14 minutes, or until golden brown. Remove and place on a cooling rack. You can store these in zipper-type bags for up to 3 days or freeze them for up to 4 months. To thaw, place in the microwave and set on Defrost for about 1 to 1½ minutes, or let sit out for about an hour.

Nutrient Values per Bar Calories: 164.1 Protein: 3.795 g. Carbohydrate: 33.2 g. Dietary Fiber: 2.589 g. Total Sugars: 5.601 g. Total Fat: 2.714 g. Saturated Fat: .233 g. Monounsaturated Fat: .304 g. Polyunsaturated Fat: 1.505 g. Cholesterol: 0 mg. Calcium: 50 mg. Potassium: 173.4 mg. Sodium: 4.026 mg. Vitamin K: 0 mcg. Folate: 34.7 mcg.

❖ DON'S DATE BARS ❖

HAND PREPARATION—OVEN BAKE
NOT ADAPTABLE FOR DIABETICS

As a youngster in southern California, I used to endure the long two-lane drive from Los Angeles to the "ranch" my father owned in the searingly hot desert of the Coachella Valley. It was in a place called Mecca, near a small town called Thermal, if that might help get the heat point across. Enroute we would stop at Hadley's Date Stop in the middle of nowhere. Date shakes were my favorite. They were cold and full of date bits, which I loved. But Hadley's also had something else I liked—date bars. This is the best replication I can come up for that bar. Either my memory serves me well, or my baking ability does. No matter, these are delicious. P.S. I prefer them made with almonds, but walnuts or coconut taste great also.

**MAKES 33 (1×2⅓-INCH) BARS   SODIUM PER RECIPE: 206.2 MG
SODIUM PER SERVING: 6.248 MG**

THE FILLING
2½ cups dates (13.3 mg) or date bits, packed tightly, soaked in hot water for 2 to 3 hours, puréed with the ingredients below (2.67 mg)
1 teaspoon ground cinnamon† (.606 mg)
1 teaspoon vanilla extract (.378 mg)

To prepare the filling, soak the dates or date bits in hot water that just covers the dates. After 2 hours, drain the water, leaving just a bit with the dates. Purée the dates with the cinnamon and vanilla.

Preheat your oven to 350°F.

Lightly grease a 7×11-inch pan or an 8×12-inch pan, then dust with whole wheat pastry flour.

THE CRUST
½ cup whole wheat pastry flour (3 mg)
½ cup oat bran (1.88 mg)
¼ teaspoon ground cloves (1.275 mg)
1¼ cups (packed) brown sugar (70.7 mg)
½ cup chopped unsalted walnuts (1.2 mg) or chopped unsalted almonds (8.52 mg), or unsalted flaked coconut (22.8 mg)*
½ cup (1 stick) unsalted butter (12.5 mg), softened, or ½ cup olive oil (trace), or 1 cup flaxseed meal (43 mg), or ⅜ cup honey (5.085 mg)
1 medium to large egg (63 mg)
1 teaspoon vanilla extract (.378 mg)
3 cups Quaker quick oats or rolled oats (11.3 mg)

To make the crust, combine the flour, bran, ground cloves, sugar, and walnuts, stirring well with a wooden spoon until mixed. Set aside.

Stir in the softened butter or oil, egg, and vanilla. If using flaxseed meal, then add either ¼ cup olive oil or water. If still more moisture is needed when using flaxseed meal, after the egg is stirred in add water 1 tablespoon at a time.

Combine the wet with the dry ingredients. Add the oats. Now mix

*Packaged coconut generally has salt added. Look for the dried sweetened flakes in a can (no salt) or in a package. Check the nutrient label for the sodium count per tablespoon.
†You can add more cinnamon to the filling.

everything together with your hands. Split the mixture in half. Press half the mixture down into the baking pan, distributing it evenly.

Spread the date purée evenly over the bottom. Crumble the balance of the crust mixture over the top evenly.

Bake at 350°F for about 38 to 40 minutes. Cut into 33 pieces while still hot or warm (cut 1 inch along the width of the pan and 3 even slices along the length). Let cool in the pan on a rack.

Serve warm or cooled from pan. Store leftovers in the refrigerator and let come to room temperature before serving.

Nutrient Values per Bar Calories: 143.3 Protein: 2.589 g. Carbohydrate: 27.9 g. Dietary Fiber: 2.975 g. Total Sugars: 17.8 g. Total Fat: 4.835 g. Saturated Fat: 2.918 g. Monounsaturated Fat: 1.171 g. Polyunsaturated Fat: .432 g. Cholesterol: 14 mg. Calcium: 18.6 mg. Potassium: 187.5 mg. Sodium: 6.248 mg. Vitamin K: 0 mcg. Folate: 8.904 mcg.

❃ SOURDOUGH DATE BARS ❃

HAND PREPARATION — OVEN BAKE
NOT ADAPTABLE FOR DIABETICS

My father owned a farm in Mecca, California. Mecca was just south of Indio, date capital of the U.S. We had date trees everywhere. They are an interesting fruit, growing high up on the trees and needing extreme heat to survive and ripen. Many varieties exist but one of my favorites is the Majoul. Today, I like cooking with dates and have created more than one recipe for them. They are without fat, without cholesterol, and are sweet-tasting. They make a terrific snack and I use them to make great cookies. Try this date bar. I've made it with as little white sugar as possible and with as little butter as possible. The first few times around I tried this without sugar, then without butter, but always had to bring some back. If you can handle the added fat and sugar, bring the sugar up to 1 cup and the unsalted butter up to ¾ cup. If you do that, leave out the applesauce. The fat will increase more than the sodium.

MAKES 32 DATE BARS   SODIUM PER RECIPE: 94.5 MG
SODIUM PER BAR: 2.658 MG

1   **cup sourdough starter* (3.489 mg), at room temperature**
½   **cup unsalted butter (12.5 mg)**

*Sourdough starter is difficult to get going if you've not done it before. You can make my Sourdough Starter (see recipe on page 57), which is the one I use for all recipes in this book. Or you can purchase a package of sourdough starter mix,

¼ **cup unsweetened applesauce or Homemade Applesauce (see page 206) (1.22 mg)**
1 **egg (63 mg)**
½ **cup granulated white sugar (1 mg)**
1 **teaspoon vanilla extract (.378 mg)**
½ **teaspoon ground allspice (1.463 mg)**
⅓ **cup whole wheat pastry flour (1.98 mg)**
2 **cups chopped pitted dates (10.7 mg)**
  Olive oil spray (trace)

Use 1 cup sourdough starter. Let it stand overnight on your kitchen countertop covered with a light cloth. Set out the butter and applesauce at this time, too. Bring an egg to the countertop for "warming" to room temperature about an hour before preparation time.

In a medium-size mixing bowl, beat together until creamy the butter, sugar, and applesauce, stirring in the vanilla and allspice (don't leave out the allspice). Beat the egg until fluffy, then stir it into the mix. Add the sourdough starter with a wooden spoon, stirring as you do. Add the flour while you stir. Set the bowl aside in a warm (about 80°F. to 90°F. location) for about ½ hour.

Preheat your oven to 375°F. Prepare a 9×13-inch baking pan by greasing with a light spray of olive oil spray, then dusting the pan with pastry flour.

When ready, pour half of the batter into the pan and spread it evenly with a rubber scraper—it will spread thinly. Drop the dates on top evenly. Pour the rest of the batter on top of this in such a way that it spreads over the entire mix. The dates will show through.

Bake at 375°F. on a middle rack for about 20 to 22 minutes, or until golden brown. Check for doneness with a toothpick. Cool in the pan on a rack. After it cools, cut the mixture into 24 bars and serve warm or cold.

Nutrient Values per Date Bar Calories: 38.5 Protein .48 g. Carbohydrate: 6.622 g. Dietary Fiber: .173 g. Total Sugars: 4.95 g. Total Fat: 1.22 g. Saturated Fat: 1.082 g. Monounsaturated Fat: .052 g. Polyunsaturated Fat: .013 g. Cholesterol: 0 mg. Calcium: .805 mg. Potassium: 17.6 mg. Sodium: 6.31 mg Vitamin K: 0 mcg. Folate: .374 mcg.

---

such as the one from Goldrush Products Company, 491 West San Carlos Street, Banjoes, CA 95110, or from Healthy Heart Market at www.healthyheartmarket.com or toll-free at 1-888-685-5988.

For this recipe, if you can't make starter successfully, you may substitute for the starter ¾ cup whole wheat pastry flour (or white unbleached flour), 1 teaspoon Featherweight Baking Powder, and ¼ cup water. If the dough becomes too thick, add water 1 tablespoon at a time until it is easily pliable.

❈ DATE NUT COOKIES ❈

I used to love a cookie from a bakery in Mendocino, California. Today, I can't eat them because of the salt, baking soda, and consequently high sodium content. However, I've managed to come close to making a low-sodium cookie with the same texture, flavor, and goodness. Kids will love these; for heart patients, this is a once-a-week treat.

MAKES 30 LARGE 3-INCH COOKIES
SODIUM PER RECIPE: 271.4 MG   SODIUM PER COOKIE: 11.3 MG

  1 **stick (8 tablespoons) unsalted butter (12.5 mg), softened**
  1 **cup (packed) light brown sugar (85.8 mg)**
 ½ **cup white granulated sugar (1 mg)**
  2 **medium eggs (110.9 mg)**
  1 **tablespoon vanilla extract (.378 mg)**
1½ **cups best for bread white flour (3.75 mg)**
  2 **teaspoons Featherweight Baking Powder (13.5 mg)**
1½ **teaspoons ground cinnamon (.908)**
  2 **cups Quaker or other quick oats (7.52 mg)**
 ½ **cup SunSweet date bits or chunks (2.67 mg)**
  1 **cup semisweet chocolate chips (32 mg)**
  1 **cup walnut halves, ground in processor, or ½ cup packaged chopped unsalted walnuts (.5 mg)**

Place the cooking rack in the middle of your oven and preheat to 350°F.

With a double beater, cream together the butter, sugars, vanilla and eggs until smooth. Sift together the flour, baking powder, and cinnamon and combine with the butter mixture. Stir in the oats, date bits, chocolate chips, and ground walnuts.

On a very lightly greased cookie sheet, spoon enough balls of batter to make eight 3-inch cookies. Press down on them with your spoon or your pancake turner to form them; they will not rise.

Bake at 350°F. for 10 minutes, then take them out and let cool on a rack. Do not bake longer than 10 minutes unless you like your cookies crispier. These will harden up after they cool. Serve hot, warm, or at room temperature. Store in zipper-type bags in the freezer.

Nutrient Values per Cookie Calories: 211.3 Protein: 3.58 g. Carbohydrate: 33.6 g. Dietary Fiber: 2.225 g. Total Sugars: 18 g. Total Fat: 8.663 g. Saturated Fat: 4.366 g. Monounsaturated Fat: 2.444 g. Polyunsaturated Fat: 1.458 g. Cholesterol: 25.9 mg. Calcium: 51 mg. Potassium: 222.4 mg. Sodium: 11.3 mg. Vitamin K: 0 mcg. Folate: 21.1 mcg.

❧ Maple Bars ❧

Look out, these are delicious and closely replicate the real thing (the real thing being maple bars deep-fat-fried and loaded with salt, much more fat, and more sugars). At first they'll just appear to be bread buns, but after you layer the maple topping on and take a bite, you'll know you're into a real buttermilk-maple bar. These are not fried like the commercial maple buns, and they are much lower in fat, sugar, and, of course, sodium.

Makes 12 bars　Sodium per Recipe: 238.3 mg
Sodium per Bar: 19.9 mg

THE DOUGH
  1　cup reduced-fat (1%) buttermilk* (130 mg)
  2　tablespoons light or standard sour cream (20 mg), at room
     temperature
  1　tablespoon apple cider vinegar (.15 mg)
  3　cups white unbleached bread flour (7.5 mg)
  2　teaspoons vital wheat gluten (1.8 mg)
  1　tablespoon grated fresh orange or lemon zest (.36 mg)
  1　tablespoon orange peel, grated (.18 mg)
  2　tablespoons white granulated sugar, Splenda or honey (.252
     mg)
  2　tablespoons extra virgin olive oil (trace)
2½　teaspoons bread machine yeast, room temperature (4.8 mg)

THE MAPLE TOPPING
  4　tablespoons unsalted butter (6.248 mg), melted in pan
  1　tablespoon maple extract (1.134 mg)
  2　tablespoons nonfat milk (15.8 mg)
  1　cup powdered (confectioners') sugar (1.2 mg)

Warm the buttermilk to about 80°F. Pour it into your bread machine basket and add the rest of the dough ingredients in the order listed. Place the yeast in a dry place.

　Set the machine on the Dough cycle.

　When ready, transfer the dough to a lightly floured breadboard and flatten with your hands to about ¾ inch high. Cut into 12 elongated bar-shaped pieces. Place these on a lightly greased cooking sheet (you may use 2 sheets if you prefer). Draw a knife lengthwise down the middle of each

*This recipe also works well using Bob's Red Mill Buttermilk Powder.

from ½ inch inside each top edge, slicing down into dough about ¼ inch. Cover with a light cloth and set in a warm place to rise for about 45 minutes.

Preheat your oven to 425°F.

When ready to bake, bake on the middle rack for about 6 to 8 minutes, or until golden brown.

To make the topping, melt the butter over low heat, add the maple extract and stir to a light boil for 2 minutes or simmer until completely dissolved. Stir in the milk, then add the confectioners' sugar. When the sugar is completely dissolved and the frosting thickens, spread it on the baked bars. Let them cool for 5 minutes before serving.

Nutrient Values per Bar Calories: 274.5 Protein: 4.497 g. Carbohydrate: 49.7 g. Dietary Fiber: 1.03 g. Total Sugars: 24.4 g. Total Fat: 7.117 g. Saturated Fat: 3.169 g. Monounsaturated Fat: 2.82 g. Polyunsaturated Fat: .467 g. Cholesterol: 13.3 mg. Calcium: 105.1 mg. Potassium: 184 mg. Sodium: 21.1 mg. Vitamin K: 1.103 mcg. Folate: 67.2 mcg.

✸ MACAROONS ✸

HAND PREPARATION — OVEN BAKE
NOT ADAPTABLE FOR DIABETICS

Coconut is sweet, but these macaroons are "sweeter." Low in fat and sodium, they hit the spot.

MAKES 30 TO 40 COOKIES   SODIUM PER RECIPE: 189.3 MG
SODIUM PER COOKIE (30): 6.31 MG
SODIUM PER COOKIE (40): 4.733 MG

  3 **egg whites (164.3 mg), well beaten**
  ¾ **cup white granulated sugar (1.5 mg)**
  1 **teaspoon vanilla extract or flavoring (.378 mg)**
1½ **cups unsweetened, unsalted dried canned or dried packaged coconut flakes (check container for low sodium) (23.1 mg)**

Preheat your oven to 300°F.

Beat the egg whites with a double beater until stiff. Slowly add the sugar and vanilla and mix while beating. When ready, fold in the coconut flakes.

Drop batter with a teaspoon onto a lightly greased cookie sheet. You will need 2 cookie sheets to complete all the cookies. Bake 1 sheet at a time on the middle rack of the oven. If you want to bake both at the same time, place 1 on the middle rack, the other on the lower rack. These will brown a bit. Bake for 28 minutes at 300°F.

Cool on rack and serve cooled. Store in airtight containers.

Nutrient Values per Cookie (30) Calories: 38.5 Protein: .48 g. Carbohydrate: 6.622 g. Dietary Fiber: .173 g. Total Sugars: 4.95 g. Total Fat: 1.22 g. Saturated Fat: 1.082 g. Monounsaturated Fat: .052 g. Polyunsaturated Fat: .013 g. Cholesterol: 0 mg. Calcium: .805 mg. Potassium: 17.6 mg. Sodium: 6.31 mg. Vitamin K: 0 mcg. Folate: .374 mcg.

✦ DELICATE COCONUT MACAROONS ✦

HAND PREPARATION — OVEN BAKE
CREATED ESPECIALLY FOR DIABETICS

Coconut has its own flavor, and I for one have always liked it. (That Helms Bakery man I mentioned earlier also had great coconut macaroons in his truck.) I got my coconut education in Tahiti, however, while filming a documentary. There are so many stages a coconut goes through before it's edible, and before the liquid in it is good enough to drink, that I'm not sure I remember which stage is which. Coconut milk, when it's ready, however, is delicious, but getting to the meat of the coconut is a terror. My Polynesian film star and guide, Rene Tupano, climbed a coconut tree for me the old-fashioned way, knocked down some coconuts, and then taught me how to open them and dig the meat out. I learned how to do that, but attempting to climb the tree barefoot and without safety lines was not to be.

They served a cookie down there that I called a macaroon (they referred to it with a name from their own 11-syllable language that I have since forgotten). This recipe is from that trip, and it's a good one. You can add some flour if you like, but I make them without. And, best of all, in our country, the coconut comes in a package, already shredded.

MAKES 6 LARGE MACAROONS   MAKES 12 MEDIUM-SIZE MACAROONS
SODIUM PER RECIPE: 180.9 MG
SODIUM PER MACAROON (6): 30.1 MG
SODIUM PER MACAROON (12): 15.1 MG

 3 **large egg whites (164.3 mg) beaten to stiff peaks**
 ½ **teaspoon cream of tartar (.78 mg) (for egg white beating)**
 1 **teaspoon vanilla extract or flavoring (.378 mg)**
 ½ **cup Splenda Sugar Substitute* (trace)**
 1 **cup low-sodium (no-salt-added) coconut flakes (15.4 mg)—the
    dried, canned ones are low in sodium**

Preheat your oven to 300°F.

In a medium-size bowl, beat the egg whites until they begin to stiffen. Add the cream of tartar and vanilla and beat until they get closer to stiff

*If you prefer granulated sugar, replace the Splenda with ½ cup (1 mg).

For another version, you can fold in ⅓ cup all-purpose flour to make these macaroons a bit crispier. This will add 8 mg sodium to the total recipe. Either way, they are delicious.

Then add in the Splenda slowly while beating. When the whites are very stiff, stir in the coconut.

Using an ice cream scoop drop the cookie batter onto a lightly greased cookie sheet, or use a cake decorating sleeve to squeeze them out, spiraling them as you do so. You will make either 6 large or 12 medium macaroons.

Bake at 300°F. for 20 to 23 minutes. Then cool on a rack. Serve cooled or at room temperature.

Nutrient Values per Macaroon (6) (Halve the figures if baking 12) Calories: 67.9 Protein: 2.187 g. Carbohydrate: 5.664 g. Dietary Fiber: .578 g. Total Sugars: 0 g. Total Fat: 4.067 g. Saturated Fat: 3.606 g. Monounsaturated Fat: .173 g. Polyunsaturated Fat: .045 g. Cholesterol: 0 mg. Calcium: 2.896 mg. Potassium: 107.7 mg. Sodium: 30.1 mg. Vitamin K: .002 mcg. Folate: 1.412 mcg.

❧ FISTFUL OF COOKIE ❧

HAND PREPARATION—OVEN BAKE
NOT ADAPTABLE FOR DIABETICS

Here's an unorthodox recipe for the holidays, created for your surprise drop-in guests but edible by you, too. If you've never cooked like this, then you just aren't having fun. This is a make-it-as-you-go recipe, but follow these instructions and the cookies will blow your guests away— and don't do this again until next holiday season.

**MAKES 20 (2½-INCH) COOKIES SODIUM PER RECIPE: 133.3 MG
SODIUM PER COOKIE: 6.667 MG**

Ready for this? Here we go!

1 **medium to large egg (55.4 mg), beaten with a whisk**
2 **tablespoons extra virgin olive oil (trace)**
1 **tablespoon unsalted butter (1.562 mg), softened or melted**
1 **fistful of white unbleached flour (2.5 mg)**
1 **fistful of quick or rolled oats (3.24 mg)**
1 **fistful of unsalted walnut halves (7.92 mg), chopped in a food processor**
1 **fistful of black seedless raisins (13 mg)**
1 **fistful of dried cranberries or Ocean Spray Craisins (6 mg)**
1 **fistful of semisweet chocolate chips (12 mg)**
1 **teaspoon Featherweight Baking Powder (9 mg)**
1 **tablespoon apple cider vinegar (trace)**
½ **teaspoon ground cinnamon (.303 mg)**
1 **teaspoon vanilla extract (.378 mg)**
½ **fistful of brown sugar (28.3 mg)**

What's a fistful equal? Well, I measured mine after my first attempt with this recipe and it grabbed up 1 cup of flour and about ⅔ cup of nuts, ¾ cup raisins, and 1 cup oats.

You can play with this one. If you like a really sweet cookie, add a bit more brown sugar. Sorry to our diabetic friends, I just didn't find these as tasty with sugar substitutes, but don't let my tastebuds stop you from trying if you can handle the sugars in the raisins and cranberries.

Preheat your oven to 350°F.

In a medium-size bowl, beat the egg with a whisk. Add the olive oil and softened or melted butter. Mix in the flour and oats and stir until crumbly. Mix in the rest of the ingredients and work it with your hands. It's a "dry" recipe. If you need to add moisture, add a touch of orange juice or water. More butter will make these crispier but fattier, too.

Drop the batter by the spoonful on a lightly greased cookie sheet. You should have 20 cookies.

Bake at 350°F. for 13 to 15 minutes on the middle rack. Cool on rack. The cookies will store in zipper-type bags on the countertop for up to 2 weeks. You can also freeze them for up to 2 months. Thaw them on the countertop to room temperature.

Nutrient Values per Cookie Using Butter and Oil Calories: 150.9 Protein: 2.505 g. Carbohydrate: 22.2 g. Dietary Fiber: 1.473 g. Total Sugars: 8.946 g. Total Fat: 6.259 g. Saturated Fat: 1.665 g. Monounsaturated Fat: 2.016 g. Polyunsaturated Fat: 2.265 g. Cholesterol: 10.9 mg. Calcium: 38 mg. Potassium: 160.5 mg. Sodium: 6.667 mg. Vitamin K: .662 mcg. Folate: 16.6 mcg.

Nutrient Values per Cookie Using Applesauce in Equal Exchange (.076 mg) for Butter and Oil Calories: 135.8 Protein: 2.504 g. Carbohydrate: 22.6 g. Dietary Fiber: 1.537 g. Total Sugars: 9.087 g. Total Fat: 4.341 g. Saturated Fat: 1.126 g. Monounsaturated Fat: .855 g. Polyunsaturated Fat: 2.133 g. Cholesterol: 9.35 mg. Calcium: 38.1 mg. Potassium: 163 mg. Sodium: 6.592 mg. Vitamin K: 0 mcg. Folate: 16.7 mcg.

GINGER COOKIES

HAND PREPARATION—OVEN BAKE
ADAPTABLE FOR DIABETICS

This cookie can be made two different ways. I use fresh ginger root and grind it down. If you don't mind a higher sugar count, you can use crystallized ginger, chopped, to replace the ginger root. (Some may label crystallized ginger as "candied ginger.") Using candied ginger lowers the fiber a bit and raises the calorie count and the sugar content. Your guests might prefer the crystallized ginger cookie over the raw ginger one for flavor and texture. However, both have excellent flavor and are great as a snack.

MAKES 24 COOKIES SODIUM PER RECIPE: 248.9 MG
SODIUM PER COOKIE: 10.4 MG

THE COOKIE DOUGH
   2 **cups whole wheat pastry flour (12 mg)**
   1 **tablespoon Featherweight Baking Powder (13.5 mg)**
   1 **teaspoon ground ginger (.584 mg)**
   1 **teaspoon ground cloves (5 mg)**
   1 **cup white granulated sugar (2 mg) or Splenda (0 mg)**
1½ **teaspoons apple cider vinegar (.075 mg)**
   4 **tablespoons unsalted butter (6.248 mg), softened**
   2 **tablespoons olive oil (trace)**
   2 **medium to large eggs (126 mg)**
   2 **tablespoons dark corn syrup (62 mg)**
   ¼ **cup (4 ounces) chopped/sliced crystallized ginger (20.5 mg)**
      or a 6-inch piece (3 ounces) fresh ginger root* (3.2 mg)

THE TOPPING
   2 **tablespoons white granulated sugar (.252 mg)**
   ½ **teaspoon ground cinnamon (.303 mg)**

In a large bowl, using a wooden spoon stir together the flour, baking powder, ground ginger, and cloves.

In a small or medium mixing bowl, using a double beater, cream the butter with the sugar, vinegar, olive oil, and eggs until fluffy. Blend in the corn syrup and crystallized ginger and mix until smooth. Mix this into the flour mixture. Using a wooden spoon, stir until well mixed.

Roll the dough out onto wax paper and form a ball. Wrap and refrigerate for about 2 hours or longer.

Preheat your oven to 350°F.

Prepare the sugar/cinnamon mix by combining the two in a small bowl. Set aside.

Prepare 2 large cookie sheets by lightly greasing them with olive oil spray. Cut the dough ball in half. From each ball pull apart 8 to 12 equal-size pieces. Roll each piece into a 2-inch ball or slightly smaller if making 24 cookies.

Roll each ball in the sugar/cinnamon mix. Place the balls on the cookie sheet about 3 inches apart and push down lightly.

Bake each cookie sheet for about 15 to 20 minutes at 350°F. (don't let them darken too much). Cool on racks. Serve these warm, cold, or at room temperature. You may freeze these cookies for up to 2 months in zipper-type bags.

Nutrient Values per Cookie Using Raw Ginger Root Calories: 96.8 Protein: 1.675 g. Carbohydrate: 18.5 g. Dietary Fiber: 1.31 g. Total Sugars: 10.6 g. Total Fat: 2.344 g. Saturated Fat: 1.299 g. Monounsaturated Fat: .66 g. Polyunsaturated Fat: .186 g. Cholesterol: 14 mg. Calcium: 33.8 mg. Potassium: 113.7 mg. Sodium: 6.986 mg. Vitamin K: 0 mcg. Folate: 5.653 mcg.

*Diabetics: Peel fresh ginger root instead of using crystallized ginger and slice it very thinly. Place this into your Braun or other food processor (or in a spice grinder) and process to about 4 tablespoons finely grated ginger—the finer, the better.

Nutrient Values per Cookie Using Crystallized Ginger Calories: 106.1 Protein 1.657 g. Carbohydrate: 20.8 g. Dietary Fiber: 1.276 g. Total Sugars: 13.2 g. Total Fat: 2.334 g. Saturated Fat: 1.297 g. Monounsaturated Fat: .659 g. Polyunsaturated Fat: .184 g. Cholesterol: 14 mg. Calcium: 144.1 mg. Potassium: 46.4 mg. Sodium. 6.956 mg. Vitamin K: C mcg. Folate: 5.541 mcg.

❖ GINGERBREAD MAN ❖

COOKIES OR REAL GINGERBREAD MAN
PREPARE THE DOUGH A DAY AHEAD OF TIME.
NOT ADAPTABLE FOR DIABETICS*

Danny Boy's Cookies provided us with this recipe, and it's so good that our grandchildren ask us to make them for them all the time. It's high in unsalted butter, but okay if you eat only one 2-inch cookie. We use this recipe for our grandchildren's school parties during the holidays. Made without salt and using a low-sodium baking powder, these are a standout. Try them with your family and your salt-free doubting friends. They make a good snack for you and a great treat for them.

MAKES 6 GINGERBREAD MAN   MAKES 36 (2-INCH) COOKIES
SODIUM PER RECIPE: 174.8 MG
SODIUM PER COOKIE (36): 4.856 MG
SODIUM PER GINGERBREAD MAN: 29.13 MG

½ **pound (2 sticks) unsalted butter (24.9 mg)**
1 **cup white granulated sugar (2 mg)**
1 **cup molasses (121.4 mg)**
2 **tablespoons hot water (trace)**
1 **tablespoon Featherweight Baking Powder (13.5 mg)**
3½ **cups white unbleached all-purpose flour (8.75 mg)**
1 **heaping tablespoon ground ginger (2.104 mg)**
1 **tablespoon ground cinnamon (2.149 mg)**

With your electric beater, cream the butter, sugar, molasses, and hot water in a medium-to-large mixing bowl.

Combine the baking powder, flour, and spices in another bowl. Gradually stir this into the butter-molasses mixture, using half or slower speed with your mixer.

Divide the dough in half into 2 round balls and place them in a bowl to chill in your refrigerator overnight or for at least 2 hours.

*Molasses presents the diabetic a challenge with this recipe. We know of no molasses substitutes. Brown Twin Sugar product doesn't work well as a replacement in this recipe.

Preheat your oven to 350°F.

Roll out the dough with a pin to about ¼ to ⅜ inch thickness (no thinner) and cut out the gingerbread men (each ball should make 3 gingerbread men). If making cookies, use a drinking glass or cookie cutter to cut out 36 of the 2-inch cookies. Place these on an ungreased cookie sheet.

Bake at 350°F. for 10 to 12 minutes (the less time the better). Cool on a rack.

If making cookies, dust with sugar, or roll in sugar when rolling dough and before flattening.

If making gingerbread "men," cool and let your children decorate them. They can use frosting, M&Ms, miniature marshmallows, raisins, or nuts.

Nutritional Values per Cookie (36) Calories: 136.8 Protein: 1.335 g. Carbohydrate: 21.6 g. Dietary Fiber: .483 g. Total Sugars: 11.2 g. Total Fat: 5.258 g. Saturated Fat: 3.207 g. Monounsaturated Fat: 1.492 g. Polyunsaturated Fat: .248 g. Cholesterol: 13.8 mg. Calcium: 43.1 mg. Potassium: 193.8 mg. Sodium: 4.856 mg. Vitamin K: 0 mcg. Folate: 19 mcg.

❂ HEART OF HEARTS ❂

HAND PREPARATION—OVEN BAKE
ADAPTABLE FOR DIABETICS

After forty-plus years of marriage I've pretty much run the gamut of what to get my wife for Valentine's Day (other than a great card). So, this year, I thought a nice wrapped gift from our local jewelry store and a heart-shaped cookie would fill the bill. Diabetics, you can use ⅔ cup Splenda Sugar Substitute to replace the sugar.

MAKES 50 HEART-SHAPED 2-INCH COOKIES
SODIUM PER RECIPE: 114.2 MG   SODIUM PER COOKIE: 2.285 MG

THE COOKIE
10½ tablespoons (⅓ pound) unsalted butter (16.6 mg)
 ⅔ cup white granulated sugar (1.32 mg)
  1 medium to large egg (63 mg)
  2 teaspoons Featherweight Baking Powder (9 mg)
1¾ teaspoons vanilla extract (.661 mg)
2⅓ cups unbleached white flour (5.832 mg)

THE FROSTING
 ½ cup confectioners' sugar (.6 mg)
  1 drop red food dye (trace)
  1 to 2 tablespoons nonfat milk (17.4 mg)

Cream the butter and sugar together. Add the egg and beat until smooth. Add the baking powder, vanilla, and flour and stir with a wooden spoon until batter is heavy but smooth.

On a lightly floured board, break or cut the dough in half. Roll each half on wax paper or a lightly floured board until about ¼ inch thick. Lift the dough with the wax paper and set each piece on a separate cookie sheet and chill in refrigerator for 30 minutes to 1 hour.

Preheat your oven to 350°F.

Bring out one sheet at a time and lift off the cookie dough with the wax paper. Remove the wax paper. Using your 2-inch heart-shaped cookie cutter, begin cutting the cookies and placing them on a lightly greased cookie sheet. Do the same with the second batch. (You can find a 2-inch heart-shaped cookie cutter at a kitchenware shop or on-line a www. surlatable.com.

Bake the cookies at 350°F for about 6 to 10 minutes. Don't let them burn. Cool on a rack.

To make the frosting, using a spoon or fork, stir the sugar with the milk. Begin with just 1 tablespoon milk. If more is needed, add it slowly. When the frosting is smooth, add the food dye.

When the cookies are cooled, use a knife to layer each cookie with a thin coating of frosting. Sprinkle multicolored "sprinkles" on each cookie, if desired. Serve warm or cooled.

Nutrient Values Per Cookie Calories: 59.8 Protein: .776 g. Carbohydrate: 8.441 g. Dietary Fiber: .162 g. Total Sugars: 3.802 g. Total Fat: 2.58 g Saturated Fat: 1.547 g. Monounsaturated Fat: .743 g. Polyunsaturated Fat: 128 g. Cholesterol: 10.8 mg. Calcium: 11.6 mg Iron: .309 mg. Potassium: 29.8 mg. Sodium: 2.285 mg. Vitamin K: 0 mcg. Folate: 9.577 mcg.

❧ HORNSWAGGLING GOOD COOKIES ❧

NOT ADAPTABLE FOR DIABETICS

While on a road trip through the northwest a few years before being diagnosed with heart failure, my wife and I stopped in a small coffeehouse in Hood River, Oregon. While there, I bought an oatmeal cookie . I'm sure it was high in sodium and fat, but, oh boy, did it taste good. I just had to try to remake that flavor while taking out much of the extra fat. My original version called for 1 cup of butter. I've cut that in half here, replacing the other half with applesauce.

These cookies have proven to be as tasty if not tastier and higher in fiber than the commercial variety I found on that trip. They are easy to make and even easier to take with you. I use a muffin ring to shape them into 4-inch cookies. You can also make them in 3-inch size without changing the baking temperature or cooking time. This recipe is not easily convertible for diabetics.

MAKES 18 (4-INCH) COOKIES   MAKES 28 (3-INCH) COOKIES
SODIUM PER RECIPE USING BUTTER: 283.4 MG
SODIUM PER COOKIE USING BUTTER (18): 15.7 MG
SODIUM PER COOKIE USING BUTTER (24): 11.8 MG
SODIUM PER COOKIE USING APPLESAUCE (18)
SODIUM PER RECIPE USING APPLESAUCE (24): 271.1 MG
SODIUM PER COOKIE USING APPLESAUCE/PRUNE PURÉE (18):
15.1 MG
SODIUM PER COOKIE USING APPLESAUCE/PRUNE PURÉE (24):
11.3 MG

1 **cup all-purpose or white unbleached flour (2.5 mg)**
½ **cup whole wheat flour (3 mg)**
1 **tablespoon Featherweight Baking Powder (13.5 mg)**
½ **teaspoon cornstarch (.072 mg)**
2 **teaspoons ground cinnamon (1.211 mg)**
3 **cups Quick Quaker Oats (9.72 mg)**
½ **cup unsalted butter (12.5)*, softened**
½ **cup white granulated sugar (1 mg)**
1 **cup (packed) brown sugar (85.8 mg)**
2 **large egg whites (109.6 mg)**
1 **teaspoon vanilla extract or flavoring (.378 mg)**
1 **tablespoon apple cider vinegar (.15 mg)**
½ **cup Homemade Applesauce (see page 206) (.218 mg)**
1 **cup semisweet chocolate chips (18.5 mg)**
½ **cup walnuts (.625 mg), finely chopped in processor**
1 **cup (not packed) seedless black raisins (17.4 mg)**
½ **cup dried coconut flakes (canned or packaged) (7.7 mg),**
   ground in processor

Preheat your oven to 350°F.

In a medium-size bowl, with a wooden spoon stir together the flours, Featherweight baking powder, cornstarch, cinnamon, and oats.

In a larger bowl, using your Braun single beater or other beater, cream together the butter, sugars, egg whites, vanilla, vinegar, and applesauce.

Add the flour mix and combine with a wooden spoon. Add the chocolate chips, walnuts, coconut, and raisins, stirring as you do.

Spoon the batter into muffin rings or other kitchen form, set on a lightly greased cookie sheet, and shape. If no form is available, spoon onto cookie sheet and flatten to the shape you want the cookie to take.

*My original recipe called for 1 cup unsalted butter. To lower the fat content per cookie, you may exchange all or part of the butter for equal parts of prune purée or Quick Applesauce. The exchange will make the cookie much softer. Total sodium levels for whole recipe in each exchange: applesauce: .218 mg; prune purée: 12.5 mg.

These will neither rise nor spread out. (What you shape is what you get.) You will have 18 of the 4-inch cookies, or 28 of the smaller 3-inch ones.

Bake at 350°F. for about 12 to 13 minutes. Cool on a rack. You may freeze these or pack them into zipper-type bags for a few days. They can also be stored in the refrigerator in zipper-type bags for up to 1 week.

Nutrient Values per Cookie with Butter (24) Calories: 228.5 Protein: 4.018 g. Carbohydrate: 36.4 g. Dietary Fiber: 2.494 g. Total Sugars: 17 g. Total Fat: 8.69 g. Saturated Fat: 4.315 g. Monounsaturated Fat: 2.372 g. Polyunsaturated Fat: 1.476 g. Cholesterol: 10.4 mg. Calcium: 52.4 mg. Potassium: 242.3 mg. Sodium: 11.8 mg. Vitamin K: 0 mcg. Folate: 15 mcg.

Nutrient Values per Cookie without Butter (24) Calories: 198.5 Protein: 3.988 g. Carbohydrate: 37.4 g. Dietary Fiber: 2.627 g. Total Sugars: 17.3 g. Total Fat: 4.871 g. Saturated Fat: 1.93 g. Monounsaturated Fat: 1.265 g. Polyunsaturated Fat: 1.339 g. Cholesterol: 0 mg. Calcium: 51.8 mg. Potassium: 246.5 mg. Sodium: 11.3 mg. Vitamin K: 0 mcg. Folate: 15 mcg.

❖ OATMEAL COOKIES ❖

HAND PREPARATION—OVEN BAKE
WITH FLAXSEED MEAL
NOT ADAPTABLE FOR DIABETICS
MAKES 18 (3-INCH) COOKIES   MAKES 36 (2-INCH) COOKIES
SODIUM PER RECIPE: 291.7 MG
SODIUM PER COOKIE (18): 16.2 MG
SODIUM PER COOKIE (36): 8.103 MG

1½ cups whole wheat pastry flour* (9 mg)
 1 tablespoon Featherweight Baking Powder (13.5 mg)
 1 cup flaxseed meal (trace)
1½ teaspoons ground cinnamon (.908 mg)
 6 tablespoons unsalted butter (9.372 mg), softened
 1 cup (firmly packed) brown sugar (85.8 mg)
 ½ cup white granulated sugar (1 mg)
 ½ cup bottled water (trace) or unsweetened orange juice (.821 mg)
 2 medium eggs (110.9 mg)
 2 teaspoons vanilla extract (.756 mg)
 3 cups rolled oats or Quaker Original Oats (7.02 mg)
 1 cup (not packed) black baking raisins (17.4 mg)
 ½ cup chopped unsalted raw almonds (.69 mg)
 1 ounce crystallized ginger† (optional) (5.2 mg)
 1 cup semisweet chocolate chips (19 mg)

*If not available in your area, use white unbleached bread flour
†Usually found in the produce or health food sections. Chop or thinly dice.

Preheat your oven to 350°F.

In a medium-size bowl, stir together the flour, baking powder, flaxseed meal, and cinnamon.

In a large bowl, beat together the butter, sugars, orange juice/water. Add the eggs and vanilla and beat until smooth. Stir in the flour/flaxseed mix. If it gets too dry, add water or olive oil (trace sodium), by the tablespoon. You don't want this "wet."

Add the oats, raisins, chopped almonds, optional crystallized ginger, and chocolate chips and stir to combine.

For standard-size (2-inch) cookies, drop the batter by spoonfuls onto the cookie sheet and press with your hands into shape you want. They won't rise or expand. For larger (3-inch) cookies, I use muffin rings; place 9 on a large cookie sheet, divide the batter into the 9 rings, and press down to form a perfectly round cookie. Two sheets are needed for this size. You can do the same with smaller rings for the smaller cookies, which I recommend. That way the calories for each are lower.

Bake large cookies for 12 minutes at 350°F on the middle rack. Smaller cookies without rings might bake in about 10 minutes. (They're done when finger pressure rises.) Cool on racks.

Serve hot, cold, or from the freezer.

Nutrient Values Per Cookie (18) Calories: 293.3 Protein: 6.017 g. Carbohydrate: 45.3 g. Dietary Fiber: 5.139 g. Total Sugars: 23 g. Total Fat: 11.9 g. Saturated Fat: 4.54 g. Monounsaturated Fat: 3.72 g. Polyunsaturated Fat: 1.032 g. Cholesterol: 34 mg. Calcium: 84.9 mg. Iron: 1.767 mg. Potassium: 335.8 mg. Sodium: 16.2 mg. Vitamin K: 0 mcg. Folate: 13.7 mcg.

Nutrient Values Per Cookie (36) Calories: 146.6 Protein: 3.008 g. Carbohydrate: 22.6 g. Dietary Fiber: 2.569 g. Total Sugars: 11.5 g. Total Fat: 5.966 g. Saturated Fat: 2.27 g. Monounsaturated Fat: 1.86 g. Polyunsaturated Fat: .516 g. Cholesterol: 17 mg. Calcium: 42.5 mg. Iron: .884 mg. Potassium: 167.9 mg. Sodium: 8.103 mg. Vitamin K: 0 mcg. Folate: 6.856 mcg.

PASTRIES

❖ ❖ ❖ ❖ ❖ ❖ ❖ ❖

❖ AEBLESKIVERS ❖

ADAPTABLE FOR DIABETICS

There's a small village in California not far from where we used to live. It's called Solvang. This is where I first tasted and fell in love with aebleskivers—small, round wafflelike balls that when served with jam or syrup are so good they can become addictive. Unfortunately, the real aebleskivers use a lot of salt, baking powder, and baking soda and the sodium count reaches upwards to more than 150 mg per small aebleskiver ball. Most people will eat about six of these for breakfast, which means they are consuming 900 mg of sodium. This recipe has about 15 mg sodium per ball, and half the fat of the original recipe we've used for years. You'll need an aebleskiver pan. These are generally available at most kitchenware stores and sell for around $15 each.

MAKES 30 TO 36 AEBLESKIVERS   SODIUM PER RECIPE: 452.8 MG
SODIUM PER AEBLESKIVER (30): 15.1 MG

2 **cups white unbleached flour (5 mg)**
1 **tablespoon Featherweight Baking Powder (13.5 mg)**
1 **teaspoon vital wheat gluten (.72 mg)**
2 **cups reduced-fat, cultured buttermilk* (260 mg)**
1 **teaspoon vanilla extract or flavoring (.378 mg)**
1 **tablespoon grated orange or lemon zest (.36 mg)**
2 **egg yolks (14.3 mg)**
3 **large egg whites (164.3 mg)**
2 **tablespoons unsalted butter (3.124 mg), melted**
½ **teaspoon extra virgin olive oil (trace)**

Mix the flour, baking powder, and gluten together with a wooden spoon (sifting is okay, but not necessary). Add the buttermilk, vanilla, zest and egg yolks. (If cholesterol is not a problem for you, add in 3 yolks, adding

---

*Use low-fat, lowered-sodium buttermilk such as Knudsen. If Knudsen not available in your area, use a local brand.

7 mg sodium for the total recipe.) Beat the egg whites until stiff. Fold this into the batter and stir in the melted butter, mixing it gently.

Lightly oil the aebleskiver pan with the olive oil over high heat. (If you just bought your new aebleskiver pan, make sure you "cure" it; most are iron and need to be "cured" over high heat with olive oil in the cups.) Pour in the batter and cook, turning the aebleskivers with a turkey skewer or butter knife or fork. When golden brown serve with jam or fruit-flavored syrup.

Nutritional Values per Aebleskiver Calories: 47.1 Protein: 2.006 g. Carbobydrate: 7.255 g. Dietary Fiber: .232 g. Total Sugars: .6 g. Total Fat: 1.601 g. Saturated Fat: .807 g. Monoun-saturated Fat: .414 g. Polyunsaturated Fat: .116 g. Cholesterol: 17.9 mg. Calcium: 46.8 mg. Potassium: 48.9 mg. Sodium: 15.2 mg. Vitamin K: .059 mcg. Folate: 14.6 mcg.

❈ ALMOND MAPLE CINNAMON BUNS ❈

A HOLIDAY TREAT
BREAD MACHINE KNEAD—OVEN BAKE
NOT ADAPTABLE FOR DIABETICS

Safe as far as sodium is concerned, each serving of this recipe is a bit higher in sugar and calories than I like to normally use, but not prohibitive per slice. Treat with care, and serve these only during holidays or on special occasions. Still need to justify this splurge? Consider that the almonds are high in monounsaturated fat—that's the good fat, the one that helps lower your cholesterol. This recipe has three times more mono than saturated fat. Another benefit is that almonds are high in Vitamin E. Enjoy! If you leave out the almonds, you extract almost all the fat.

MAKES 24 BUNS, ROLLS, OR MUFFIN-SIZE CUPS
SODIUM PER RECIPE: 411.3 MG   SODIUM PER BUN: 17.1 MG

THE DOUGH
1¾ **cups low-fat, low-sodium buttermilk* (227.5 mg), at room temperature (70°F. to 80°F.)**
  1 **tablespoon extra virgin olive oil (trace)**
  2 **teaspoons apple cider vinegar (trace)**
 ¼ **teaspoon almond extract (trace)**
  4 **cups best for bread white unbleached flour (10 mg)**
  1 **cup best for bread whole wheat pastry (or standard) flour (6 mg)**

*Use Knudsen's or another local brand with the same low-fat, low-sodium content.

1 tablespoon vital wheat gluten (.2.25 mg)
1 tablespoon grated orange or lemon zest (trace)
1 tablespoon white granulated sugar (.126 mg)
1 medium to large egg (55.4 mg)
1 tablespoon bread machine yeast (6 mg)
½ cup unsalted, chopped almonds (7.59 mg)
1 cup (not packed) black seedless raisins (17.4 mg)

Place all the dough ingredients except the almonds and raisins into your bread machine pan in the order listed, or in the order your machine recommends. Set on the Dough cycle. When the raisin buzzer sounds, add the chopped almonds and the seedless raisins.

Lightly grease two 9×13-inch baking dishes.

THE FILLING
4 tablespoons unsalted butter (6.248 mg), melted in pan
1 cup (unpacked) brown sugar (Sugar Twin brown is also acceptable) (56.6 mg)
2 tablespoons nonfat milk (15.8 mg)
2 tablespoons sweet white syrup (.72 mg)
4 teaspoons maple extract or imitation flavoring (1.8 mg)

To prepare the filling, heat all the ingredients together, stirring often over a low flame or heat. When it just begins to boil, remove the pan from the heat and let it stand until the dough is ready.

THE TOPPING*
1 cup confectioners' sugar (1.2 mg)
2 teaspoons maple extract (1 mg)
2 tablespoons natural maple syrup (3.6 mg)

To prepare the topping, stir together all the ingredients. If you need more liquid, add additional maple syrup 1 teaspoon at a time. Let stand.

When the dough is ready, turn it out onto a lightly floured breadboard. Cut it in half. Flatten it with your hands until about ⅜ inch thick. Shape it

*OPTIONAL TOPPING

Sodium per Recipe: 2.266 mg

1 cup confectioners' sugar (1.2 mg)
2 tablespoons orange juice (.31 mg)
2 teaspoons vanilla extract (.756 mg)

Stir the ingredients together. If you need more liquid, add more orange juice 1 teaspoon at a time.

to about 6×12×14 inches. Spread half the filling on the dough evenly. Roll it up lengthwise into a log. Slice crosswise, making about 12 pieces.

Place the slices into a 9×13-inch lightly greased pan with "rings" facing up. Set about ⅛ inch apart. Repeat with the second half of the recipe in a second pan.

Cover with a light cloth or wax paper and set in a warm place to rise for about 45 minutes. About 15 minutes before the buns are risen, preheat your oven to 350°F.

Bake at 350°F. for about 20 minutes. When done, spread the topping evenly over the buns.

Note to diabetics: This didn't work well with Splenda Sugar Substitute.

Nutrient Values per Bun with Filling and Topping Calories: 243.6 Protein: 6.799 g. Carbohydrate: 41.7 g. Dietary Fiber: 3.962 g. Total Sugars: 7.125 g. Total Fat: 6.305 g. Saturated Fat: .728 g. Monounsaturated Fat: 1.918 g. Polyunsaturated Fat: 3.183 g. Cholesterol: 0 mg. Calcium: 49.5 mg. Iron: 2.24 mg. Potassium: 230.5 mg. Sodium: 5.652 mg. Vitamin K: .911 mcg. Folate: 98.2 mcg.

❖ BEAR CLAWS ❖

BREAD MACHINE KNEAD—HAND SHAPE—OVEN BAKE
ADAPTABLE FOR DIABETICS

Not the fatty, butter-produced crescent dough bear claws, but just as good. Guaranteed. And with very little total fat and hardly any sodium. You'll love these!
MAKES 32 (3-INCH) BEAR CLAWS*   SODIUM PER RECIPE: 59.5 MG
SODIUM PER BEAR CLAW: 1.86 MG

THE CLAW DOUGH
1¾ **cups plus 2 tablespoons unsweetened orange juice with calcium (3.109 mg)**
  4 **cups unbleached best for bread machine flour (10 mg)**
  1 **cup best for bread whole wheat flour (6 mg)**
  2 **level teaspoons vital wheat gluten (1.62 mg)**
  2 **tablespoons white granulated sugar (.252 mg)**
1½ **tablespoons olive oil (trace)**
   Zest from 1 orange (.54 mg)
  1 **teaspoon ground cinnamon (.606 mg)**

*I often make 16 claws with half the dough, and a loaf of "cinnamon" bread or twist bread with the other half. To make the bread from second half of dough: Roll the dough ball into a 9-inch loaf pan and bake at a lower temperature of 350°F for about 20 to 25 minutes. If you want cinnamon bread, sprinkle cinnamon and sugar on the flattened dough, then roll over into a loaf. If making the loaf of bread, halve the filling/topping recipes above.

1 teaspoon almond extract (trace)
1 tablespoon bread machine yeast (6 mg)
1 cup (not packed) raisins (17.4 mg)

2 tablespoons cornmeal (trace)
   or olive oil spray (trace)

THE FILLING
½ cup marzipan or almond paste (10.2 mg) or Homemade
    Almond Paste (see page 205) (.778 mg)
½ teaspoon ground cinnamon (.303 mg)
1 teaspoon white granulated sugar (.042 mg)

THE TOPPING
¾ cup sliced unsalted almonds (2.07 mg)
6 tablespoons confectioners' sugar (.96 mg)
1 tablespoon fresh orange juice from the orange used for the
   zest (.619 mg)

Place the orange juice, flours, gluten, sugar, oil, orange zest, cinnamon, almond extract, and yeast, at room temperature (70°F. to 80°F.) into the bread machine pan and set for Dough cycle. Add the the raisins at the sound of the raisin buzzer (at about 30 minutes for the Breadman TR810). When the dough is ready, spread it out on a breadboard, cut the ball in half, and flatten the first ball with a rolling pin. You'll have to flour your breadboard with some whole wheat flour. Roll it until it's square and about ¼ inch thick.

Working with one half of the dough at a time, spread half of the marzipan or almond paste on top. Mix together the cinnamon and sugar and sprinkle half on the marzipan. Fold the dough over, covering the filling and making a rectangular shape. Pinch closed. Using a sharp knife, slice the dough lengthwise down the center. You should now have two 12-inch to 14-inch long, 1½-inch strips of double-laid-over dough (with the filling in the center). Pinch the open sides closed. Cut these strips into 8 slightly rectangular pieces, for a total of 16 pieces. Cut the toes into claws (they'll be very small cuts). The claws will not be the shape of commercial claws, but they will expand in size during rising.

Now do the second half the same way. (See footnote on page 196 about using the second half of dough for a loaf of cinnamon bread.) Spray the cookie sheets with oil and evenly spread cornmeal on pan, or oil.

Transfer the claws to a cookie sheet at room temperature (70°F. to 80°F.). Cover with a light cloth and place in warm place (I use my warmed oven), to rise for about 45 minutes to 1 hour. (Or, if you prefer, use the dough of the second ball to make rolls, buns, or a single loaf in your loaf pan. If making rolls, bake for 1 minute longer than the claws when the time comes.)

Preheat your oven to 425°F.

After rising, bake the claws at 425°F. for 4 to 6 minutes or until golden brown.

To prepare the topping, slightly toast the almonds (about 1 minute). Mix the sugar with the orange juice. Mix the toasted almonds into the sugar/orange juice mixture. When the claws come out of the oven, spread this topping on top while still hot. Cool on a cooling rack or serve hot. They may be reheated in the microwave. They may also be frozen for future use.

Nutrient Values per Bear Claw Calories: 149.6 Protein: 3.936 g. Carbohydrate: 25.2 g. Dietary Fiber: 1.972 g. Total Sugars: 2.606 g. Total Fat: 4.176 g. Saturated Fat: .401 g. Monounsaturated Fat: 2.592 g. Polyunsaturated Fat: .908 g. Cholesterol: 0 mg. Calcium: 43.6 mg. Iron: 1.667 mg. Potassium: 146.2 mg. Sodium: 1.859 mg. Vitamin K: .31 mcg. Folate: 45.2 mcg.

❖ SPECIAL SUNDAY MORNING BEAR CLAWS ❖

BREAD MACHINE PREP—OVEN BAKE
NOT ADAPTABLE FOR DIABETICS

This is my richer version of bear claws. It's closer to the real thing, which also means it has more fat, a bit more sodium, and more sugar. It's a great treat once a year or so. Make this recipe when you have the whole gang over for breakfast or a holiday.

MAKES 24 BEAR CLAWS SODIUM PER RECIPE: 467.3 MG
SODIUM PER BEAR CLAW: 19.5 MG

1¼ cups reduced-fat, cultured buttermilk (162.5 mg), warmed to about 80°F.
 6 tablespoons extra virgin olive oil (trace)
 2 tablespoons unsalted butter (3.124 mg)
 1 tablespoon apple cider vinegar (.15 mg)
 1 teaspoon pure vanilla extract (.378 mg)
 1 teaspoon almond extract (.378 mg)
 3 medium to large eggs (189 mg)
 5 cups best for bread white flour (12.5 mg)
 2 tablespoons vital wheat gluten (4.5 mg)
 ½ level teaspoon ground cinnamon (.303 mg)
 ⅓ cup white granulated sugar (.66 mg)
 1 tablespoon plus ½ teaspoon bread machine yeast or active dry yeast (7.98 mg)

Warm the buttermilk and place into your bread machine basket. Add the rest of the ingredients in the order listed or according to your manufacturer's instructions. Set the machine on the Dough cycle.

For the filling, while the dough is rising in the machine, prepare your Homemade Almond Paste (see page 000) and set it aside in the refrigerator.

When the dough is ready, roll it onto a lightly floured bread board. Slice this very light and spongy dough into four sections. Set three pieces aside on a lightly flour dusted surface. With your palms or a rolling pin, press down on the first section, making a rectangle about the size of your large breadboard (14×18 inches) and about ⅛ inch thick. You will repeat this with each section of dough. Trust me, this dough will spring up, making larger bear claws appear the size of a huge fist. So thin is what we want.

Spread a quarter of the almond paste filling you've set aside and put it on the top half of the dough, working lengthwise. Fold over the uncovered dough and pinch the open side closed.

Cut 3-inch-square sections out. Make three or four 1-inch cuts about 1 inch into the side of each claw—along the folded edge of each section—and gently pull it apart, shaping the bear claw into a quarter-moon shape. Set each claw on your lightly greased cooking sheet about 2 to 3 inches apart. Now repeat the process with the other dough sections. You may need as many as four baking sheets.

Cover the sheets with lightly oil-spritzed wax paper or a very light cloth, and set in a warm place to rise for about 45 minutes to 1 hour. They will double or triple in size and then double again while baking.

Preheat oven to 425°F. Bake at 425°F. 4 to 6 minutes or until golden brown.

THE TOPPING
   1 cup confectioners' sugar (1.2 mg)
   ½ to 1 tablespoon orange juice fortified with calcium (.149 mg)
   ½ cup sliced unsalted almonds (7.59 mg)
   ½ teaspoon almond extract (.189 mg)

Mix the topping ingredients together with a wooden spoon, then spread the topping on the hot claws just out of oven.

Nutrient Values per Bear Claw Calories: 287.7 Protein: 7.523 g. Carbohydrate: 37.1 g Dietary Fiber: 2.55 g. Total Sugars: 13.8 g. Total Fat: 13.2 g. Saturated Fat: 2.036 g. Monounsaturated Fat: 7.915 g. Polyunsaturated Fat: 2.338 g. Cholesterol: 30.5 mg. Calcium: 61.4 mg. Potassium: 182.8 mg. Sodium: 19.3 mg. Vitamin K: 1.654 mcg. Folate: 64.6 mcg.

❄ EGG BREAD CINNAMON BUNS ❄

LIKE THE REAL THING
BREAD MACHINE KNEAD—HAND SHAPE—OVEN BAKE
NOT ADAPTABLE FOR DIABETICS

These are a sure bet to win over friends who don't believe you can cook without salt. Bake this one for special holidays. I like to call these my "mile-high cinnamon buns."

MAKES 24 CINNAMON BUNS   SODIUM PER RECIPE: 267 MG
SODIUM PER CINNAMON BUN: 11.1 MG

THE DOUGH
- 1 **cup orange juice fortified with calcium (2.488 mg), at room temperature (70°F. to 80°F.)**
- ¼ **cup honey (3.39 mg), at room temperature (70°F. to 80°F.)**
- 1 **tablespoon apple cider vinegar (.15 mg)**
- 2 **large eggs (126 mg)**
- 3 **tablespoons extra virgin olive oil (trace)**
- 1 **teaspoon white granulated sugar (.042 mg)**
- 4 **cups bread machine flour (10 mg)**
- 1 **teaspoon vital wheat gluten (.72 mg)**
  Grated zest of ½ large orange (.12 mg)
- 1 **tablespoon bread machine yeast (6 mg)**

MAPLE SYRUP FILLING
- ¼ **cup natural maple syrup (7.088 mg)**
- 1 **cup (packed) light brown sugar (85.8 mg)**
- 2 **teaspoons white granulated sugar (.252 mg)**
- 2 **tablespoons unsalted butter (3.124 mg)**
- 2 **tablespoons orange juice, fortified with calcium (.311 mg)**
- 2 **teaspoons ground cinnamon (1.211 mg)**
- 1 **cup (not packed) golden seedless raisins (17.4 mg)**

GLAZE OR TOPPING
- 2 **cups confectioners' sugar (2.4 mg)**
  Grated zest of ½ large orange (.18 mg)
- 1 **teaspoon vanilla extract (.378 mg)**
- 2 **to 3 tablespoons orange juice, fortified with calcium (.498 mg)**

This recipe will work in most bread makers that have a Dough cycle. Place all the dough ingredients in your machine in the order listed or according to your manufacturer's recommendation, but with the liquid first in any case. Set on Dough cycle. After the paddles are finished kneading, remove the dough from the machine and place it in a large mixing bowl that is lightly greased and at room temperature (70°F. to 80°F.). Cover with a lightly oil-spritzed wax paper and place in a warm place for 2 to 2½ hours. When it has risen, press down on it, reaching to the bottom of the pan (but don't "punch it" down), cover with wax paper, and let it rise for another hour.

When ready (about two to three times the size), roll it out onto a lightly floured breadboard. Cut it in half so you can work with smaller pieces. Set aside one half. Roll the other half out by pressing down and shaping it into a piece that is about 5 to 6 inches wide and about 12 to 14 inches long. Spread the filling lengthwise across half the dough. When ready, roll up the dough into a log.

You will need a 13×9.5-inch baking dish. Lightly grease it.

Using a sharp knife, slice off 1-inch to 1¼-inch pieces and lay these in your prepared baking dish, with the concentric circles showing upwards. Set them in the dish about ½ inch apart. Prepare the second half and fill the baking dish. If you end up with more buns than baking dish, use a cake pan or an 8×8-inch pan for the extras and prepare them in the same way.

Cover with wax paper (or a very light cloth) and set aside for about 30 to 40 minutes.

While the bread is in its second rise, place syrup, brown sugar white sugar, butter, and orange juice into a saucepan. Heat, stirring constantly, while the butter melts. Add the cinnamon and raisins when nearly done. Set aside on the stovetop. (You may have to reheat this before using.)

Preheat your oven to 350°F. about 10 minutes before the buns have finished rising.

Bake at 350°F. for about 16 to 20 minutes, or a bit longer, on the lower third of your oven. They may not brown but instead turn a cream color.

In a small bowl, using a wooden spoon, mix the ingredients together while the bread is baking. When the buns are out of the oven, leave them in the baking dish and spread the glaze across the top. Serve from dish warm, hot, or reheated. These will keep in refrigerator overnight, covered, or in zipper-type bags. You may freeze leftovers in sealed zipper-type freezer bags; thaw in the microwave for about 10 to 20 seconds only.

Nutrient Values per Bun Calories: 226.1 Protein: 3.19 g. Carbohydrate 46.8 g. Dietary Fiber: .997 g. Total Sugars: 28.3 g. Total Fat: 3.346 g. Saturated Fat: 1.093 g. Monounsaturated Fat: 1.719 g. Polyunsaturated Fat: .339 g. Cholesterol: 20.3 mg. Calcium: 36.8 mg. Potassium: 171.8 mg. Sodium: 11.1 mg. Vitamin K: .827 mcg. Folate: 52.3 mcg.

❖ PENUCHE (AKA STICKY BUNS) ❖

BREAD MACHINE KNEAD—OVEN BAKE
NOT ADAPTABLE FOR DIABETICS

For the past twenty years my wife and I would take time off and visit Mendocino, California. There's a neat little bakery called Tote Feté that makes a sticky bun that I always enjoyed. It was slightly overdone most of the time, which gave it its richness. After my CHF diagnosis, I mused I could reproduce it without sodium. It's a good thing I can, because now I spend my summers in that cooler climate and the temptation might weaken my otherwise perfect low-sodium diet. Here it is for you, too. Rich, tasty, low in sodium but a bit high in calories—this one is a "treat."

MAKES 12 TO 24 BUNS   SODIUM PER RECIPE: 200.3 MG
SODIUM PER TEXAS-SIZE BUN (12): 16.7 MG
SODIUM PER BUN (24): 8.347 MG

THE DOUGH
- ½ cup natural maple syrup (14.2 mg) at room temperature (70°F. to 80°F.)
- ½ cup prune juice (5.12 mg), at room temperature (70°F. to 80°F.)
- ½ cup low-fat, lowered-sodium buttermilk (65 mg), at room temperature (70°F. to 80°F.)
- ¼ cup bottled water (trace), heated to 115°F. to 125°F.
- 2 tablespoons olive oil (trace)
- 2½ cups whole wheat pastry flour (15 mg)
- 2½ cups unbleached white bread flour (6.25 mg)
- 1 tablespoon vital wheat gluten (2.25 mg)
- 3 tablespoons (packed) brown sugar (16.1 mg)
- 1 level tablespoon ground cinnamon (1.791 mg)
- 1 tablespoon apple cider vinegar (.15 mg)
- 1 tablespoon bread machine yeast (6 mg)

THE FILLING
- ½ cup (packed) raisins (9.9 mg)
- ¼ cup chopped unsalted walnuts or pecans (.312 mg)
- 1 teaspoon ground cinnamon (.606 mg)
- 2 tablespoons corn syrup (31 mg)
- 2 teaspoons (packed) brown sugar (3.754 mg)
- 2 tablespoons unsalted butter (3.124 mg), melted

THE TOPPING
- 2 tablespoons unsalted butter (3.124 mg), melted
- 2 tablespoons (packed) brown sugar (10.8 mg)
- 2 tablespoons corn syrup (31 mg)
- ⅓ cup half-chopped unsalted walnuts or pecans (.312 mg)

Place all the dough ingredients in your bread machine in the order listed. Make sure you heat the liquids to their appropriate temperature, and that the yeast is at least at room temperature (70°F.) but not warmer than 80°F. Set the machine on the Dough cycle (approximately 1½ hours).

Note: This is considered a "heavy" dough.

To prepare the filling, mix the raisins, nuts, cinnamon, corn syrup, and sugar together in a small bowl using a wooden or metal spoon. Just before the dough has reached its full rise, melt the butter, and stir into the mix just before brushing on the dough.

When the dough is ready, preheat your oven to between 80°F. and 100°F. and turn it off. Keep the door closed.

You must prepare the muffin tins. Because these muffins will stick to the pan, and to the paper cups, lightly spray the tins and paper cups with olive oil spray (trace sodium).

Roll the dough out on a large breadboard floured with whole-wheat flour to 11 × 17 inches. Using your hands, flatten the dough on the board. This dough, although considered "heavy," is also pliable and will stretch for you to great lengths—but don't overstretch it. If you do, let it rest for a few minutes. The gluten in the bread will bring it back. You can use a rolling pin to roll it out to about ⅜ inch thick or even ¼ inch thick, if you want to make more buns.

Spread the raisin mixture on the dough evenly. Roll the dough up lengthwise tightly, so that you have a long log. Use a sharp knife and slice the log so that you obtain either 12 or 24 pieces. Place these into cups with the concentric rings facing upwards. (**Note:** Texas-size muffins are twice the size of the standard ones.)

Cover the muffins with a light cloth and let rise in the warmed oven for about 30 to 45 minutes. Remove them gently from the oven if you have only one oven, then set it to 350°F.

Bake at 350°F. for about 20 minutes, or until the muffins begin to turn dark.

While the buns are baking, heat the topping ingredients together in a small saucepan. When buns are out of the oven, drizzle this mixture onto them.

Nutrient Values per Bun (24) Calories: 183.2 Protein: 4.488 g. Carbohydrate: 32 g. Dietary Fiber: 2.509 g. Total Sugars: 8.177 g. Total Fat: 5.054 g. Saturated Fat: 1.577 g. Monounsaturated Fat: 1.776 g. Polyunsaturated Fat: 1.307 g. Cholesterol: 5.704 mg. Calcium: 29.1 mg. Iron: 2.4 mg. Potassium: 161.5 mg. Sodium: 8.347 mg. Vitamin K: .583 mcg. Folate: 39.3 mcg.

Nutrient Values per Bun (12) Calories: 366.4 Protein: 8.977 g. Carbohydrate: 64 g. Dietary Fiber: 5.017 g. Total Sugars: 16.4 g. Total Fat: 10.1 g. Saturated Fat: 3.155 g. Monounsaturated Fat: 3.552 g. Polyunsaturated Fat: 2.614 g. Cholesterol: 11.4 mg. Calcium: 58.1 mg. Iron: 4.799 mg. Potassium: 323 mg. Sodium: 16.7 mg. Vitamin K: 1.167 mcg. Folate: 78.6 mcg.

TOPPINGS AND FILLINGS

❖ HOMEMADE ALMOND PASTE ❖

You can use marzipan or store-bought almond paste that comes without salt and, if you like, a tablespoon of powdered sugar, if you can find it. But this homemade version is easy to make, stores well in freezer or refrigerator, and tastes fresher.

MAKES 32 TABLESPOONS   SODIUM PER RECIPE: 6.226 MG
SODIUM PER TABLESPOON: .195 MG

- 2 **cups whole unsalted almonds (2.76 mg)**
- 2 **cups confectioners' sugar (2.4 mg)**
- 2 **tablespoons orange juice* (.311 mg)**
- 2 **teaspoons almond extract (.756 mg)**

Using your food processor's steel cutting blade (a high-powered Braun 550 hand mixer works well), grind the unsalted almonds down. Add ½ cup sugar and chop some more. Add the orange juice or the corn syrup and almond extract and the rest of the sugar and continue to process until you have a smooth paste. The almond skins will show as tiny specs, but they only add to the flavor.

You can use this paste for breakfast rolls, such as bear claws, almond croissants, etc.

Nutrient Values per Tablespoon Calories: 81.9 Protein: 1.912 g. Carbohydrate: 9.264 g. Dietary Fiber: 1.02 g. Total Sugars: 7.848 g. Total Fat: 4.565 g. Saturated Fat: .35 g. Monounsaturated Fat: 2.906 g. Polyunsaturated Fat: 1.095 g. Cholesterol: 0 mg. Calcium: 24.2 mg. Iron: .395 mg. Potassium: 66.7 mg. Sodium: .195 mg. Vitamin K: 0 mcg. Folate: 3.27 mcg.

*You may substitute light corn syrup (48.4 mg for the recipe).

❖ HOMEMADE APPLESAUCE ❖

*Quick and light on the sugar, this sauce can be whipped
up in a hurry for adding to recipes calling for homemade
applesauce.*

MAKES 2 CUPS   SODIUM PER RECIPE WITH SUGAR: *.325 MG*
SODIUM PER CUP: *.162 MG*   SODIUM PER TABLESPOON: *.101 MG*

  3 **medium-size ripe apples (trace)**
  ½ **cup bottled water (0 mg)**
  1 **tablespoon granulated white sugar* (.126 mg) or Splenda**
      Sugar Substitute (9 mg)
  ¼ **teaspoon ground cinnamon (.151 mg)**
      Spritz of lemon juice† (trace)

Clean the apples, slice in half, and core. Cut apples into slices or chunks
and place into a medium-size stovetop pan. Add the water. Bring to a
rapid boil and boil for 4 minutes while stirring constantly. Reduce the heat
to medium and stir frequently while apples continue to cook. Reduce the
heat to low and simmer for 8 to 10 minutes. Add the sugar (or sugar substitute) and cinnamon, and stir for another minute. Cool in the pan. Serve
hot, warm, or use in recipes that call for homemade applesauce.

*Nutrient Values per Cup with Sugar Calories: 147.9 Protein:.414 g. Carbohydrate: 38.3 g.
Dietary Fiber: 5.755 g. Total Sugars: 6.237 g. Total Fat: .754 g. Saturated Fat: .122 g.
Monounsaturated Fat: .032 g. Polyunsaturated Fat: .219 g. Cholesterol: 0 mg. Calcium:
18.3 mg. Iron: .487 mg. Potassium: 242.7 mg. Sodium: .162 mg. Vitamin K: 0 mcg. Folate:
6.615 mcg.*

*Nutrient Values per Cup with Sugar Substitute Calories: 123.5 Protein: .414 g. Carbohy-
drate: 32 g. Dietary Fiber: 5.755 g. Total Sugars: 0 g. Total Fat: .754 g. Saturated Fat: .122
g. Monounsaturated Fat: .032 g. Polyunsaturated Fat: .219 g. Cholesterol: 0 mg. Calcium:
18.2 mg. Iron: .483 mg. Potassium: 242.6 mg. Sodium: .1 mg. Vitamin K: 0 mcg. Folate:
6.615 mcg.*

*Begin by using only 1 tablespoon of sugar. Some apples are sweeter than others
and may not need much. Sugar substitutes can be added in the same manner;
however, I cooked Delicious Apples without sugar or sugar substitutes and found
they didn't need any at all. You may want to test your apples before you add in the
sweetener.
†I often add a dash of lemon juice to the mix, but if you're using this right away,
it's not necessary.

❖ DON'S SWEET CHOCOLATE MIX ❖

MAKES 3 CUPS   MAKES 48 TABLESPOONS
SODIUM PER CUP: 14.2 MG   SODIUM PER TABLESPOON: .837

1 **cup cocoa powder (hot cocoa mix) (16.3 mg)**
1 **cup ground semisweet (not milk chocolate) chocolate (24 mg)**
2 **cups white granulated sugar (2 mg)**
2 **teaspoons powdered vanilla (.252 mg)**

Mix all the ingredients together in a food processor. Store what you don't use for future use. It can be used for brownies or cakes, or you can make a delicious hot chocolate drink using 2 or 3 tablespoons per cup of warm nonfat milk.

APPENDIX

MEASUREMENT CONVERSIONS

❖ ❖ ❖ ❖ ❖ ❖ ❖ ❖

MEASUREMENT CONVERSIONS

- 1 ounce dry yeast is equivalent to 3 tablespoons dry yeast (granules)
- One .25-ounce envelope of yeast equals 2¼ teaspoons
- 1 ounce fresh yeast is equivalent to 1 tablespoon plus ¼ teaspoon dry yeast
- 1 fluid ounce (of anything) is equivalent to 2 tablespoons
- 1 ounce flour is equivalent to ¼ cup. If a recipe calls for more yeast than seems normal, it may be because you are making a rich pastry or a sweet bread dough.

CONVERSIONS FROM U.S. TO METRIC

VOLUME

1 teaspoon = 5 milliliters
1 tablespoon = 15 milliliters
1 dram = 3.7 milliliters
1 fluid ounce = 30 milliliters
1 cup = 8 oz., and .24 liters
1 gill = 118.3 milliliters
1 gill = 1.18 deciliters
1 gill = 0.118 liters
1 pint = 0.47 liters
1 quart = .95 liters

WEIGHT

1 ounce = 28.35 grams
1 pound = 453.59 grams
1 pound = 0.454 kilograms

Supporting
Research

❖ ❖ ❖ ❖ ❖ ❖ ❖ ❖

Anderson, J.W., et al. Oat-bran cereal lowers serum total and LDL cholesterol in hypercholesterolemic men. *Am J Clin Nutr*. 1990; 52: 495–499.

Anderson, J.W., et al. Hypocholesterolemic effects of different bulk-forming hydrophilic fibers as adjuncts to dietary therapy in mild to moderate hypercholesterolemia. *Arch Intern Med*. 1991; 151: 1597–1602.

Brodribb, A.J.; Humphreys, D.M. Diverticular disease: three studies Part I: Relation to other disorders and fibre intake. *Br Med J*. 1976; 1: 424–425.

Brown D.D.; Juhl, R.P.; Warner, S.L. Decreased bioavailability of digoxin due to hypocholesterolemic interventions. *Circ*. 1978; 58 (1): 164–172.

Gazzaniga J.M.; Lupton, J.R. The dilution effect of dietary fiber sources. *Nutr Res*. 1987; 7: 1261–1268.

Graedon, J.; Graedon, T. *Deadly Drug Interactions: The People's Pharmacy Guide*. New York: St. Martin's Griffin; 1995: 4, 5.

Huupponen, R.; Seppala, P.; Iisalo, E. Effect of guar gum, a fibre preparation, on digoxin and penicillin absorption in man. *Eur J Clin Pharmacol*. 1984; 26 (2): 279–281.

Jenkins, D.J.; Jenkins, A.L. Dietary fiber and the glycemic response. *Proc Soc Exp Biol Med*. Dec 1985; 180 (3): 422–431.

Johnson, B.F.; Rodin, S.M.; Hoch, K.; Shakar, V. The effect of dietary fiber on the bioavailability of digoxin in capsules. *J Clin Pharmacol*. 1987; 27 (7): 487–490.

Katz, D.L. *Nutrition in Clinical Practice*. Philadelphia: Lippincott, Williams & Wilkins; 2001.

Kenji, T., et al. Dietary factors and prevention of colon cancer. *Nippon Geka Gakkai Zasshi*. 1999; (6): 368–372. In Japanese.

Kritchevsky, D. Dietary fibre and cancer. *Eur J Cancer Prev*. 1997; 6: 435–441.

Lanza, E., et al. Dietary fiber intake in the US population. *Am J Clin Nutr.* 1987; 46: 790–797.

Marlett, J.A., et al. Mechanism of serum cholesterol reduction by oat bran. *Hepatology.* 1994; 20: 1450–1457.

Shils, M.E.; Olson, J.A., Shike, M., eds. *Modern Nutrition in Health and Disease.* 8th ed. Media, Pa: Williams & Wilkins; 1994: 89, 92–98.

Whitney E.N.; Hamilton, E.N. *Understanding Nutrition.* 3rd ed. New York: West Publishing Company; 1979: 69.

INDEX

Acidity ingredient, low-sodium
    substitute, 33
Aebleskivers, 193–194
Air pressure, 25–27
Almond biscotti
    chocolate dipped, 164–165
    poppy seed, 161–162
Almond incredible cookies, 167
Almond maple cinnamon buns,
    194–196
Almond meringue cookies, 168
Almond paste, 205
Altitude, 25–27
Anise biscotti, 162–163
Apple cider vinegar, 14
Apple crisp cookies, 170
Apples, diabetes, 39
Applesauce, homemade, 206
Applesauce bread
    cinnamon raisin, 72–73
    with shredded carrots, 71–72
Apple streusel muffins, 144–145
Apricot dinner rolls, 111–112

Bagels, poppy seed, 125–126
Baguettes
    French, 45–46
    sourdough, 59–60
Baking powder/soda
    low-sodium substitute, 33
    specialty, 18
    whole wheat flour, 11, 12
    working with, 13–14
Banana bread
    basic recipe, 76–77
    oatmeal with orange zest, 77–78
Beans, dietary fiber, 2
Bear claws
    basic recipe, 196–198
    special Sunday morning, 198–199

Becky's bran muffins, 140–141
Belgian waffles supreme, 160. *See also*
    Waffles
Biscotti
    almond poppy seed, 161–162
    anise, 162–163
    chocolate chip, 165–166
    chocolate dipped almond, 164–165
    ginger with almonds, 163–164
Biscuits, Don's, 118–119. *See also*
    Muffins, rolls and biscuits
Black seedless raisins, low-sodium
    substitute, 33
Blueberry muffins
    basic recipe, 139–140
    bran, 138–139
Braided orange cinnamon twist, 81
Bran muffins
    Becky's, 140–141
    blueberry, 138–139
    chocolate chip, 141–142
    hearty, high-fiber, 135–136
    long-lasting, 134–135
    oat bran and date, 137–138
    pineapple prune, 136–137
Bread(s), 45–101. *See also* Hamburger
    buns
    applesauce, 71–72
    applesauce cinnamon raisin bread,
        72–73
    banana bread, 76–77
    banana oatmeal bread, 77–78
    braided orange cinnamon twist, 81
    bread dough enhancer, 100–101
    calzone y empanadas, 98–100
    cinnamon bread (hearty), 70–71
    cinnamon raisin bread (standard),
        67–68
    cinnamon raisin bread with
        cranberry raisins, 69

Bread(s) (*continued*)
  Don's bread dough enhancer,
    100–101
  Don's secret bread recipe, 82–83
  English muffin bread, 83–84
  flaxseed buns, rolls, and bread,
    84–85
  flour tortillas, 95–96
  focaccia a la garlic cheese, 54–56
  French bread and baguettes, 45–46
  French bread (Fleischmann's), 47–48
  French onion bread, 48–49
  impossible bread, 92–94
  Irish soda bread, 56–57
  Italian garlic toast, 53–54
  maple walnut, 75–76
  Musketeers bread, 87–88
  nutty date bread, 80
  oats, dates, and prune bread, 78–79
  orange anise bread, 90–91
  orange currant bread, 91–92
  panettone, 50–51
  panettone (holiday), 51–53
  pizza dough, 97–98
  pumpernickel (quick and easy), 63
  pumpernickel raisin rye, 62–63
  raisin rye, 64–65
  sandwich bread (high-grain, low-fat,
    low-sugar), 86
  seven-grain with orange zest, 66–67
  sourdough baguettes, 59–60
  sourdough (old-fashioned Italian),
    60–61
  sourdough starter, 57–59
  ten-grain with walnuts, 65–66
  trail mix bread, 94–95
  walnut raisin, 74–75
  whole wheat and orange bread,
    89–90
Bread dough enhancer
  advantages of, 19–20
  low-sodium substitute, 33
  recipe for, 100–101
Bread machines, 5–9
  advantages of, 5–6
  dough rising, 8–9
  hand-knead bread compared, 7–8
  recommendations for, 20
  use of, 6–7
  whole wheat flour, 11–12
  yeasts, 13
Breadsticks
  soft, 119–121
  soft cheddar, 121–122

Browning, troubleshooting, 30
Brown sugar
  low-sodium substitute, 33, 35
  sweeteners, 16
Butter
  fats, 16
  low-sodium substitute, 33
Buttermilk
  diabetes, 39
  low-sodium substitute, 33–34
  types of, 17–18
Buttermilk bars, 82–83
Buttermilk egg buns, 104–105
Buttermilk waffles, old-fashioned,
    158–159

Calzone, 98–100
Canola oil, 16
Carbohydrates, diabetes, 38
Carbon dioxide, yeast, 11, 12
Carrot muffins, 142–143
Cereals, low-sodium substitute, 34
Cheddar breadsticks, soft, 121–122
Cheese, low-sodium substitute, 34
Chocolate chip biscotti, 165–166
Chocolate chip bran muffins, 141–142
Chocolate dipped almond biscotti,
    164–165
Chocolate meringue cookies, 169
Chocolate mix, sweet, Don's, 207
Chocolate oat and honey cookies, 171
Cholesterol
  dietary fiber, 1
  eggs, 15
Cinnamon bread (hearty), 70–71
Cinnamon buns
  almond maple, 194–196
  egg bread, 200–201
Cinnamon raisin bread
  applesauce, 72–73
  with cranberry raisins, 69
  standard, 67–68
Coarse bread, troubleshooting, 30
Collapsed bread, troubleshooting, 30
Colorectal cancer, dietary fiber, 1
Convection ovens, 23
Conversions, measurement, 211
Cookies, 161–192
  almond incredibles, 167
  apple crisp, 170
  biscotti (almond poppy seed),
    161–162
  biscotti (anise), 162–163
  biscotti (chocolate chip), 165–166

biscotti (chocolate dipped almond), 164–165
biscotti (ginger with almonds), 163–164
chocolate oat and honey, 171
cowboy, 173–174
cranberry cookies, holiday, 174–175
date bars (Don's), 176–178
date bars (sourdough), 178–179
date nut, 180
Don's energy bars, 175–176
fistful of cookies, 184–185
ginger, 185–187
gingerbread man, 187–188
heart of hearts, 188–189
macaroons (basic recipe), 132
macaroons (delicate coconut), 183–184
maple bars, 181–182
meringue (almond), 168
meringue (chocolate), 169
oatmeal (basic recipe), 191–192
oatmeal (hornswaggling good), 189–191
oatmeal (sugarless strawberry), 172–173
Corn flours, 12
Cowboy cookies, 173–174
Cracked bread, troubleshooting, 31
Cranberry cookies, holiday, 174–175
Cranberry raisin muffins, 147–148
Cranberry streusel, holiday, 145–147
Crust, troubleshooting, 31

Date bars
    Don's, 176–178
    sourdough, 178–179
Date muffins with pineapple, 148–149
Date nut cookies, 180
Dates, diabetes, 40
Dense bread, troubleshooting, 31
Diabetes
    bread recipes for, 37–40
    dietary fiber, 1
    fiber supplements, 2–3
    low-sodium substitute, 34
Diet
    diabetes, 37–40
    health and, 41
    sodium retention, xi–xiii
Dietary fiber, importance of, 1–3
Digoxin, fiber supplements, 2
Dinner rolls, apricot, 111–112
Diuretics, xi, xii, xiii

Don's best soft pretzels, 122–124
Don's biscuits, 118–119
Don's date bars, 176–178
Don's energy bars, 175–176
Don's pizza dough, 97–98
Don's pumpkin muffin, 149–150
Don's secret bread recipe, 82–83
Don's sweet chocolate mix, 207
Double-action baking powder, 14. See also Baking powder/soda
Dough rising
    bread machines, 8–9
    troubleshooting, 31
Doughy bread, troubleshooting, 30
Dried fruits sweeteners, 16
Dry bread, troubleshooting, 30
Dry milk solids, low-sodium substitute, 34

Egg bread cinnamon buns, 200–201
Eggs
    Ener-G egg replacer, 19
    low-sodium substitute, 34
    use of, 15
Empanadas, 98–100
Ener-G baking soda
    low-sodium substitute, 33
    working with, 18
Ener-G egg replacer, use of, 19
Energy bars, Don's, 175–176
English muffin bread, 83–84
English muffins
    basic recipe, 113–114
    raisin cinnamon, 126–127
Equipment, 20
Eskimo hamburger buns, 106–107

Fats and oils
    choices of, 16
    low-sodium substitute, 35
Featherweight baking powder
    ingredients, 18
    low-sodium substitute, 33
Fermentation, salt, 6
Fiber. See Dietary fiber
Fiber supplements, 2–3
Fillings. See Toppings and fillings
Fistful of cookies, 184–185
Flat bread, troubleshooting, 29
Flavorings, recommendations for, 15, 20
Flaxseed buns, rolls, and bread, 84–85
Flaxseed meal
    fats, 16
    working with, 18–19

Flour, types of, 11–12, 19
Flour tortillas, 95–96
Fluid intake, dietary fiber, 2
Fluid retention, sodium, xi
Focaccia a la garlic cheese, 54–56
Food and Drug Administration (FDA)
  labeling, 38
  nutrient data, 21
French bread, 45–46
French bread (Fleischmann's), 47–48
French onion bread, 48–49
Fruits
  diabetes, 38, 39–40
  sweeteners, 16
Fruits and vegetables, dietary fiber, 2

Garlic cheese focaccia, 54–56
Garlic toast (French), 48
Garlic toast (Italian), 53–54
Ginger biscotti with almonds, 163–164
Gingerbread man, 187–188
Ginger cookies, 185–187
Glucose tolerance
  dietary fiber, 1
  fiber supplements, 2–3
Gluten
  flours, 11, 12
  liquids and, 14
Glyburide, fiber supplements, 3
Grains, low-sodium substitute, 34

Hamburger buns
  buttermilk egg buns, 104–105
  Eskimo, 106–107
  oatmeal raisin buns, 109–110
  whole wheat 'n white buns, 107–108
Hand-knead bread, bread machines
  compared, 7–8
Health, diet and, 41
Heart disease
  sodium retention, xi–xiii
  symptoms of, xi
Heart of hearts cookies, 188–189
Hearty, high-fiber bran muffins,
  135–136
Hearty cinnamon bread, 70–71
High altitude, 25–27
High-grain, low-fat, low-sugar
  sandwich bread, 86
Holes in bread, troubleshooting, 29
Holiday cranberry cookies, 174–175
Holiday cranberry streusel, 145–147
Holiday panettone, 51–53
Honey, sweeteners, 16

Hornswaggling good oatmeal cookies,
  189–191

Impossible bread, 92–94
Ingredients, 11–21
  altitude effects, 26–27
  baking powder/soda, 13–14
  bread dough enhancer, 19–20
  buttermilk, 17–18
  eggs, 15
  Ener-G Baking Soda, 18
  Ener-G egg replacer, 19
  fats and oils, 16
  featherweight baking powder, 18
  flavorings, 15, 20
  flaxseed meal, 18–19
  flours, 11–12, 19
  liquids, 14–15
  nutrient data, 21
  resources for, 11
  sourdough starter, 19
  sweeteners, 16
  yeast, 12–13
Irish soda bread, 56–57
Italian garlic toast, 53–54

Jams, sweeteners, 16
Jam surprise wheat muffins, 154–155

Ketchup, low-sodium substitute, 34
Kneading, bread machines, 5

Labeling (FDA), 38
Lemons, diabetes, 40
Liquids
  fats, 16
  low-sodium substitute, 34
  working with, 14–15
Long-lasting bran muffins, 134–135
Low-sodium substitutes, listed, 33–35

Macaroons
  basic recipe, 182
  delicate coconut, 183–184
Maple bars, 181–182
Maple syrup, low-sodium substitute, 34
Maple walnut bread, 75–76
Margarine, fats, 16
Measurement conversions, 211
Medications, fiber supplement
  interactions, 2–3
Meringue cookies
  almond, 168
  chocolate, 169

Metformin, fiber supplements, 3
Metric measurement conversions, 211
Molasses
  low-sodium substitute, 35
  sweeteners, 16
Monounsaturated fats, 16
Muffins, rolls, and biscuits, 103–156.
    See also Hamburger buns
  apple streusel muffins, 144–145
  apricot dinner rolls, 111–112
  bagels (poppy seed), 125–126
  blueberry muffins, 139–140
  bran muffins (Becky's), 140–141
  bran muffins (blueberry), 138–139
  bran muffins (chocolate chip),
    141–142
  bran muffins (hearty, high-fiber),
    135–136
  bran muffins (long-lasting), 134–135
  bran muffins (oat bran and date),
    137–138
  bran muffins (pineapple prune),
    136–137
  breadsticks (soft), 119–121
  breadsticks (soft cheddar), 121–122
  buttermilk egg buns, 104–105
  carrot muffins, 142–143
  cranberry raisin muffins, 147–148
  cranberry streusel (holiday), 145–147
  date muffins with pineapple, 148–149
  Don's best soft pretzels, 122–124
  Don's biscuits, 118–119
  Don's pumpkin muffin, 149–150
  English muffins (basic recipe),
    113–114
  English muffins (raisin cinnamon),
    126–127
  hamburger buns, Eskimo, 106–107
  jam surprise wheat muffins, 154–155
  oatmeal raisin buns, 109–110
  oat muffins, 132–133
  pineapple muffin tops, 150–152
  polenta muffins (with currants),
    130–131
  polenta muffins (high-fiber low-fat),
    131–132
  poppy seed puff-ups, 152–154
  raisin apple juice buns, 127–128
  Sandwich buns, San Francisco,
    103–104
  scones (basic recipe), 114–115
  scones (street vendor scones with
    orange zest), 115–116
  scones (whole wheat), 116–118

sopaipillas, 128–130
vanilla raisin buns, 110–111
whole wheat 'n white buns, 107–108
yam muffins, 155–156
Musketeers bread, 87–88
Mustard, low-sodium substitute, 35

Nutrient data, sources of, 21
Nutty date bread, 80

Oat bran and date muffins, 137–138
Oat flours, 12, 19
Oatmeal cookies
  basic recipe, 191–192
  sugarless strawberry, 172–173
Oatmeal raisin buns, 109–110
Oat muffins, 132–133
Oats, dates, and prune bread, 78–79
Oils. See Fats and oils
Old-fashioned buttermilk waffles,
    158–159
Old-fashioned Italian sourdough, 60–61
Olive oil, 16
Onion bread, French, 48–49
Orange anise bread, 90–91
Orange bread, whole wheat, 89–90
Orange cinnamon twist bread, braided,
    81
Orange currant bread, 91–92
Orange juice
  diabetes, 39
  liquids, 14
Orange peel, diabetes, 39
Ovens, 23

Panettone
  basic recipe, 50–51
  holiday, 51–53
Pastries, 193–203
  aebleskivers, 193–194
  almond maple cinnamon buns,
    194–196
  bear claws (basic recipe), 196–198
  bear claws (special Sunday morning),
    198–199
  egg bread cinnamon buns, 200–201
  penuche (sticky buns) 201–203
Penuche (sticky buns), 201–203
Pineapple muffin tops, 150–152
Pineapple prune bran muffins, 136–137
Pizza dough, Don's 97–98
Polenta muffins
  with currants, 130–131
  high-fiber low-fat, 131–132

Poppy seed bagels, 125–126
Poppy seed puff-ups, 152–154
Pretzels, Don's best soft, 122–124
Prunes, diabetes, 40
Pumpernickel bread
    quick and easy, 63
    raisin rye, 62–63
Pumpkin muffin, Don's, 149–150

Raisin apple juice buns, 127–128
Raisin cinnamon English muffins,
    126–127
Raisin rye bread, 64–65
Raisin rye pumpernickel bread, 62–63
Raisins, low-sodium substitute, 33, 35
Rice flours, 12
Rising. See Dough rising
Rolls. See Muffins, rolls, and biscuits
Rye flours, 12

Salt. See also Sodium
    bread flavor, 5–6
    low-sodium substitute, 35
Salt substitutes, bread making, 6, 35
Sandwich bread, high-grain, low-fat,
    low-sugar, 86
Sandwich buns. See also Hamburger
    buns
    oatmeal raisin buns, 109–110
    San Francisco, 103–104
    vanilla raisin buns, 110–111
San Francisco sandwich buns, 103–104
Saturated fats, 16
Scones
    basic recipe, 114–115
    street vendor scones with orange
        zest, 115–116
    whole wheat, 116–118
Seedless raisins, low-sodium substitute,
    33
Seven-grain bread with orange zest,
    66–67
Small bread, troubleshooting, 32
Soda bread, 56–57
Sodium
    eggs, 15
    fats, 16
    low-sodium substitutes, 33–35
Sodium retention
    fluid retention, xi
    treatment of, xi–xii
Soft breadsticks, 119–121
Soft cheddar breadsticks, 121–122
Soft pretzels, Don's, 122–124

Sopaipillas, 128–130
Sourdough breads
    baguettes, 59–60
    old-fashioned Italian, 60–61
Sourdough date bars, 178–179
Sourdough sandwich buns, San
    Francisco, 103–104
Sourdough starter
    low-sodium substitute, 35
    recipe for, 57–59
    working with, 19
Sourdough waffles, 159
Standard cinnamon raisin bread, 67–68
Sticky buns (penuche), 201–203
Sugar substitutes
    diabetes, 37–38, 39
    low-sodium substitute, 35
    sweeteners, 16
Sweet chocolate mix, Don's, 207
Sweeteners, types of, 16

Temperature
    dough rising, 8–9
    liquids, 15
    ovens, 23
Ten-grain bread with walnuts, 65–66
Thick crust, troubleshooting, 31
Toppings and fillings, 205–207
    almond paste, 205
    applesauce, 206
    chocolate mix, Don's sweet, 207
Tortillas, flour, 95–96
Trail mix bread, 94–95
Triglycerides, olive oil, 16
Troubleshooting, 29–32

United States Department of
    Agriculture (USDA), nutrient data,
    21
United States measurement
    conversions, 211

Vanilla raisin buns, 110–111
Vegetables, diabetes, 38

Waffles, 157–160
    basic recipe, 157–158
    Belgian waffles supreme, 160
    buttermilk waffles, old-fashioned,
        158–159
    sourdough waffles, 159
Walnut raisin bread, 74–75
Water retention. See Fluid retention;
    Sodium retention

Weather effects, 25–27
Wet bread, troubleshooting, 30
Wheat flours, 11
White flour, whole wheat flour and, 11, 12
Whole grains, dietary fiber, 2
Whole wheat and orange bread, 89–90
Whole wheat flour, properties of, 11–12, 19
Whole wheat 'n white buns, 107–108

Whole wheat pastry flour, 12
Whole wheat scones, 116–118

Yam muffins, 155–156
Yeast
  carbon dioxide, 11, 12
  salt, 6
  sugar substitutes, 38
  sweeteners, 16
  working with, 12–13